FAR FROM HOME

FAR

LILLIAN SCHLISSEL
BYRD GIBBENS
ELIZABETH HAMPSTEN

FOREWORD BY ROBERT COLES

FROM HOME

Families of the Westward Journey

SCHOCKEN BOOKS • NEW YORK

 Published in the United States by Schocken Books Inc., New York, and simultaneously in Canada by Random House of Canada Limited, Toronto. Distributed by Pantheon Books, a division of Random House, Inc., New York.

LIBRARY OF CONGRESS CATALOGING-IN-PUBLICATON DATA
Schlissel, Lillian.
Far from home.
Includes index.
1. Frontier and pioneer life—West (U.S.)
2. Family—West (U.S.)—History. 3. West (U.S.)—
Social life and customs. 4. Pioneers—West (U.S.)—
Family relationships—History. I. Gibbens, Byrd,
1936– . II. Hampsten, Elizabeth, 1932– .
III. Title.
F596.S28 1989 978 88-42685
ISBN0-8052-4052-7

Designed by Beth Tondreau Design/Jane Treuhaft

Manufactured in the United States of America

CONTENTS

FOREWORD BY ROBERT COLES

Each of these three narrative presentations brings us back to a question central to our nature, a question as old, no doubt, as the human cerebral cortex, with its biologically enabled capacity for consciousness and for speculation through language: How does one make sense of all the woe this world puts in our way between our first and last moments? Surely Abigail Malick must have made such inquiry during her years in the Oregon Territory; and Maggie Brown, especially, must have wondered aloud in such a vein at one or another point in time as she and her husband moved through Colorado and New Mexico; and similarly with the Nehers and the Martins in North Dakota, as they tried to figure out not only how to survive from season to season, but how to think about a life so unremittingly tough, demanding, frustrating, burdensome.

This book, in essence, offers three tales of immense suffering—yet, also, of obvious endurance. Families left home (Pennsylvania and Illinois, Virginia, czarist Russia) in order to find the proverbial new life, only to experience hunger, sickness, the loss of loved ones, and day in, day out, a seemingly endless expanse of backbreaking toil, with no sign that even a modest good fortune was forthcoming. Under such circumstances, one may wonder *why*—to what purpose, and for how long. Perhaps one doesn't stop and ask such introspective questions, though; perhaps the terrible press of life wears down that kind of meditative impulse. *We*, as the Malicks and Browns and Nehers and Martins come to our attention, most certainly stop turning pages and have our moral reveries on their behalf, and no doubt, imagine ourselves wanting to turn around and go back pronto to Illinois or Virginia, or incredibly, even to Odessa or Hamburg. But *they*—what did they make of their ongoing experience? True, we know of their thoughts through their letters, or the remembered moments of one of the Neher children—yet we try to imagine what they may not have shared with anyone, maybe even themselves: those Job-like times when terrible pain and the bleakest of prospects and the worst disappointments must have seemed like nothing compared with the peculiarly human curse of awareness. How often, if ever, did *they* really stop and think about this life's apparently interminable opportunities for more and more trouble?

After spending two years talking with migrant farm families in the late 1960s—men and women who also went with seasonal regularity "far from home"—I returned to New England, where I hoped to make sense of what I'd seen and heard. Those families continue to be our nation's most hard-pressed ones, and their agricultural work connects them, somewhat at least, to the families we meet in the pages that follow. I well remember a discussion I had with Erik H. Erikson about those migrant lives. I was wondering then, as I did more recently, when I read the galleys of this book, how it is that people can keep putting up with so much tragedy, and yet seem strong enough to live through their allotted span with dignity and poise, and even a modest amount of hope. After all, throughout my years spent in medicine and psychiatry I had seen many a person who had faltered badly in response to one or another set of difficulties, and though it is foolish to compare human misery and tribulation, those contemporary psychiatric patients surely have had an easier life than that of some of the people who figure in the stories of *Far from Home*. Put differently, how does one compare contemporary American patients, who may have an emotional illness, or a physical one, with those who lived in the mid-nineteenth-century world of desperation familiar, say, to the Malicks, the Browns, the Nehers, and the Martins? Similarly, as I talked with Professor Erikson about the migrant families I'd come to know, I found myself amazed by their ability simply to survive, especially when I recalled the trouble doing just that experienced by well-to-do patients I'd met in the course of my pediatric and psychiatric residencies—families utterly devastated, it seemed, by a particular setback, to the point that all of us doctors and nurses seemed helpless as we tried to encourage and explain and exhort.

The more Professor Erikson and I talked, the more I began to realize that suffering can sometimes generate its own energy, even resourcefulness, provided it is a suffering that connects in a certain way with a particular person's (family's) heart, mind, soul. I am being a bit murky and evasive here, even as I was when talking to Erik Erikson. I well remember his prompting: "You are talking about a psychology of suffering, and we'd best try to comprehend it psychoanalytically." No, I averred—I didn't think I knew how to do so. He gave me a sharp look, then pulled back a bit, or maybe moved forward: "All right, phenomenologically."

I assented—by presenting to him my individual "case histories," a term I then used to describe the life stories I had come to know. In particularly, I told him of some migrant families I knew, their relentless, everyday search for a better life, a search that never seemed even remotely within sight of achievement, yet a search constantly pursued, never mind the disappointments and disasters which life kept presenting. Had I ever discussed that matter with the particular migrants I knew, Erikson kept wondering—and yes, I kept saying, of course I had: my job was precisely to do so, to put such essentially psychological questions to men and women, fathers and mothers, even as I was learning how their children understood a world of constant travel and travail.

One day we both listened to some tapes my wife and I had made early in our work with Florida migrants (1963). These families went up and down the Atlantic coast states, harvesting crops, and we'd met them because they were kin to some of the black families we'd met in Louisiana and Georgia while studying school desegregation. We found such lives almost beyond our comprehension, try though we did to make an effort of the mind's imagination. Yet as we heard particular migrants talk, it became clear that they, for their part, did not feel as down-and-out as we felt them to be, and also did not feel as gloomy as we did about their overall prospects, notwithstanding their clear sense of being in a tough predicament.

Put differently, these were men and women who were in a great deal of difficulty, and who knew such to be the case (they were *not* fooling themselves by whistling Dixie), yet who also found within themselves the capacity—the will, the determination—to keep going, or as people put it today, to keep trucking. Whence such psychological energy? That question was Erikson's, of course, and mine, too. We both, I think, received the beginning of an answer from one migrant woman, and here is part of her explanation—her *raison d'être*, really:

I try to get from sunup to sundown. That's my hope, that I can do so. After night comes, I stop trying and worrying; I fall asleep, and then time goes racing by, and I'm not counting the crops and figuring how much cash I'll be collecting. My bones be tired by nighttime, and I let them get their rest. All day I bend and pick, and my mind tries to do the best—to cut the celery right, and stack them up right. I try to keep the kids moving along, and being helpful. I talks to them, and I sings with them. Their father, he'll keep them in line, if they don't pay attention to me. He'll come charging at them, and they look like the Lord has come to take them away!

We don't "plan" too much, no. [I had asked.] We try to clear some money by the end of the season; but it's hard, because you never know if you'll get the pay they promise. We try to keep going, and we pray to God that He'll give us the strength to keep going. When I'm low, I turn to Him, and that's when I say my prayers, and sing a few songs my momma taught me. Yes, they are "spirituals." We hear them in church, and we remember them. I'll break out with them in the fields, or someone else will, and next thing you know, we's all singing. We're talking to the Lord, and He's hearing, I know, because He's sending us energy, lots of it, and He's making us smile, while we work our burden, and you know, it's just a few minutes we're here, and then we pass through, and it's the long time afterwards that counts, and not whether you're a bossman down here on the earth. Jesus told us that the bossmen fall real low, and the ones way down bottom, they'll get way up there. Hereabouts—it's a long way from His home, and that's what you've got to remember, and when you go to meet Him, He'll not shake His head because you are doing shares or picking crops; He'll smile, and say come on and settle down, now that you've come where the Lord's place is, and no more wandering to here and to there; you can stay put forever. I'll say amen to that, and I'll be dreaming more about meeting Him, but then I'll wake up, or scratch myself if I've been letting my mind wander.

We sat there, two psychoanalytically trained white men living in the second half of the twentieth century in relative comfort, and wondered how a woman who spoke such words actually managed to keep her spirits high, as she claimed she could, given all the turmoil and misery of her life and that of her family. Surely she was in some way fooling herself, thereby masking a despair that must have been a constant presence in her life, however unrecognized or unacknowledged. Surely, too, she must have known many moments of doubt; must have had numerous misgivings; must have given vent at times to rage—spells of anger and resentment that her fate should be as it is. As for her much-espoused Christian faith, and the blues and work songs and spirituals to which she'd give voice—how far a net can they cast? Sometimes, somewhere, she must have wanted to forget all those topsy-turvy promises of Jesus, those life-everlasting declarations uttered so hard and long in the Sunday excesses of passion called churchgoing, and instead break down in a rage of bitter tears: it is a lousy deal, this life, and I know it, and I'd do anything to change things, but I can't, and so all I can do now is say what I feel in my rock-bottom heart of hearts, namely, that I hate so much of what passes for life, and if I keep getting up, still, it's because I'm trapped and I have no choice.

But such words are mine, needless to say, and were never uttered by that migrant farm worker. Nor, I suspect, did those "far from home" in the nineteenth century whom we meet in these pages have such words with themselves, for themselves. My hunch is that it is we, the observers or doctors or historians, who wonder how others have managed to go through the kinds of hell we document or analyze or try to survey in all its horror and terror—whereas those going through such experiences find their own reasons and routines to get through time, to stay alive, to keep picking crops or clearing land or betting on one or another dream coming true. When Erik Erikson and I had finished listening to my tapes of migrant farm life in America, and read my typed notes, we both were ready to throw our hands up in the air, though he did have this to say: "People don't 'examine' life the way you and I do—not if they live as they [the migrants] do, and it's just as well, I suppose. But they do have their hopes, and some they tell to others, and some they must keep to themselves."

The more I work with extremely vulnerable people living at the edges of one or another society, the more I realize that such hopes, put forward or kept in the heart's more remote chambers, offer their own energy—keep bodies going, keep minds as alert and steady as possible. I used to be stunned at the resourcefulness and persistence of certain agricultural workers, who were quite aware—I knew, for I'd talked with them at length—how bleak their future, immediate or long-term, would end up being. The harder I tried to figure out what kept such families in the ring, punching away by the hour, the day, the week, and it turned out cumulatively, year after year, the more perplexed I became—unless, of course, I settled for easy psychiatric or sociological truisms: they are "victims" of a "culture of poverty," or they resort to various psychological defense mechanisms. Yet the migrant woman I have quoted here had her own forthright, vigorous life, and her words and deeds deserve as much respect as those of the rest of us, including the writers and social critics and psychological observers among us.

Similarly with the Malicks and the Browns, the Nehers and Martins: they who left one world to explore and tame another; they who held out great hopes for themselves, and saw them turn into the grinding disappointments of a mean life; they who yearned for a bright future that eluded them, to be sure, but never stopped beckoning them, it seems. The stories that follow tell us about the American frontier, about the yearning of those who took it on, and with their lives, made it part of the nation we now take for granted. The stories that follow also give us our history in the most compelling manner possible—the incidents of life, the details, the accidents, surprises, trials which letter writers recall or survivors remember and tell those interested in hearing. Even as particular migrant farm workers are ever so important parts of a sum called "American agricultural abundance," these nineteenth-century families who ventured far from home are part of what the rest of us now rather too readily think of as our nation's westward triumph. It is good, then, that we are asked in a book such as this to forsake the mind's larger grasp, its conceptual hurry, in favor of a while spent with those whose sweat and blood and considerable heartache and assertions of courage and honor and perseverance and lapses into illusion if not delusion all amounted to lives spent making a wilderness become a nation's safe and secure territory. These are our American heroes too, as surely as our generals and politicians and businessmen and writers and inventors. These families went far from home in order to further their own chances in a life that seemed all too tenaciously unyielding, and so doing, particular men and women gave us, today, a homeland that is wonderfully far-flung. So it is that one generation falters and seems almost ready to fall down badly, never to stand up again—yet, in the long run of things, turns out to have taken us who have followed upon its broad and hard-worked shoulders.

Cambridge, Massachusetts
November 1988

ACKNOWLEDGMENTS

The editors came to the writing of this book in agreement on its structure and message, but working with letters and reminiscences over the years presented thorny problems. It took revisions, persistence, precision, and good will to bring the manuscript into its final form. At the end, we find we share a new respect for each other born of time and process and mutual assistance.

Each of us has incurred debts to friends and colleagues who helped along the way. I want to thank Kenneth L. Holmes, who shared his research with me and showed me how generous the exchange among scholars can be; Stephen Dow Beckham, who checked maps and census records for traces of the Malicks in Oregon and Washington; Stephen Biles in Portland, who helped me to trace the history of his family; Mrs. Jackie Roszel, a great-great-granddaughter of the Albright family in Illinois, who was my co-researcher and guide. Ms. Loree Bergerhouse of the Tazewell County Historical Society, and George Miles, Curator of Western Americana, Beinecke Library, Yale University, were unfailing in their courtesy and patience.

Rachel Burd, who has been my student, research assistant, and copy editor, has contributed more to this book than those tasks suggest. Brooklyn College gave me a semester's leave to write the final draft of the manuscript. And Bonny Fetterman of Schocken Books provided a steady head and hand when the editing seemed full of detours. My daughter and son have been cheerful and encouraging through the years of writing, and my mother has given me a strong belief in the value of family history.

LILLIAN SCHLISSEL

My gratitude is to Mary Brown Gose, who retrieved the letters of her parents from old desk drawers and attic trunks and began the work of transcribing and editing; to Mrs. Lolita Cox Smith, who recognized the letters' value, and after Mary's death, donated the collection to the University of New Mexico archives; to Mrs. Lillian Keller Peters, a distant relative of Maggie Keller Brown, who gave me contemporary information about the Keller family in Virginia; to Stella de Sa Rego, photoarchivist in the Special Collections Library of that university, who has been unfailingly helpful in locating photographs and permissions.

Marta Weigle, Ferenc Szasz, and Ann Boylan at the University of New Mexico brought their scholarly expertise to bear on my editing and reading of the Brown letters. English department secretary Veneta Hines assisted me with typing and printing. In addition, I am indebted to Rowena Rivers, Arthur and Henrietta Loy and Jan Commings, Vivien Michals, Patricia Alley, Ben Wren, Ken Ackron, and my loving family.

BYRD GIBBENS

I am indebted to Pauline Neher Diede for permission to quote from *Homesteading on the Knife River Prairies*, and for reading the final manuscript. I should also like to thank the Germans from Russia Heritage Society for their sponsorship of *Homesteading* when it was originally edited and published in 1983.

ELIZABETH HAMPSTEN

INTRODUCTION

Eastward I go only by force; but westward I go free. . . . I should not lay so much stress on this fact, if I did not believe that something like this is the prevailing tendency of my countrymen. I must walk toward Oregon. . . . And that way the nation is moving. . . .

HENRY DAVID THOREAU, "Walking"

We Americans are the pioneers of the world; the advance-guard sent on through the wilderness of untried things, to break a new path in the New World that is ours.

HERMAN MELVILLE, *White Jacket*

When *Women's Diaries of the Westward Journey* was published in 1982, the project that had taken seven years to finish was at last done. The difficulty had been in making one narrative out of so many fragments—diaries, letters, journals—each single story the same and yet so unlike the others. But though *Diaries* had become a book with a life of its own, the women's words would not leave my mind. I kept wondering what lay in store for the women after that long and arduous journey.

The diaries taught me that a family on an American frontier—wherever that frontier might be—was a family separated from some part of itself. Frontier settlers were fragments of families, maintaining outposts on uncharted land. Far from home, they yearned to connect with those who had been left behind, through memory, through photographs, through letters that carried seeds from old gardens, clippings from hometown newspapers, swatches of fabric from dresses, stories of old friends—anything out of which to weave continuity over the distances and the separations. "Somehow [the women] found the time to write the letters back home and to keep track of birthdays, marriages, and deaths. They simply refused to sever the framework of their old lives as they began to build anew." (*Diaries*, p. 149) The women had not been able to refuse the journey, which was often filled with regrets, but they "refused to sever the framework of their old lives." That was a haunting idea.

In our national passion for frontiers, we have not considered very much how frontiers affected family life. Our disposition has been to know the western experience through expansive and self-realizing acts—through exploration and "conquests" of people and of resources. Our penchant has been for studies of farming and ranching, railroading and mining, for stories of mountain men and cowboys, for accounts of empires of land and of water. We are slower to look for the stuff of history in the lives of plain people who wanted not much more than to live in ordinary ways and to build again in a new land the remnant of their old homes.

In three hundred years of American migrations, families have been routinely "dis-assembled." The individualism we are justly proud of, our national celebration of separation and autonomy, these have also given us the justifications for taking families apart. American families grow the best they can, some part of them in California, some in Colorado, and some in Massachusetts and New York. And we have grown accustomed to the "dis-assembled" condition. It has become our special accommodation, over time, to the fact of frontiers in our lives. We hold our reunions by telephone and greeting cards. We yearn for home, but we don't live there. We contemplate rootedness, but we fight free of its hold. The geography of American families is spelled out across the face of the land.

It became important to find out what had happened to those frontier families who moved west, to see how—and if—they survived over time. I did not want statistical norms; I wanted to touch the unadorned lives of ordinary people. One solution was to locate case histories that were somehow representative of life as it was actually lived. Byrd Gibbens, then in New Mexico, was editing a large collection of letters of a Virginia family that went west to Colorado and New Mexico. Elizabeth Hampsten had been working with the personal narratives of settlers in North Dakota. Each agreed to contribute a chapter for the book that was beginning to take form.

The sources for my own chapter were the last to be found. It took a year's search to discover the Malick letters in the Beinecke Library of Yale University, where they had been stored and almost forgotten. Most archives collect the papers of prominent families; those who acquire the papers of "anonymous" Americans usually file them away under "miscellaneous." For my purposes, files marked "miscellaneous" and "anonymous" are the jewel cases of American history.

The construction of this book has been serendipitous. We could not have predicted that the range of history from 1848 to 1909 would be represented so clearly or so neatly. Each family history was chosen because it revealed the lives of everyday people who lived for an extended period of time on some part of the western frontier: the Malicks, a nineteenth-century family that made the overland journey in 1848 looking for free land in Oregon; the Browns, who left Virginia after the Civil War to find quick wealth in Colorado mining camps; the Nehers and the Martins, Germans from Russia who traveled halfway around the world in 1909 to escape the czar's army, ending up on the awesome prairies of North Dakota. The surprise was that there would be so many parallels in these disparate histories.

Each chapter has a different voice and is composed of different kinds of sources. Byrd Gibbens and I have worked with collections of letters. Elizabeth Hampsten has drawn upon the published reminiscences of Pauline Neher Diede, the daughter of the family whose story is here retold. I am profoundly grateful to my coeditors for their patient and careful scholarship and for their insightful shaping of those sources into cohesive chapters for this book. The introduction and the concluding chapter are mine.

In working with the original letters, we have attempted, as far as possible, to present them just as they were written. For the sake of clarity and readability, however, we have allowed occasional editing: correction of the spelling of a word where it was misleading, or insertion of punctuation where the lack of it seemed likely to confuse the reader. Such changes have been kept to a minimum, and are usually not indicated in any way in the text.

The undertaking that began with the diaries of the women who made the westward journey is completed in this book about families and their frontier years. These histories are not heroic; on the contrary, they tend to flatten out much of what we have learned about pioneering. The frontier family, remembered with nostalgia as a model of ordered simplicity, was neither simple nor orderly, but full of changes and abrupt transitions. Yet, in all its permutations, the frontier family is also our own. In their self-willed dislocations and discontinuities are the outlines of our own lives. They are us in other clothes, where we began and where our dreams were given form. On the broad spaces of the unformed frontiers, in the curious destinies of these families, is something that speaks to us of what it means to be a family in America today.

LILLIAN SCHLISSEL

FAR FROM HOME

1. The Malick Family in Oregon Territory

1848–1867

The children . . . Are Not Like children Raised in the States . . . they have no Father And they Will Not Mind Me.
ABIGAIL MALICK

George and Abigail Malick came from Sunbury, Pennsylvania. Abigail's predecessors represented the British East India Company in the colonies; George's family stood with Washington through the cruel winter at Valley Forge. In 1836 they sold their land in Pennsylvania and, with four children, traveled by wagon to Illinois. They had three children more, farmed in Illinois about a dozen years, and then, in 1848, even before Congress declared the Oregon Territory part of the United States, they set out, almost two thousand miles, for the Pacific slopes. They left behind a married daughter, her husband, and their children, hoping the families would be reunited the next season. The Malicks filed a claim on the shore of the Columbia River, on land that would become part of the state of Washington. The climate was milder and the land richer than any they had ever known.

In the course of time, however, the new land showed a more savage face, taking the lives of George Malick, his two grown sons, and a daughter. The younger children, like the frontier that formed them, were wild and uncontrollable. The Illinois branch of the family never came west. When Abigail Malick died, at sixty, she was alone on her land except for the tenants who rented half her house. She had conquered the frontier in every way except the ways in which it changed her children and took them from her.

I. Leave-Taking, *1848*

When seventeen-year-old Hiram Malick wrote to his sister and brother-in-law in Tazewell County, Illinois, that his father and mother and five sisters and brothers were preparing "to leave the States" for Oregon Territory, he couldn't know the families would never see each other again. The Malicks were pulling up stakes, and starting for the Pacific Northwest. On a day in April, the air still sharp and the sun barely strong enough to melt the snow, his family set out for the new country. In muddy little towns along the Missouri River, jumping-off places like St. Joe and Council Bluffs, other farm families were setting out to claim free land. Pennants to the wind, a quarter of a million men, women, and children between 1840 and 1860 would cross some two thousand miles of this broad American continent looking for a better home, looking to make a better life. Helter-skelter, children crying, dogs barking, chickens flying, oxen bellowing, cows mooing, torn clothes, irritable voices, belly-aches and heartaches, laugher and hope, families carried the flag.

Abigail Jackson and George Malick were married in Pennsylvania. Abigail was a self-willed young woman who married against her family's wishes. The Malicks (Mölichs) were German Lutherans, God-fearing land-holders and merchants, strong and hardworking people. In 1836 George and Abigail bundled their four small children into a wagon with no springs and only a canvas cover to keep out the rain, and journeyed over bumpy roads—or no roads at all—from Sunbury, Pennsylvania, to Tazewell County, Illinois.[1]

The Malicks lived in Illinois a dozen years.[2] Their eldest daughter,

Mary Ann, married the eldest son of Jacob Albright, a Kentucky abolitionist who left the South in 1829 because he did not believe in holding slaves. The Albrights had three children of their own and another about to be born when the Malicks set out for Oregon.

Word of the mild climate and the rich soil of the Pacific territories stirred Midwest farmers in the 1840s. In 1841 Jesse Applegate led 900 people overland to the Pacific slopes; the very next season, 1,200 more followed. There was talk that Congress would "donate" a whole section of land, 640 acres, to families that would settle the new country, and land-hungry farmers saw the chance to shake loose from Illinois snows and winter miseries ("Mother was sick with . . . a very sore coff she was obleged to take medason"). It meant escape from the bad debts that had plagued them since the panic of 1837. But for some, it was more than the promise of free land or escape from debts and hard weather. It was time to move on. Time to try something new. That, after all, was what America was all about—the moving on. The vision in the mind of "somewhere else," the disposition to pick up and go.

> Dear Brother and Sister
>
> . . .
>
> I must tel you that Charles and old Roesin is almost redy to start. Mother is agoin' to make the wagon cover tomorow and I want you to wright to us just as quick as you get this because I want to hear from you before I go.
>
> (MARCH 20, 1848)[3]

Hiram Malick's sweetheart broke their engagement. If she wanted Hiram, she would have to leave her family, just as the Malicks were leaving Michael and Mary Ann Albright. Hiram was disappointed, but he was also excited about the adventure that lay ahead. "I must [tell] you that I don't ever expect to come thare [to his fiancée's home] again. I like the far west."

It was Ho! for the westward journey, for new places, for a mild climate and a new beginning. And it was also an ending. Abigail would not speak of the departure to her daughter, nine months pregnant. Not one word. She couldn't bring herself to say goodbye. She left Mary Ann's house, closed the door behind her, and told herself that the Albrights would follow the very next summer, bringing her grandchildren with them.

The Albrights, for their part, must have known for a while that the families were separating. Farmers spent months building sturdy wagons of seasoned hardwood. They tarred the sides of their wagons so they could be lifted off the wheelbase and floated across the rivers. Each family supplied itself with 200 pounds of flour, 150 pounds of bacon, 10 pounds of coffee, 20 pounds of sugar, 10 pounds of salt. Additional supplies included chipped beef, rice, tea, dried beans and fruit, baking soda, vinegar, pickles, tallow, and gunpowder. The basic kitchenware was a kettle, a fry pan, coffee pot, tin plates, cups, knives, and forks. Supplies for a large family weighed in at more than a ton, and a fully loaded wagon needed four yoke of oxen to pull it. Wagons, oxen, and gear could cost over $400, supplies another $200, and powder and shot $75 more. Families needed cash for repairs and supplies on the crossing and for food during the first winter. They needed cash to build a house and to start new crops the following spring. Resettling was an expensive business.[4]

Most important on the journey was something you could not pack—or buy: the knowledge of the road. Men had to know how to repair wagons when there was no new wood and nothing on the horizon but sky and wind. They had to know how to drive four or five yoke of oxen and then swim the terrified animals through swollen rivers. They had to reset iron tires, take the wheels off, soak them overnight, and then grease and replace them. Broken axles had to be repaired. Broken locks had to be tightened, whiplashes cut and spliced. One had to know at a glance which grasses the cattle could eat and where the water was poisonous. Wagons could make only ten to thirteen miles a day, and the travel took six months' time in the first years; everyone feared the early snows of the Rockies and the cold of the Cascade and the Sierra Nevada mountains.

For women the overland journey meant six months' stooping over smoking coals on the ground to make a small fire. It meant cooking in the wind and rain, with only weeds and "buffalo chips" for fuel. It took all a woman's patience to deal with the common complaints of infants and small children—diapers, coughs, teething, colic, rashes, measles, whooping cough, irritability, high spirits, mischief. The uncommon dangers—cholera and dysentery and the continual fear of Indian attacks—strung out the nerves of every man and woman on the road.

When George and Abigail Malick set out in March of 1848, Congress had not even declared the Northwest a territorial possession. The 3,000 people who traveled with them that summer headed for a land that was poorly mapped, over distances that had no roads and only a handful of U.S. forts across 1,800 miles. There was no one to help if they were tired, or sick, or if the oxen died. No towns, no houses, no supplies along the way. They could as well be traveling over the sea, the land was that empty.

At first, the wagons followed the rivers, the Missouri, the Platte, the Sweetwater. They stopped for supplies at Fort Kearney in central Nebraska, and then in Wyoming at Fort Laramie. They passed landmarks such as Court House Rock, Chimney Rock, and Scotts Bluff, and they took the South Pass comfortably through the first rise of the Rocky Mountains. They were about three and a half months and 1,200 miles from their starting point.

By August they reached the fierce terrain of the Blue Mountains, where they had to lift the wagons up the mountain walls with ropes and pulleys. The men and boys pulled the heavy wagons up and the women and children set blocks behind the rear wheels so the wagons would not slide backward. On the other side, it was muscle and prayer to hold the wagons in check as they slid and catapulted down the steep declines.

More than physical hardship, the road in the 1840s was filled with uncertainties. No map was trustworthy. A piece of paper nailed to a tree or an arrow painted with tar on a rock pointing to a new cutoff was enough to split parties that had traveled together for five hundred miles. A rumor could set some wagons one way, some another. Every journey was a history of false starts and near disasters. Sooner or later there was bound to be foul weather and mishap. And as the days of August and September came on, fear overtook even the stouthearted. A mistaken road, a broken axle, a disabled draft animal, a lost child, a layover to recover from "mountain fever" or dysentery or malaria or cholera, an Indian skirmish, a rainstorm—anything might happen on the road. Emigrants perpetually worried about finding safe grass and water for their oxen. The last weeks of the journey were the desperate efforts of sheer will.

After two hundred miles of straining and rising panic in the mountains, travelers finally reached The Dalles, almost the end of the journey. But that river was known as an "evil" branch of the Columbia, with steep cliff walls and swirling waters. The emigrants loaded their possessions onto canoes or improvised rafts and paid Indians to take them through the rapids. Some tied their children and what they still had left onto pack mules. Others left everything behind them and made the last miles on foot.

The Indians in the Willamette Valley of Oregon stared in wide-eyed amazement at the men and women who came stumbling into the land.

All things considered, it was astonishing that there were already generations for whom the moving on had become a habit of life. Emigrant farmers, like itinerant soldiers of fortune, boasted that they had been "raised on the road."

George and Abigail Malick started out with six children in a stout wagon. Three older children—Charles, Hiram, and Rachel—were almost full grown, at nineteen, seventeen, and fourteen years old. They were strong enough to help on the crossing, to pitch in with the hard work. Peter Shindel, Abigail Jane, and Nancy Susan were still young, but not infants; they were big enough for chores. This was a seasoned party. They had been on the road before and they looked sharp for the troubles they could reasonably expect.

But how could they or anyone imagine that a young man like Hiram would drown on a summer day? The Platte River, in late summer so low and muddy that you could walk through it, swelled and raced from the April rains. Hiram, seventeen years old, joyful with the thought of adven-

Children on a Colorado homestead. Some, for whom the moving on became a way of life, remembered as grown men and women how they had been "raised on the road."

ture before him, who would think he would be dead in three months' time?

It was a year and a half before Abigail Malick would write the story of their terrible journey.

> I never shal see eney of you eny More in this world. We Are Almost three thousand Miles apart. I would like to see My sweet littl Ann And Homer And the other two but I never Shall. . . . And you never Will see Hiram. . . . Hiram drounded in [the] Plat River At the Mouth of Dear Krick. He went Aswiming with some other boys of the Compeny that we Trailed with And he swum Acrost the river and the Water run very fast And he could not reach this side. The young Men tried to save him but he [had the Cramp] And Could swim no more. And they Said o hiram do swim but he said I cannot swim eney More. And one young Man took A pole And started to him And the water ran so fast that he thought he Could not swim eney more so he returned And left him to his fate. And the other boys Called to him and said O hiram O swim. And he said o my god I cannot eney More. They said that he went down in the water seven or eight times before he drounded. And then he said o my god O lord gesus receive My Soul for I am no More. Oyes I think that if ever A young Man went to their lord gesus that he Did for he Always Was A very good boy and that [all who] knew him liked him. So you know All about Hiram's death now. So you need not ask eneything About him eney More for it will not do us eney Good to trouble ourselves About him eney More. It has Almost kild Me but I have to bear it. And if we Are good perhapes then we can meete him in heven. (OCTOBER 10, 1850)[5]

The Malicks wrote letters home over the next seventeen years, and Hiram's drowning was always there—a hand clawing at memory. He was only seventeen. Too young to die, swimming with friends on a mild afternoon.

Abigail's letters were written with dogged determination. All the news, the everyday life, the everyday burdens. She meant the letters to hold the family together, part of them in Oregon Territory, part of them back in "the States." Abigail wrote also to convince herself that distance did not matter, that they were still one family, whole and unbroken, and that they would be reunited. Each season she coaxed and urged and wheedled the Albrights to leave Illinois and make the journey west. She reassured them that prosperity was theirs if they would come: "My o dere children. I wish that you were heare." (JANUARY 31, 1850)

II. Staking a Claim, *1848–1855*

The Malicks' claim in Oregon Territory bordered the Columbia River, a mile from Fort Vancouver.[6] Only a year before, Cayuse Indians burned the Whitman Mission in Walla Walla, killing fourteen people, including Marcus and Narcissa Whitman, and it seemed to new arrivals that it was prudent to settle close to the protection of the fort. The Whitman massacre moved Congress to place the Northwest territories under the protection of the American flag just months before the Malicks arrived. Oregon Territory was a fragile outpost of America, some 5,400 men and 3,600 women, scattered through the expanse of what would eventually become the two states of Washington and Oregon. For the purposes of the territorial government, Congress set aside $26,000 for public buildings, a library, a few lighthouses, and the salaries of all officeholders and legislators.[7]

But the Malicks were satisfied. Their land was rich and high enough not to be flooded by the river. They had more salmon than they could eat and enough lumber to sell. There were neighbors within a few miles so they did not feel alone. Abigail wrote, "We have got Abutiful Claim near fourt vancover on the Coulumbia River. A whol sexsion of land, and theare is ships asailing every day on the greate Columbia right befoure our dore." (OCTOBER 10, 1850)

The mouth of the Columbia River was a bustling cross section of interests and peoples. The British were there, operating the Hudson's Bay Company under a grant from the Crown that dated back to 1670. French-Canadian trappers, "Kanakas" married to Indian women, lived in some thirty cabins just beyond the stockade at Fort Vancouver. The fort itself held 250 officers and enlisted men drawn from almost every state in the nation. Negroes and mulattoes, legally forbidden residence by the legislation that formed the Oregon Territory, were part of the population, most of them servants bravely named, like Man o' War and Margaret Lord and Rogue Duehamay. And there were Chinese and Hawaiian laborers with even more exotic-sounding names: Treheward Owyhee, Henry Honolulu, James Molaly, Opumi Maioui.[8] And there were the Cayuse and the Klickitat Indians at some distance from the settlements. Columbia City, later to be called Vancouver, was a strange mix of peoples and races. A town, a port of call for Pacific packet boats and fur traders, it was no simple farming community, but an exciting and a precarious place to build a new home.

In 1850, two years after the territory was created, Congress passed the Donation Act whereby a settler and his wife would have 640 acres "donated" after four years' residence. The Donation Act was what the emigrants were waiting for. Farmers filed claims for as much land as they could find, hoping to become rich by selling off the unused acres. But the claims would not be finalized until the region could be surveyed, which could not happen until the Hudson's Bay Company's title expired or was extinguished by the federal government in treaty or by purchase. None of these conditions were met until 1860. In the interim, for over a decade, no one held clear title to the land, and the region became a maze of claims, counterclaims, and "jumped" claims. The Oregon Territory would be one of the most litigious regions in the nation. The practice of law in Vancouver was as profitable as mining and a lot less strenuous. George and Abigail

Oregon City, photographed in 1858, lay at the end of the Oregon Trail, near the falls of the Willamette River, called The Dalles. Columbia City, where the Malicks made their claim, and Oregon City were seen as major sites of the new territory; Portland, however, would outgrow them both.

Malick filed their claim and turned their attention to tending crops and feeding livestock.

But then, hardly giving the travelers time to recover their senses after the long journey, came word of the discovery of gold at Sutter's Mill, a few hundred miles south near Sacramento. By the spring of 1849, news of gold had circled the world, and able-bodied men set out to make claims along the rivers and the hills of northern California. Steamers and clipper ships, railroads and wagons, horses and mules—anything and everything that could move—brought men smitten by the "California fever." "A great elemental force swept tens of thousands into a wild and forbidding country that, but for the abnormal call of gold . . . would have been left to the Indians and to a scattering of hardscrabble farmers."[9] Even seasoned farmers like George Malick and his eldest son Charles took a turn at the mines and came back with enough gold to astonish the family. Abigail wrote to Michael and Mary Ann, "If you did not wish to stay heare you coud leve your family with us and go to the Gold Mines and get all that you ever would want." (JANUARY 31, 1850)

But mining brought hardship and danger. The men who filled the "rag towns" along the rivers and in the hills were an unstable crowd from as far away as the Hawaiian Islands, Mexico, Peru, Chile, Australia, China. California's population, before the strike probably no more than 14,000 people, swelled by the end of 1849 to more than 100,000.[10] And these men, sleeping in wet tents and often hungry, following rumors upriver or down, lived in the hope of finding gold and in fear that what they found would be stolen.

Nineteen-year-old Charles Malick came home with five thousand dollars in gold dust in the first months of the gold rush and almost immediately went back to find more. For George, however, once to the mines was enough; he and Abigail were satisfied to find wealth under the plow. Abigail wrote, "We have an exceedingly Butiful Winter. . . . It is aGreat Country for wheat and the prettiest wheat that ever I seen." There were "fir tres very tall and o they make a most butiful lumber."

For her part, Abigail, an "old" woman in her forties, was falling in love with the new landscape. She had farmed in Pennsylvania, she had farmed in Illinois, but here she was, hardly knowing it, putting down roots. This Pacific landscape filled her heart. "We milked eight cows late last sommer And we got A half A dollar Apound for butter." All she needed to complete her happiness were the children she left behind. Prosperity, she assured Michael and Mary Ann, was there for the asking if they would just come and join the rest of the family. "O if you was hear with your Cows you could make A great Deal of money, " she wrote. "Butter is now one dollar And A half A pound. Eggs Are A dollar and Ahalf per doson And Chickins A half A dollar apeice and American cows are fifty dollars apeice. . . . Shipps sails on the Columbia River . . . with store goods of All kinds. . . . O it will be one of the gratest places in the whole world sur." (JANUARY 31, 1850)

Abigail tried to put Hiram's death behind her and wrote that Columbia City (Vancouver) would soon "mak Atown As good As Chicago." "Thear is Agoing to be Alarge town built write hear At Vancover gest two miles from hear As [soon] as the hudson bay Compeney is don living heare." (OCTOBER 10, 1850)

George set about clearing the land, selling the timber, and building them a home.

> Father has built Anice Milk house an now he is Abuilding A very nice porch Cleare Acrost the rooms And Kitchin. . . . Our house is ful of good things And I have Made two new bedes cince we have bin in oregon.
>
> (JUNE 24, 1851)

The letters went back and forth, full of the news of farming and prosperity. Days settled down to commonplace concerns. The family was being recognized in the community; George was chosen to be a judge in a local election at their neighbor's house and was paid six dollars for his services. And Abigail tried to explain to Mary Ann why, almost two years earlier, she had not said goodbye: "You was not in A situation to bare mutch At that time and I thought that if you did not know it that when you would hear it that you Could bare it better. My Dear Child O I want to se you and dear Michael again." (OCTOBER 10, 1850)

Almost from the first, Abigail sent her younger children to school. Abigail Jane and Nancy Susan, who came into the territory when they were eight and three, were in school in only two years' time. Peter Shindel, who was ten when he arrived in Columbia City, preferred to help his father cut and haul timber. Abigail even had an Indian girl named Mary to help with the chores: "She is a Very good girl but she could not talk English."

Pa was plowing potatoes and spring wheat. "He is very well and in Agood humor." (NO MONTH, 1850)

Then, just as they were beginning to take comfort in the ordinary rhythms of life, just as the family was getting used to the rewards of this new land, they met calamity again.

Abruptly, Abigail wrote to Illinois, "Your brother Charles he is Dead to. He Died in California the thirteenth of August of Abrain fever in the gre[e]n Valley. He was on his way A coming home." There had been a letter from Charles's friend Franklin Kincaid. The Malicks tried to piece together the events that led to Charles's death, but there were conflicting stories. They heard that he had died of a brain fever, that he was set upon by thieves who stole his gold, and, contrary to all these stories, that he was living in California, out of touch with the family.

> Thare was peopple Came that knew Charles And said that Charles had Agreate deal of money. One said that he [had] seven thousand dollars. And thare was one young Man Came home from there And told us that Charles was on his way home And got in to green wood valley And was Robed. And that was the Caus of his death. It hurt him so mutch that he took the brain fever And died. . . . Franklin kincade wrote to us that there was onley Monney enough to bury him. (OCTOBER 10, 1850)

Charles "drowned" in the gold rush as Hiram had drowned in the Platte River. Charles was swallowed up; he would have been only nineteen or twenty when he disappeared. He went away, like other young men, to look for gold to make his fortune. And then his letters stopped coming. How many weeks, waiting, did Abigail tell herself that the packet boats were slow, that he was a long way from any place where he could post the mail, that young men were poor correspondents. And all the time, Charles was likely dead. Alone, feverish, set upon by thieves, murdered? How would they know for sure? There was no way of going to look for him. Charles was with them one moment, a strong young man, and then gone, with only a letter from a companion telling them that he had died. Hiram's death had been etched so sharply; they would live forever with the image of his drowning. But Charles's death left only lingering doubt. A vacant place.

> O trouble Attendes Me. Trouble trouble trouble. O lord when will it be over.
> (OCTOBER 10, 1850)

Now there were two young men gone.

Rachel took up the task of writing the family's letters. Covering Abigail's silence, Rachel poured out her own news. She had just turned sixteen and was being courted by more suitors than she could tell about: "There is a great many young men loves me about Hear." (MARCH 5, 1852)

When Congress passed the Donation Act in 1850, providing that a married woman could enter her own claim to a half-section of land, the lawmakers unwittingly turned Oregon Territory into a marriage market. No girl over twelve was safe from young farmers looking to double their land. Rachel did not need to be pretty or wealthy; by historical accident, she was matrimonially desirable. And just a mile from her home, in Fort Vancouver, were 234 young bachelors, not counting officers, whiling away their time, with no Indians to fight. With few young women in the territory, Rachel had suitors to turn away. She wrote to Mary Ann:

> You stated that Edward C[ornelius] was a coming out here in the spring & that he intends to have one of Fathers girls. As for that I don't know but as for my self he shal not get [me] because I wont have him, nor mr. Phiester wont get me [either]. Although as far as I know they both are very respectable young men but they dont suit my taste. (JANUARY 24, 1852)

Among all her suitors, Rachel Henrietta gave her heart to a young man from Pennsylvania, where her mother and father came from and she had been born. John DeNormandy Biles (Byles) was born in Bucks County in 1827. He ran away to join the army and arrived in Oregon Territory the spring following the Malicks' arrival. Rachel was fourteen when he began to send her flowery, elegant letters.

> Dear Rachel,
> It is long since we first met and long since we last parted. It may be long ere we meet again but I hope nevertheless heaven speed me wherever I am and haste me on my journey and bestow me with calm water and swelling sail to meet you again. . . . In all I have loved and esteemed there is not one that

> can compete with you where the hart pours forth its tender feelings and where love and friendship mingle together and flow in one ever sparkling stream.
> (NOVEMBER 24, 1850)

John Biles had competition, as other young men outdid each other in sending Rachel gifts. Abigail wrote that one gave her a watch and another a new silk dress. Still another "gave her thre or four gold rings and a yong Doctor gave her another dress and Abutiful Collar and I do not know how mutch money." Young men who came courting even brought presents to Abigail—"twenty Pounds of coffee and that Mutch shougar." (OCTOBER 10, 1850)

John Biles, however, was more educated than most young men in the territory, and he courted Rachel with sentimental, romantic, thrilling letters declaring his loyalty and his love: "The Columbia whose name sounds sweet and rolls between its shores and no hopes of its ever failing so may our love ever roll between us and never be forsaken by each other. . . . I long to see you once more . . . my love for you is greater than ever and [I] will render all in my power to come soon." (OCTOBER 24, 1850) His letters were decorated with drawings of flowers and birds; they were enough to turn the head of any girl. His pet name for Rachel was "Musha," the country translation of "ma chère," and he teased her that their courtship was so unhurried by frontier standards that soon "you will know how to get married" merely by having witnessed the weddings of so many of their friends. (MARCH 24, 1851)

Biles waited two years before he proposed, knowing that Rachel's father would not give permission until he was out of the army. No Malick daughter would marry a soldier. Biles confessed his impetuous youth: "I left my parents without them knowing wither I went or what had become of me. . . . About 20 months after my absence from home I wrote to my parents & asked my father to liberate me from the sirvice of the U.S. army." His father did not rail against his wandering son, but "tryed every way to clear me from the Army & at last my discharge was affected by civil process & I was discharged." (COLUMBIA CITY, NO MONTH, 1851)

Until Biles was out of the army, and had properly received George Malick's permission, Abigail cautioned the Albrights to make no mention of any wedding in their letters, "until you should here from us that him And Rachel is married for fere that father should scold me And brok up the Match. And I would not like to have it brok up for he is a very nice

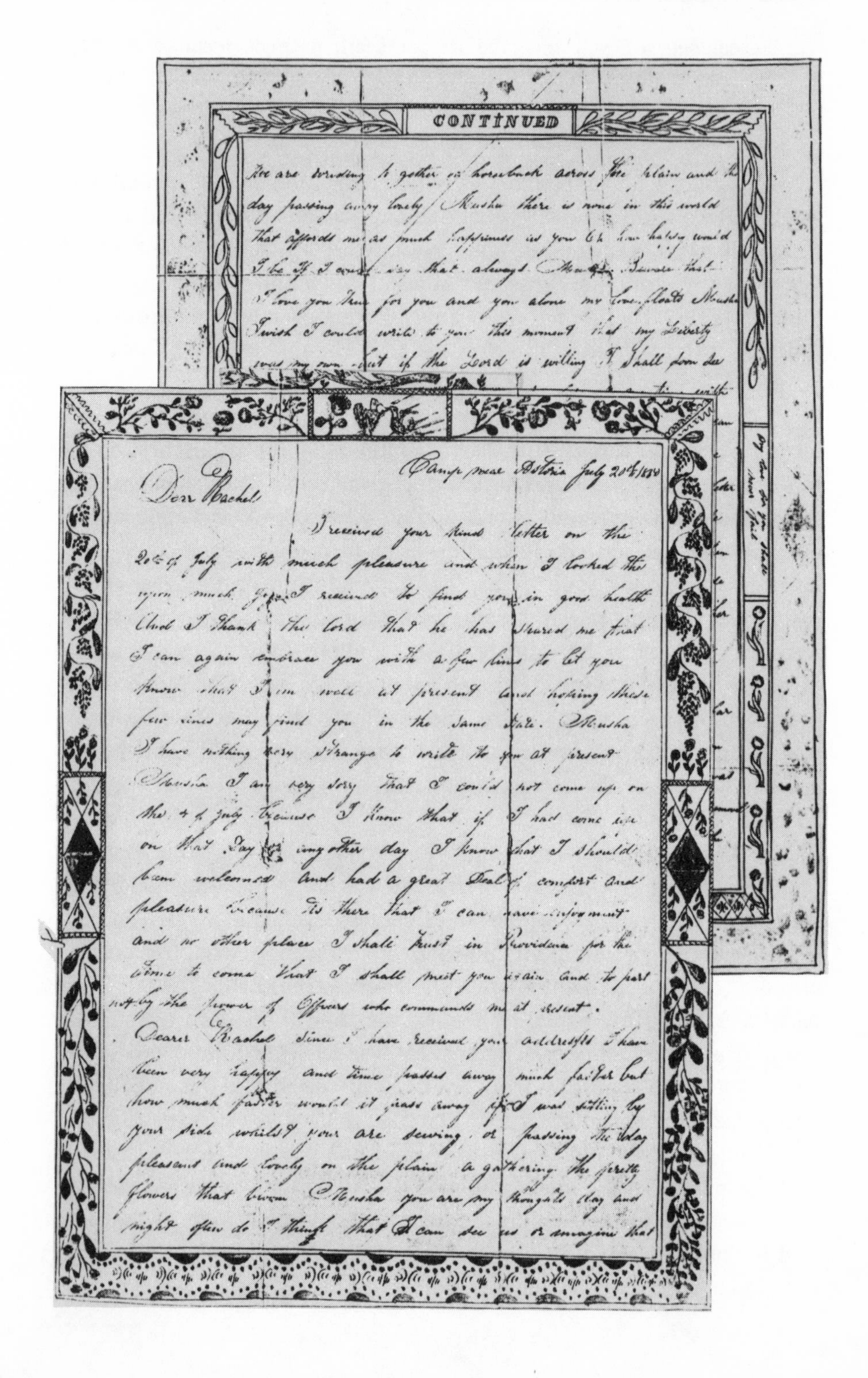

CONTINUED

We are winding to gether on horseback across the plain and the
day passing away lovely Musha there is none in this world
that affords me as much happiness as you Oh how happy would
I be If I could say that always [illegible] Because that
I love you there for you and you alone my love floats Musha
I wish I could write to you this moment that my Liberty
was my own but if the Lord is willing I Shall soon see

Camp near Astoria July 20th/18[illegible]

Dear Rachel

I received your kind letter on the
20th of July with much pleasure and when I looked the
upon much joy I received to find you in good health
And I thank the Lord that he has spared me that
I can again embrace you with a few lines to let you
know that I am well at present and hoping these
few lines may find you in the same state. Musha
I have nothing very strange to write to you at present
Musha I am very sorry that I could not come up on
the 4th of July because I know that if I had come up
on that day or any other day I know that I should
been welcomed and had a great deal of comfort and
pleasure because tis there that I can have enjoyment
and no other place I shall trust in Providence for the
time to come that I shall meet you again and to part
not by the power of Officers who commands me at present.
Dearest Rachel since I have received your addresses I have
been very happy and time passes away much faster but
how much faster would it pass away if I was sitting by
your side whilst you are sewing or passing the day
pleasant and lovely on the plain a gathering the pretty
flowers that bloom Musha you are my thoughts day and
night often do I think that I can see you or imagine that

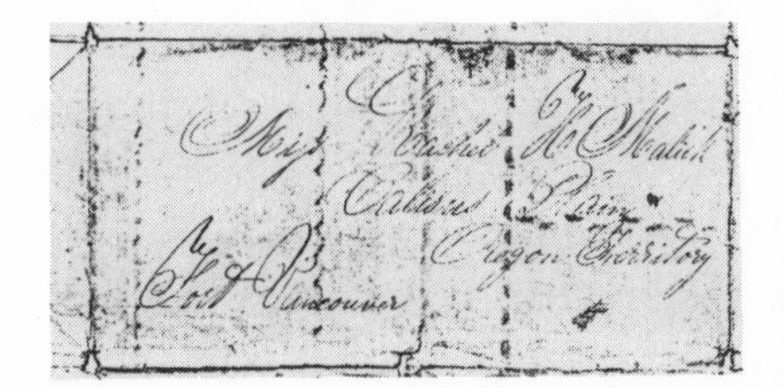

Miss Rachel M. Malick
Chalises Prairie
Oregon Territory
Fort Vancouver

Letter from John D. Biles to Rachel Malick, July 20, 1850. Elaborately drawn courtship letters, filled with poetry and expressions of faithful love, were rare on western frontiers.

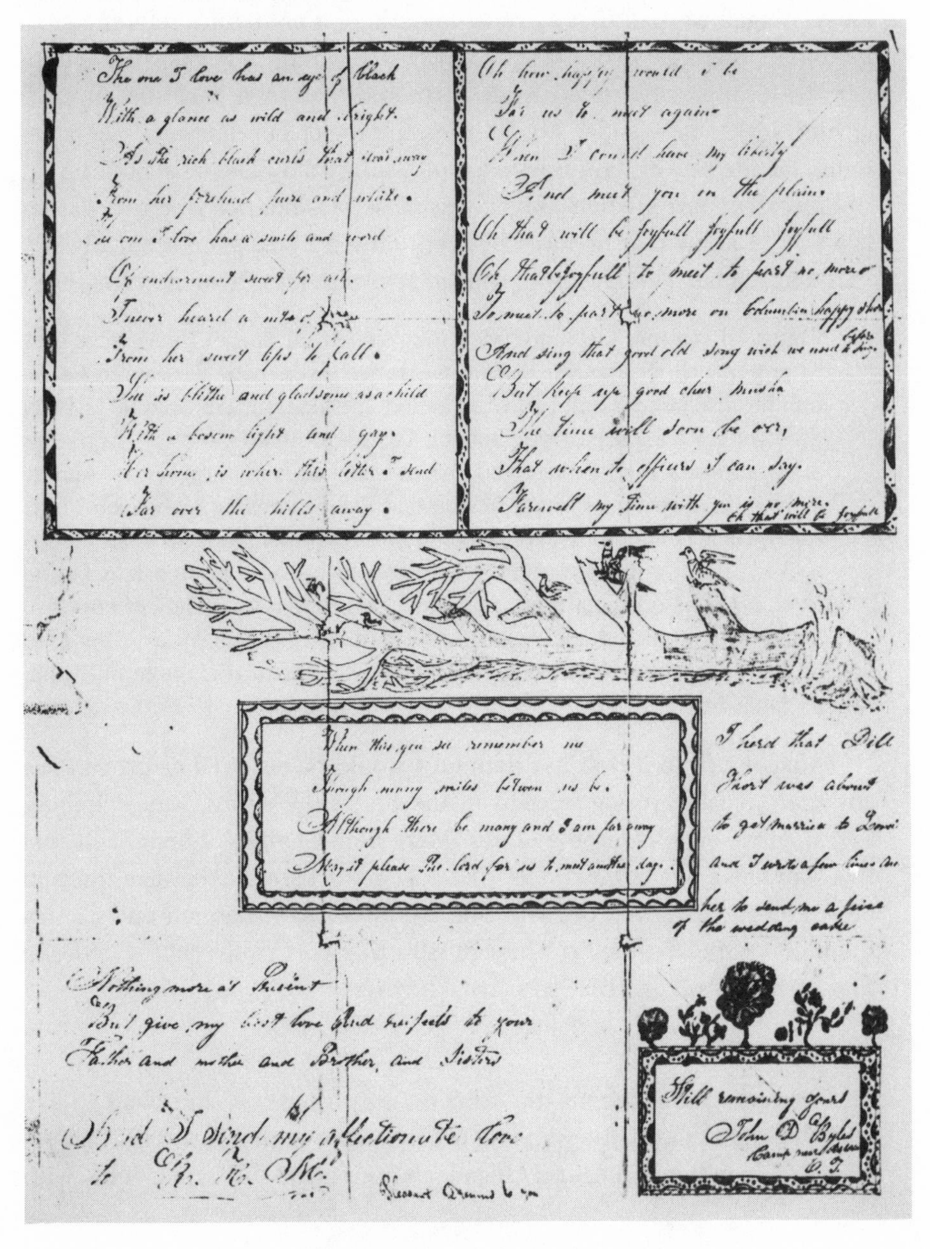

The one I love has an eye of black
With a glance as wild and bright.
As the rich black curls that wave away
From her forehead pure and white.
The one I love has a smile and word
Of endearment sweet for all.
I never heard a ...
From her sweet lips to fall.
She is blithe and gladsome as a child
With a bosom light and gay.
Her home is where this letter I send
Far over the hills away.

Oh how happy would I be
For us to meet again
When I could have my liberty
And meet you on the plain.
Oh that will be joyfull joyfull joyfull
Oh that will be joyfull to meet to part no more
To meet to part no more on Columbia happy shore
And sing that good old song wich we used to sing
But keep up good cheer Rachel
The time will soon be over,
That when to officers I can say.
Farewell my time with you is no more.
Oh that will be joyfull

When this you see remember me
Though many miles between us be.
Although there be many and I am far away
May it please the lord for us to meet another day.

I herd that Bill Short was about to get married to Louisa
And I write a few lines to her to send me a piece of the wedding cake

Nothing more at present
But give my best love and respects to your
Father and mother and Brother and Sisters
And I send my affectionate love
to R. M. M.

Still remaining yours
John D. Byles
Camp near ... O. T.

young man and not gelous harted. . . . I have knowed him this two years. We came here in the fall [of 1848] and he in the spring of 1849." (UNDATED LETTER)

George cast a long shadow over the comings and goings of his family. Abigail's earlier note that Pa was in a "good humor" was the first hint that his family took great care not to disturb him. Now, over a thousand miles away, Abigail worried that a casual remark, or a premature reference to a betrothal, might provoke George's anger. The family gave his volatile temper and disapproving ways a wide berth and tried their best to steer clear of him. It was no wonder Abigail tried to protect her daughter's engagement, for she saw in John Biles a loving young man—"he dose nothing . . . But kises her" even when Abigail was close by, "but not when yor father is by. . . . I know that he loves her very Mutch." (DECEMBER 10, 1851)

And Rachel, at sixteen, was all "in snaird in love." (NO MONTH, 1851)

> I must tel you that the young Man that is courting Rachel Henrietta is here At present. He has got his discharge. He has Avery good father And he got him his discharg for him two years be fore his time was out. And he is Avery good work Man. I supose you know what sort of Atraid he has. His traid is A wagon And Coach maker. And he can make all kind of furneture. And he is Avery in dustru[ous] young Man and is well be loved by All hoo knos him. And he is very handsom. He has blue eyes And light hair And is very pretty spoken. He dose not Sware nore Spake eney bad wordes And is A butiful form. Nore he dose not drink nor play cards nor is not guiltey of eney bad habits what ever And is very saving. I think that he will Make Avery good husband for hooever gets him. He is a pennsylvanian. He is from near philadelphia. he is Ahelping father to Make the poarch now. (UNDATED LETTER)

Abigail saw to it that her daughter would be outfitted as properly as any marriageable young woman in the States. "We have more clothing now than we ever had in the States. More ritch Clothing. I bought Rachel this sommer a new straw bonet that cost six dollars. Rachel has thirteen new dreses. And seven of them She has never had them on onley to try them on. One of them is white Muslin that cost twelv dollars and one that cost ten And one that cost five." (OCTOBER 10, 1850)

Biles was discharged from the army on July 14, 1851, and went to live with the Malicks until the wedding the following spring. It was like having another son in her home, and Abigail felt once again the tempo of life with a house full of young people. On New Year's Day 1852, the family celebrated. The Edward Cornelius in Rachel's letter had indeed come west to look over "pa's little girls." Abigail thought him a

> Nice young Man from the Sitey of Chicago. . . . Now I suppose you Would Wish to know What We Had for Dinner. . . . [And] I must tel you . . . so you May Think We Do Not Have to Starve away Here in a Teritory so Far From the States. . . .
>
> Well We had Rosted Ducks . . . And Fat Chickens And Rosted pig and Sausages And green Apl pie And Mince pies and Custard pies And Cakes of difrent kindes [and] Inglish goosburyes And Plums Blue And green gages And Siberian crab Apples And oregon Apples. . . . Like wise Buter And Sturson pikles and Beet pickles And Sauce And Bread and Mashed potatoes and Oister pie And Coffe And Tea to be shore. Now I Must tel you What other preserves that I have. I have peaches And citrons And Sweet Aples, Crab Aples Jelley And Tomatoes And Mince And pairs and Aple Butter. And now I will Tel you of the Rest of My Winter Suplies. I have A plentey of Butter And Milk And a Thousand poundes of Salman And plentey Cabage And Turnips And A Bout A Hundred and Fiftey Bushel of potatoes And plentey of dried fruits—Aples and Black Buryes the Best that I evr saw. . . . I never Saw Sutch Black Buryes And Ras Bryes As There Is in this Countrey in All My Life Time. . . . O yes I Have plentey Shougar Laid in For Winter This Year Two, And Salt. (NEW YEAR'S DAY, NO YEAR, PROBABLY 1852)

They might be far from home, but they were gathering in the rewards of hard work and good farmland.

But though her table was laden with food, Abigail kept seeing the empty places of her missing children. "How I Did Wish you Had Bin There. Your Places Ware Set. . . . All of My Children Ware Here Except you—All That Are A living." Those who had died were never far from her mind.

John Biles, now formally betrothed, became a regular correspondent to his soon-to-be-in-laws in Illinois. He urged them:

> If you should come you would relieve a heavy weight of trouble & grief from your affectionate mother-in-law. This I know by experience. There is not hardly an hour but what your mother speaks of your welfare and oft times tears flow in streams down her warm cheek. (COLUMBIA CITY, 1851)

And Rachel wrote to her older sister:

> I imagine your Neat white [plastered] rooms and your Neat kitchen and your nice looking stove and all your bright Things and that dark eyed man reading a newspaper at the table. . . . I should like very much to see my brother-in-law. I should Much like to see that pretty little woman that you are talking About for I expect she is some Pumkin. . . . When I write I realy dont think I am a writing to old people . . . the father and mother of four dear children.
>
> (NO MONTH, 1852)

Curiously, "home" still seemed to be back in Illinois where family was gathered around: "Your nice looking stove and all your bright Things and [Michael] reading a newspaper at the table." On the frontier, out of "the States," they had become vulnerable. Hiram and Charles were dead and they were somehow naked in their prosperity. Rachel shrugged off such thoughts. Her wedding was set for April of 1852.

The winter was a time for poring over the pattern books that came from England by steamer to San Francisco and then up to Vancouver. "In this letter I will enclose some of My white Matrimonial Robe but I haint Maryed yet. . . . I can't send you any of the flowerd part in the same letter but the flowerd part is around the botom of my dress. All Flowerd in white up as high as the waist Almost. . . . The waist part is Not flowerd just plain." (JANUARY 24, 1852) Rachel mentioned in passing that a ship had been wrecked on the Columbia River with the loss of forty-two lives, but her trousseau was more interesting.

The wedding party was to be held "at the residence of George Malick near Columbia City Clark County Oregon Territory. Hurah for your slippers. . . . If your foot is a little two large for them just cut a little piece off your toes and heels." (MARCH 5, 1852) Rachel promised to send "wedding tickets" to all the family in Illinois who would come.

On the wedding day, forty guests—such a large party—filled the Malick house. It was a joyful reception. The *Columbia City Spectator* noted, "At Columbia City Oregon on Sunday April the 4th 1852 by John Allman Esq. Probate Judge of Clark County Oregon Mr. John Denormandie Biles late of Bucks County Pennsylvania to Miss Rachel Henrietta Daughter of George M. Malick Esq of Northumberland County Pennsylvania." To the news of the marriage the newspaper added a poem:

Oh Happy Swain Oh happy bride
Two hearts by sweetest Love Allied
Youth, love and beauty joind in one
Make heaven itself on earth begun!

Rachel was exuberant. "I am Maryed to Mr. John D. Biles," she wrote, and "everybody says we were the Pretyest Couple They ever saw. . . . I will enclose a small piece of . . . my wedding cake. We had all kinds of cakes and roasts and different kinds of preserves and pies and pickles and all kinds of things." The future was unlimited. "Mr Biles is agoing soon to build a house on this claim for us to live in. We are all very hapy Making [a] garden at present. . . . Everything is agrowing very nicely." (APRIL 23, 1852)

This was happiness. You could feel it in the air. Rachel was a buoyant seventeen-year-old bride: "Mr. Biles and Me Had a Nice ride on horse back last Sunday about 8 Miles from Hear to see a friend of Mine." She asked for flower seeds and photographs and sent evidence of her new life. (APRIL 23, 1852) In June she wrote of fashion—frontier dresses and bonnets. "I shall be pleased to send you the patrns of every new thing that Comes in fashion such as wearing aparal. . . . I have got me some peach Cambric of which I am making a sun bonet . . . and a small peace of dark Calico for aprons." (JUNE 28, 1852) John Biles took his new post as son-in-law with high seriousness, writing to Michael and Mary Ann and urging them to bring the family together again:

> One thing I deeply regret is that I did not observe in your letter one word concerning your mind for emigrateing to Oregon. . . . I am unacquainted with the land route yet I believe a man is well paid for his trouble if he arives here in good health. No doubt the journey is a great one to surmount [but] Oregon is still progressing with rapture.

John Biles had a way with words.

> Crops in general looks exceedingly well. . . . Father & I have very near all the crop in. I have been very busy all winter repairing wagons. . . . I intend to commence building a new house for my "frow" and self. I have a beautiful place selected for my house . . . surrounded with a beautiful grove of small live Oak. (MAY 23, 1852)

He wrote of skirmishes with the Indians. Six men of the artillery "came on the Indians unawares [and] the indians . . . discharged about sixty arrows and four struck the Sergant in command. . . . Two companys of Dragoons heard the report of the gun and immediately run across the point of land and came upon the Indians and without any hesitation began to slaughter them & killed every Indian on the ground, about four hundred in all." (MAY 23, 1852) The account sounded the grand exaggerations of most Indian encounters, but John also balanced the excitement of frontier life with assurances that danger was more than two hundred miles to the north. Rachel's postscript drew accounts of Indian attacks into a family scale: "Alas How often is the case of poor young men dying far from their homes and relations." They were Hiram and Charles and all the other brothers who died unexpectedly. Between news of ribbons and radishes, parsley and celery seeds, there was the memory of two brothers dead.

Abigail watched the crystalline light of September making the morning leaves transparently green. She watched Rachel's happy face, and the addition of John Biles to the family was like having Charles and Hiram back again. Life was seasons. Abigail was planting and repairing what had been lost in the dark days of their arrival.

The letters flew between Oregon Territory and Illinois. Rachel reassured her sister, "You think Papa has forgotten you Becaus he has not writen so long but you are mistaken. For if you knew how much he talks of you and wants to see you in the countrey you would not think he has forgotten. You know he is very neglecting about writing and he thinks as he can hear from you it is no use for him to write." George's reticence reflected a masculine discomfort with letter writing. "I would be glad to see you hear and I know you would be Plest with the country. . . . The climet is plesent sumer and winter. All the winter we have seen fore three years was but a very few freces, sometimes a little snow and it melts as fast as it falls. Never cold enuf to frece the ground much. . . . I do not know what more to say to you. Mamey sade all. I remane your father until death george Malick." (UNDATED, PROBABLY NOVEMBER 1852)

Through most of 1852 it was Rachel who wrote the letters, a young matron eager to share her new life. "We have had a very fine circus held here at Columbia City held for three knights. . . . Mr. Biles took me thursday knight. It was 2 dollars a person. . . . The emigrants are coming on very thick and fast. The people says the streets in portland and Oregon City are crowded with them as much as any streets in the city of St. Louis." (OCTOBER 2, 1852)

In October the newly married couple moved into their own house.

> We are now living by ourselves. We moved in our new house last wednesday. We have everything fixed very nice. . . . My husband . . . is very kind to me in every respect. . . . We have plenty to eat, drink and wear and every thing in pleanty. . . . [We are] right across the field from fathers. . . . The next day after I moved I had a maryed lady and a young ladey in to see me. We have a very nice new cooking stove and a very nice new bedstead and a nice new cuphord and very nice glass wear and queens wear [queen's ware, glazed earthenware imported from England] of every kind. (OCTOBER 30, 1852)

In November Rachel was four months pregnant. "I [have been] quite unwell at this time [and] I have a young girl a living with me and that come through the fall." (DECEMBER 19, 1852) Biles was a generous husband to hire a farm girl to help Rachel with the chores in her first pregnancy. There were no other children to care for, but he wanted her to have all the comfort he could provide. He reassured his young wife and Illinois relatives, "I have one of the best companions in existence, one whose sight is always pleasing, one who comforts me in every way, one who's actions and ways are far above reproach. . . . Rachel is all my comfort & joy around my home." (JANUARY 19, 1853) Among farm people little given to praise, his words were sheer extravagance. In response to her husband's tribute, Rachel added, "Mr. Biles is a very excellent provider. I would not wish a beter and then he is so very kind to me. I wish you could see him. [Then] you could examine [him] for yourself." (UNDATED LETTER)

When Rachel was feeling unwell, Abigail took back the writing of the letters. She provided a tougher appraisal of their condition and their prospects. The gold rush brought cholera across the nation, the dread disease sweeping through the wagon trains. Among the emigrants coming through in the early winter many were ravaged and dying. "A grate meney died this yeare And A grate meney since their Arrival in oregon." John Biles wrote the same thing: "Emigrants are still coming in & great Distress still prevails among them. The major part of them are destitute of provisions & in fact everything else some half naked. The inhabitants of Oregon are doing all in their Power for their relief. It is said that one half of those that did reach this Place have died soon after arriving." (NOVEMBER 8, 1852) No one was urging the Albrights to come west any more. It was a terrible thing to die on the open road, the only grave marker a pile of rocks, coyote and wolf waiting to dig up the corpse.

Crops were having only mixed success. "First planting was nearley All drowned in the spring And the next planting did not Do so wel," wrote Abigail. "We had nearley every thing drowned out in the spring ocasioned by the unusal Rise of the columbia river. [But] we made a bout A hundred dollars that we have in gold and silver."

Abigail reported that "Johney D. Biles is A doing very well. He has worked for the Quarter Master And got five dollars a Day. He worked two Weeks And got the Cash at Reparing Wagones and he has Made Agreate deal of Money this Sommer A re paring carriages and Waggones and Carts and Making other things for he is very Handey." (NOVEMBER 8, 1852) John Biles added, "I am about to build a shop & expect to have it finished in about two weeks."

Abigail admired nothing so much as industry, and the more she applauded Biles's achievements, the more she saw that their new home was working changes in her youngest son, Peter Shindel: "He is a very rued boy And I Cannot do eney thing with him." Since they had come to Oregon Territory, Shin had grown harder to handle. He spent long days at the fort with the soldiers, who raced horses and gambled when there was nothing else to do. At fourteen he was not much younger than the raw recruits, and Abigail had misgivings about his future. "Perhaps when he gets older And knows better he will do better." But she could not ignore Shindel's behavior, and a tug-of-war between mother and son was beginning in earnest.

Ironically, Fort Vancouver, whose protection they clung to when they arrived, drew away the youngest children one by one, first Shin, and later even the girls, Jane and Susan. Abigail called them her "frontier children," and they were certainly different from Mary Ann and Charles and Hiram and Rachel, raised in Pennsylvania and in Illinois. But now Hiram and Charles were dead. And Shin was balking at being kept on the farm. He ran off to the company of other young men to escape hearing his mother eternally comparing him with his dead—and more virtuous—brothers.

I have had so Mutch trouble Aloosing Hiram and Charles that it has Al most put Me be side my self. Oh there is non no not one who knows what trouble I endure when I think of them. (UNDATED LETTER, STARTED BY GEORGE MALICK AND COMPLETED BY ABIGAIL)

With John Biles out of the house, there were only one old man and one young boy to work the claim, to haul the wood, to care for the animals, to turn the land, to plant and harvest, to repair and to build. And Abigail could be harsh and unrelenting where Shindel was concerned. "Shindel groes very fast. He will soon be a Man, but I am mutch afraid he never [will] be as good a boy as Hiram and Charles." (NOVEMBER 8, 1852)

To cover Shindel's refusal to help with the farm, George and Abigail hired Indians and grudgingly saw every dollar they had to pay out as evidence of their son's defection. "We have Indians to work for us," Abigail wrote. "Both women and men. There is two here now A beging for work. We have them A diging potatoes." (NOVEMBER 8, 1852)

Day by day, the letters were written. Rachel wrote, "They have changed the name of oregon territory to washington territory. This side of the Columbia river is washington territory and the other side of the river is oregon territory." (FEBRUARY 25, 1853) Rachel was moving into social circles and attending "grand quiltens" with as many as "15 ladeys" attending. She and Biles were living like "the highest grandees."

Letters became a way of life. They wrote about everything. Abigail had a sick headache, Mary Ann a toothache, and Nancy a "foul stumach." Susan "received a letter and she liked to jump over the Moon for Joy." They sent each other swatches of new dresses and bonnets, slices of cake, photographs, coins, local newspapers from Oregon and Pennsylvania. Abigail wrote about the new clothes she bought for the girls: "A pare of Leather Shoes" for Jane that cost $1.25 and for Nancy Susan "two pare of sealskin Moroco." Prudent Abigail bought extravagant gifts for Susan—another pair of shoes of "California gold leaf" for summer. "I went to town to get her A pair of Leather Shows and so I saw them too. And I thought she never had eney sutch shoes As them And I thought they would plees her." (MARCH 20, 1853) Susan was eight years old, Abigail's baby.

All of them were feeling expansive.

we have sowed Spring wheat and oats and onion seed and Made a garden and Put out lettus sead and Cabage sead and Radish seed. [And] Oyes Papa wantes Me to tel you that we have bought a Littl Adishon to our stock. . . . The first one [a] hors we paid seventeen dollars and Two cows for fiftey dollars Apeice and one hog we paid twentey dollars and for thre hogs we gave ten dollars and for two hogs we gave five dollars Apeice. And in Adishon to our house hold furniture we have got A new Clock. It cost 15 dollars. And Avery handsom looking glas to set on a beaurough or on a Table and it Caust fourteen dollars and Another that Caust thre dollars. Those things we bought Within this year or within A yeare and ahalf. A dosen Chairs they Cost seven dollars. (MARCH 20, 1853)

Out there on the Pacific frontier, Abigail was exchanging pioneer scarcity for middle-class accumulation. Letters describe a proliferation of goods—clothing, and rings, and shoes, and dishes, and beds, and store-bought chairs, and a bureau. They had a porch clear around the house and a fine kitchen. They had bounty that was solid and tangible. Making things, buying things, growing things, the Malicks were becoming a prosperous middle-class family.

Jane and Nancy Susan were kept in school, learning reading, writing, and geography. Jane wrote that the schoolteacher "sayed that nobody Can read your bad writing." (JANUARY 9, 1853) Nine-year-old Susan told the older sister she remembered less and less clearly that she could "Milk a grate big American Cow." (MAY 18, 1853)

Rachel continued to urge the Albrights to come west. "I am very anxious to see you all again. . . . You ought to make haste and come for you know life is precious. I know not what day nor what Hour our aged Parents are called away to their eternal home so you ought to make haste so as to make their last days Happy." And John Biles added, "You don't know how bad we want to see you. *Come, come, come* you will find in me an affectionate Brother." (FEBRUARY 25, 1853)

The real news came on March 10, when Rachel gave birth to a new son, Charles Esmond Biles, one of the "prettiest boys in existence." Rachel wrote to her sister:

There is no baby as good as little Charley. . . . We are all vaccinated and the little babe has a very sore arm now. They vaccinated when the babe was 1 weeke old. He weighed onley 7 pounds. He has blue eyes and light hair. . . . I will put a little of it in this letter so you and the children can see it. The spring is delitful. All the flouers are springing every where and the Birds are singing swetely. (APRIL 3, 1853)

The family's ultimate possession was Rachel's son, the first frontier grandchild, joyously acclaimed in a family that had lost too many sons already. Abigail concluded, "Biles and Rachel are Both well And there love toy [too]."

In April 1853, Mount St. Helens erupted. The newspapers carried accounts of that rare phenomenon, but nothing in the letters remarked on the great event less than a hundred miles away. Family absorbed all their attention. Rachel and Biles attended the "grand theatre" in Columbia City. And Rachel sent a swatch of satin from Charley's bonnet. John Biles became a justice of the peace. (MAY 4, 1853)

Letters went back and forth, an astonishing number of letters, considering that the mails were irregular and the time for writing brief. Letters told that Little Charley was cutting his first teeth. Abigail sent gifts to her grandchildren in Illinois and worried they would not arrive safely. "I would send you A twenty dollar gold peice if I could but know that it would be safe. . . . But it is two heavey to send in a letter." She sent five-dollar gold pieces and apologized that her gifts were so small. (APRIL 3, 1853) There were endless requests for seeds to make the garden in Oregon more like gardens in Illinois. Abigail asked for "cantelope seades," and "muskmellone, greap, cabage, parcely, and flour seades." "I want you to send som good redish An Lettus and shougar peas and Cabag seades and bunch peas and enney sort of seades you have. . . . I am Agoing to Get som seades sent from pennsylvania. . . . People come here from All directions to se My garden for they say They never Saw sutch Anice Garden as I had." (JUNE 26, 1853)

Letters were filled with news about crops and livestock and the price of wheat. Potatoes, chickens, hens, and calves filled the farm with work and life and profit.

A neighbor's wedding kept Abigail busy with preparations and brought unexpected income. The neighbor, "not a married man," had a

> ladey A Keeping house for him. . . . She was Agoing to get maried to a gentle Man in Port land and [her employer] provided everything that he could for her Weding. He sent A barrel of flour And forty pounds of Coffee and rice and . . . shoger as white as snow and brown Shougar and salt and dride Apples And a bushel of gren Apples and a box of sperm Candels and pepper and Alspice and soap and salortis [saleratus, or baking soda] and nut meges and ginger and sinamon Soda and . . . raisens And All kindes of thinges too

[numerous] to mention. And four large hams and two piges—very fat ones—And two salmon too. . . . And after the Weding she went Away and All the thinges was left for us. And gues what I got for Cooking her Weding soupper, why fiftey dollars. And after All was over, her husband Came to Me at the milk house And gave Me A ten dollar gold peice and said Mrs. malick you have had A good deal of trouble And I want to give you a present. I want you to buy something to remember Me by. [And there was even more.] She for her preasents gave Me A pare of nice gator Boots which I have on now and Calico for two dresses for My self And each of the little girles. A dress A peice And A half dosen of chairs and A half dosen of Stone China tea Cups. And I made her weding dress And her second day dress for five dollars Apeice which I will send you A peice in this letter . . . so that you Can se it.

(APRIL 3, 1853)

Mary Ann (Malick) Albright, the eldest daughter of George and Abigail Malick, raised eight children, six of whom lived to maturity. Family names—Ann, Homer, Esther Abigail, Rachel Jane, Charles, and George—recur in both families.

Letters carried photographs from John Biles's sister and brother in Pennsylvania, from the Albrights in Illinois, and from the Malicks in Washington Territory. Always there was the powerful need to put the family back together, to put their lives into harmony, and to bridge the gulf of separation. There was nothing in the whole world so exciting as the arrival of mail from home. Abigail wrote that she had been in bed when John Biles "cam to the Doar And Caled Mama Mama I have got a Letter. . . . I Arose Amidately out of Bed and dresed My self and Let him in And Lited a Candel And sat down And open it And found some greape seades in it and some sea shell squash seades in It." (MARCH 20, 1853)

In September 1853, war to the north with the Rogue River Indians was vaguely unsettling to residents.

Michael Albright was the eldest son of Jacob Albright, who left Kentucky in 1829 because he opposed slavery. Strong abolitionists, the Albrights joined the Republican party in 1856, and two sons fought with the Union Army.

> I was Out Atending to My soap and I got very wet. . . . I have not had to work very hard this sommer. Since spring I have had an Indian girl Aliveing With Me . . . which took A good deal of hard work off of me but She is gone home now. Her sister Was taken With the small pox And she was oblegged to go home to take care of her. And so I told her [not] to dare to Come here untill her sister would get perfectly Well or die. . . . The Indians Are very good and kind here And they Would Not do enney thing to the Americans here. But the Rogue River Indians are At War with the Americans And the Miners, but that is three hundred Miles from here. (SEPTEMBER 28, 1853)

Sometimes, letters touched subjects even more sensitive than war, and then the sentences become hard to fathom. Abigail wrote that she wanted to send Mary Ann a five-dollar gold piece, wrapped in two pieces of dress cloth, but

> I do not Want your father to know enney thing About it As it is not his Monney. You know that I alwais hav a little money at My own Command And if he should know it he mite scold Me and perhapse he would not but it will not hirt him And he kneed not know enny thing About [it]. . . . Mary Ann you Alwais was A very good girl to me and never got half so Mutch from home As rachel and you diserve As Mutch As her. I do not begrudge rachel enney thing . . . but we was not Able to give you enney More Wen you Married than we did. (SEPTEMBER 28, 1853)

This was curious information to put into a letter that was not private. Letters were always read by an assortment of people, both family and friends, but Abigail was trying to say something to her daughter alone, something about old feelings of guilt because a long time ago Mary Ann had not received her proper marriage portion. Farm ledgers or children, Abigail had a powerful need to balance the record, and here she was stumbling over an old transaction that was unconcluded or concluded unfairly.

She was also telling Mary Ann, as one woman to another, something of her life married to George. She kept secrets from him—"I do not Want your father to know enney thing About it." Her troubles with George's temper were mixed with her concern for Shindel.

> As for Shindel I do not know wot he will Make. I am Afraid not Mutch. . . . He is so wild. . . . Perhaps when he groes up And gets good Learning he will Learn that he Aught to Mind his Father And his Mother better. His father

> treats him A good deal like he youst to hiram so that he is often A good deal discouraged. Poor hiram, he never sene Meney good days And I often tel his father so. And god knew what Was for the best And took him timley away. . . . Perhaps it will go so with shindle for he has never bin very healthe And Not Able to work very hard. And I Alwais would go to his Asistance until I can not do it No longer when his father would give him hard work to do for fear his father would scold him. And I Never Could bare Scolding . . . but the older your father gets the More he likes to scold if everything dose not pleas him. And it is im posibel to pleas him so we do the best we Can And let him scold. But if papa knew that I wrote this he would be very Angry with me but it is the truth. . . . You know how he is as well as I do and I have not Mutch Com Fourt with him but he is the father of All My Children And so it is and I have to Beare it. (NOVEMBER 1, 1853)

"I have not Mutch Com Fourt with him." No wonder Abigail wanted Rachel to have her love match. A woman had a right to a loving husband if she could find one. George was a hard man to live with, a prickly man with a short temper. But, "he is the father of All My Children." In the eyes of the church and the community George was a good provider and a good Christian, but Abigail assessed her marriage with sober realism. Distance made it easier to confess intimate truths. She would never have said such things to Mary Ann—or to anyone—face to face, and even in letters she was groping her way.

> I wish you Could sit down in your fathers House for My Dear you Never sat down in your fathers house my dear. But Now if you was to Come now you Could sit in your father's hous And no one to hender you from it. And you would [have] as good A right As enney other person to sit down in there Father's house. (JUNE 26, 1853)

Had George opposed Mary Ann's marriage? Was that the reason Michael would not bring his family—Abigail's daughter and her grandchildren—out to Washington Territory? Would she never see them again because of some long-held hurt or angry words? Did all her pleadings and encouragements and proofs of prosperity founder on old grudges and harsh words said long ago? Out in Washington Territory, where according to the Donation Law, half of their stake was in Abigail's name, things were different than they had been in Illinois. It was still "your father's house," but now no one could "hender you from it." (JUNE 26, 1853)

In the simplest of letters lay feelings shut up in bent phrases and shortened allusions. Abigail assured Mary Ann, "I have not forgot you nor never Can for get My Children. A Mother cannot forget her children."

At the end of the summer of 1853, John Biles joined a surveying expedition and would be away for four months—a long time to leave Rachel alone. Little Charley was cutting his first teeth. "He is not really well all the time. You know it makes children very cross when they are teething. He can sit alone and tryes to creepe." (AUGUST 28, 1853) Photographs were exchanged, and more photographs were asked for, from the Albrights, from old friends in Tazewell County, "Mrs. Lindsey's people," and from the Judeys.

In October Rachel complained that she was alone, a "grass widow": "It haint as much fun as I thought it would be all though I haint the onley one about here. There is more than one that there husbands has gone on the expedition. . . . I guess you are tired a hearing about grass widows." Rachel went to the theater to while away the time: "It is very amusing. They have good musick. The infaintry brass band plays in the theatre whenever there is one. Every wednesday knight they act."

But when the steamer carrying the mail came into the harbor, the very audiences ran out into the streets.

> Last Tuesday night when [the ship] came rolling in the peopel were all in the theatre and as soon as she fired the cannon it roused all the people out of the theatre and they all charged out and the actors had to stop their peices on the stage until some of them came back. . . . Out of a hundred they had no more than a dosen left in the theatre. (OCTOBER 24, 1853)

Even the stage was no match for the mail steamer and letters from home—words awkwardly scrawled on a page with the most ordinary news, half-spelled sentences that made home seem closer: "The steemer that youst to fire a Cannon when it youst to Com with the Mail from the states. . . . We Alwais Will know When the Mail is A Coming for . . . we Can hear that boat As mutch as ten Miles off And we Can sea her A grate wais down the river if it is day Light. . . . We know the sound of her from enney other Boat." (DECEMBER 26, 1853) Rachel closed her letter with a bit of doggerel, deeply felt: "As the ship on the sea, think of think oh think of me."

And she took comfort in her baby. "My Boy grows very much and he is a fine Boy and he is a great pet hear being the onley little babe in the famely." She waited with increasing impatience for Biles's return: "I bought the other day a fine oil that flowd very nice for our floor and a great many nice things to welcome his return comfortabley and also myself a brown Meerino dress and I will put up a peice of it in this letter." (OCTOBER 10, 1853) The weeks wound slowly on. Their land was fertile. The climate was mild. Prosperity was all around them.

In November 1853, there was news that Mary Ann and Michael welcomed the birth of a new baby daughter. "The Mail Came in Last night At Twelve oClock Abaring The strong News That you had a young Daughter," wrote Abigail. She agreed that "you Don Wisley by not Letting Me know enney thing About it before for I should have bin so oneasey that I should not sleep." "Oho My Dear Mary Ann . . . when [you] get Write sick it is oh Mother Mother. If I could onley se you it would All be right but that Never will be My Dear Mary Ann." (NOVEMBER 1, 1853) Abigail thought of the new grandchild she would never hold in her arms.

When John Biles returned from his expedition Abigail described his homecoming. "And I tel you there was Joy when he Come. . . . Rachel fretid A great deal for him."

> It was two oclock when he Come home and he Came rite over to see us. . . . He had Come home in an open bote Al the way from the Caskades thru the dredfulist Rain. It Raind As hard as it could All day and night And was As wet As water. And when he Came on the pourch he Cald Ma Ma Are you Asleep. Biles has come. Dont you want to see Biles. I want to seyou. Wont you get up and let Me in. I told him to push open the dor. And he Came in And I told him to Come to me. . . . I put my arm A Round his neck And puld him to Me. He was gone four months And you know that is a long time for one to begone out of our familey . . . since our Boys Are no more. . . . When Hiram youst to go to Chicago And was not at hom at three or four oclock we ware oneasey About him. And if Charles woud begone onley one day we ware Alwais oneasy. . . . But when he went to California it was Along time that we . . . could not write to him Which made us very oneasey. And Biles seemes so Mutch Like one of our Children. He has lived so long with us
>
> (NOVEMBER 26, 1853)

It was all wrapped up together, the son you hugged for joy and the son you would never hug again. Families clung to each other in a big, almost empty, land.

And even as Abigail wrote, she wondered if distance—and time—had changed them. It was five years since they had been together.

> When I sit down to write I always think that I cannot Write half enough. . . . Per haps I weary you with what I do write. Perhaps you do Not Care About what I do write. . . . I am A get ing old And have had so Mutch trouble A bout Loosing yur brothers and other things that it often seams As tho I had not half the sense enney More. But it is As it is And it Cannot be helped. (DECEMBER 26, 1853)

Back in Illinois Michael's mother died, and even as Abigail sent her condolences, she seized the chance to draw them out to Washington Territory. She would be a mother to Michael: "I wish I had A Chance to be A Mother in her sted." But with that wonderful clarity of hers, she knew that while "one May think A greate deal of there Mother in Law . . . there is none like their one Mother to a child." She tried, though: "Now Michael, I think you would better get ready and Come out here and Live As Long with Me or us As Mary Ann has Lived with your people." (NOVEMBER 26, 1853)

George was persuaded to put down a few words to his daughter and son-in-law: "I wish I could see you here. . . . You can see that I am allife yet. My love to all of yore deer children. . . . George Malick." Abigail added that George "Cannot hardly sea to write enney more. . . . We are very buisey Afatning our hogs." (DECEMBER 26, 1853)

George was also hauling a hundred cords of wood to a steamboat for six dollars a cord. It was heavy work, but it added cash to the household. Abigail added, "We have a very Nice young Man A bording With us And he is Acuting timber in our timber for Another Man and yur Father Hauls that for two dollars A Cord. . . . We are . . . All as one with Indian Tribes in Oregon." (MARCH 1, 1854)

Biles was a dutiful correspondent. He wrote that he had been away on "meterological business" for five months and twenty-four days, but had been paid $696 and board and travel as well. He was taking his wages and "building a large wagon & carpenter shop. . . . It is raining like blue blazes," and had been raining straight through Christmas and New Year's. His son, he modestly confessed, was "one of the prettiest boys I ever saw." (JANUARY 8, 1854)

At the end of January, John Biles was elected to the first legislative assembly in Washington Territory. Rachel wrote that "he got more votes than aney other man on the ticket . . . and so he gained it. He has to start now for Puget Sound on the 19th of this month . . . to go to the house of representatives to make law for this territory." (FEBRUARY 12, 1854) The territorial legislature would meet in Olympia, the new capital to the north. "I will have to lose my old man for a short wile again," Rachel moaned. But she was proud of her husband and she was proud of the status she was acquiring as his wife. "I have a good husband, one that supplies my every want and wish as far as possible." Rachel and John were starting to look like a middle-class couple, a step up from their rural beginnings.

The younger children were back in school. Abigail was proud of the girls—and critical of Shindel.

> They lern very fast. They go to school to Asoldier And he is Avery good teacher. Jane larnes Arithmatic And readeing And writeing And geography and grammar. She stands at the head of the school she does, And susan learnes very fast two. Shindel Learnes fast but not so fast as Jane. He is to dumb ever to Learn Mutch. I am Afraid he wil not nevr Make Mutch of a scholler. Perhaps he May After A while but he has went to school so Mutch And is not a schollar yet. (MARCH 1, 1854)

Jane sent a book of Indian language, "one half Indian And one half in english."[11]

Nothing in Abigail's letters suggested she saw storm clouds gathering. She sent Jane and Susan to school at the fort, to "Asoldier [who] is Avery good teacher." But girls who were children in their mother's eyes were sexually provocative to young soldiers billeted far from home. Jane was fourteen and already the object of interest in a circle of young men known for their wild ways. All Abigail saw was that her outlay of money for school was having uncertain returns where Shin was concerned. He was coaxed to write to Mary Ann and Michael in Illinois. His short letters bespoke his own uncertainties: "Excuse mistakes and blots." (MARCH 13, 1854) Letters and book learning were not for him. Neither, for that matter, was work on the farm—or his mother's scolding.

In April, Biles was still away in Olympia, "making laws." He tried to secure a government post at home, and had letters from "lawyers and judges and assemblymen" petitioning that he be appointed a "survaior of customs" at Columbia City, but the post did not come through. Abigail and Nancy Susan stayed with Rachel, keeping her company while Biles was gone. "We hear the Indians haller every hour in the knight, passing the rode drunk. But we hant afrade of them. They do not come in the yeard." (APRIL 22, 1854) Jane wrote that there was no school in the winter, but the girls intended to return by early May. In the meantime, Jane planned on spending her birthday "over the river," "for you know that I have some acquaintance over there." (UNDATED)

Like Shindel, Jane was a headstrong child. She liked riding and fine dresses. Abigail tried to see that the proprieties were maintained—she had Rachel chaperone Jane, but that amounted only to providing an eighteen-year-old matron to a fourteen-year-old schoolgirl! Both girls were "geting Ready to go riding down on the plain on horse back. And Little Charles re Manes At home with Nancy Susan and Me." (APRIL 23, 1854)

Abigail loved to have her grandson by her side. She worked hard and tried to keep her children and her homestead in good order. She did not notice that Jane was already leaving the safe harbor of home.

But was their home ever a "safe harbor"? Even in their tranquil days, the family geography was extraordinarily extended. John Biles was in Olympia and his wife and son were in Columbia City (Vancouver). Shin was most often in town. The girls were in town or at home, depending on the school year. They couldn't seem to put themselves together very long in one place, and if briefly they found themselves together, they soon came apart again.

In spite of that, Abigail's dream was that they would live as one family. She was so sensitive to the lives of her distant children that even in the ebb and flow of letters she could sense when something was wrong back in Illinois: "I Wish that you Would write. . . . We are so oneasy About you. We Canot tel or imagin What is the Matter. I fear that Some Thing Serious is the Matter With Som of you that you Do not Want us to know About. . . . O Mary Ann Do Not Forget A Mother that Loves you so Much and Wantes to se you so Much My Dear Child. With tears in My eyes I write this." (MAY 5, 1854)

Abigail sent five gold quarters for each of her five grandchildren, but it was not the same as being with them: "Oho I wish I Could be there to se the Children. . . . If I onley Could se you All. If I had it All in My possession, but Alas that is not Fore Me. But perhaps if we Never meet on this earth . . . we Will Meet togeather in heven whare Children And parentes Meet to part No more. Oh that will be Joiful Joiful Joiful to Meet and part no more."

To calm her anxiety, Abigail wrote about small things. She bought some poplin and calico, to make summer dresses for Jane and Susan and herself, and promised to send samples "so you Can se what sort of Cloaths we ware in Oregon. . . . Your Father has as nice Cloathes As enney man both fine and Corse." Men's clothing was store-bought: "It is Cheaper to buy them Made up than to Buy the Cloath and Make them for We do not Make enney Cloath in this Country. And I am glad . . . for we Can buy it Cheper than Make it and . . . I have so Mutch elce to do." (MAY 5, 1854)

She was in good health, but "for fretting So Mutch About the Loss of your Brouthers . . . And you A being so far Away. Now Mary Ann and Michael Do by No meanes Do not forget to write. . . . For I do want to hear from you so bad." (MAY 5, 1854)

Three mail ships arrived and no letter came from Illinois, and this time Rachel took up the chain of letters. "Pap he has been very sick . . . in the stomache." Little Charley, who was toddling and talking, was not yet weaned: "He still nurses but I think I shall [wean him] before two much warm weather comes." (MAY 28, 1854)

John Biles added, "Father has for the last week been exceedingly ill. . . . [He has] a violent pain in his head and [is] sick in the stomache." "Old age & hard work has destroyed his once hardy constitution; his working days are about ended." As summer came on, the children pitched in to help and John wrote that Jane and Susan were working on the farm. "Jane is one of the best girls to work in existence—always ready & willing. Susan is not large enough to do much but what she can do does it willingly. Shindle is a good boy & does a great deal [but] is not very robust, rather delicate." (JULY 26, 1854) John was the family diplomat, schooled in legislative nuances. Shindel was his mother's despair, never more so than now, when George was ill.

When the mail finally arrived from Illinois in July it brought word from Mary Ann that her baby had been sick. Abigail wrote back, "I condole with it. I do Wish that you Ware here With your Familey." How could she help them so far away?

The Fourth of July 1854 was celebrated in Washington Territory with cannons firing throughout the day; in the evening there was a theatrical performance. "The family All went," except Abigail, who stayed at home with George.

In September George was still ill. Abigail took care of him and did his share of the chores. John Biles wrote:

> Mama . . . does a great amount of work. She has got a very beautiful garden this season, but [it] has cost her much hard labour. You know nobody can fix it to suit her taste and if she dont like the work of others in her garden why she undoes it & does it over herself. . . . Pap is not able to do any more work. . . . He is getting very feeble. (SEPTEMBER 4, 1854)

He wrote of Indians near Fort Boise, who attacked a company of emigrants and killed eight men and took women prisoners. "A company of artillery was immediately sent from this post to their relief." Rachel, in her turn, sent home a sample of Indian beadwork.

On September 24 a letter came with word that Mary Ann's baby was dead, and Rachel wrote, "the minete I heart the news I burst in a flood of tears and grief. . . . So the world goes—one minute in good health and the next in eturnity."

Three weeks later, George Malick had a stroke and died. Rachel wrote:

> We ware called a few evenings ago to Witness the death of our dear father who gave up all earthy toils an troubles off this world on the 18th morning at quarter past three o'clock. . . . Oh dear sister it is so hart rendering to think off. . . . He was taken sick on the 15th and was buryed on the 19th October. I was to methodist church and hearing a good sermon and then went to the church yard and viseted papas grave. . . . Mama takes it very hard and so does the children. Although mama is pretty well considering pa's death, . . . she is very frail and so we doo all that we can to lighten her wearied hart. . . . [Ma] will send some of our morning dresses and some of his shroud. He was struck with the Palsey. One whole side was numb and useless. . . . There were about 2 Hundred people in atendance to the burying. He was buryed with every respect. (OCTOBER 29, 1854)

Death took the eldest and youngest. Separated by a thousand miles, the families were living the same griefs.

But there was hardly time to stop, as life renewed itself. In November Rachel was pregnant again, and John Biles wrote to his sister- and brother-in-law in Illinois that they were all well, "with the acception of Rachel who has been very ill. . . . Rachel is at present at Mothers where all care & attention is paid her. . . . I am also at mothers now. I am building a new Chimney for her and laying a new floor in her house." And word had come that Mary Ann and Michael "had been blessed again with another fine Boy." (NOVEMBER 24, 1854) Biles did not mention that Mary Ann would have buried one child only a few short weeks before giving birth to a new son. He did chide them for not "guess[ing] accurately when I said Rachel was 'tolerable well.' " That allusion, in the language of letters, was the closest a husband would come to the news of his wife's new pregnancy. It was Thanksgiving time in Illinois and in Washington Territory.

In December 1854, Abigail wrote about Rachel:

> I have had Rachel here for three Weeks sick And Litle Charles both sick. . . . All sick At the same time and I hardley knew What to do. I thought We never would get over having sick People. And gest About three Weakes be fore your Father had died and I thought that Rachel would die too. (DECEMBER 10, 1854)

The girls were back at school, boarding away from home. "I shall be very Loansom," Abigail wrote. "They have went one Weak to school Alreadey And I Mean to send them All the time that I can for I can get them Schooled for four dollars A year. That is My School tax." She meant her frontier children to be educated. Her Illinois children had been—Charles, Hiram, Mary Ann, and Rachel had all gone to school. But these frontier children were harder to handle, and George, the disciplinarian, was dead.

Abigail also had her hands full paying off bills: "I do wish to make our funarel expenses And your fathers docter Bill With out tuching the real estate. The expenses Are very great in Sutch Cases in the Country, Althou I paid the doctor bill And his Cofin." (DECEMBER 10, 1854)

George left no written will, and the law required that Abigail appear before the court and petition to be appointed administratrix of his estate. Then the property would be divided and each child would receive a share: "Your Fathers Half Can be sold and then the Children wil get A good deal for this Land [which] wil Bring A great deal of Monney, but the Law provides A half section to the wife in her own write." She also receives a portion equal to the children's, as "one of the Hairs." (DECEMBER 10, 1854) There were legalities to be settled and matters to be arranged. But because the territory had not been surveyed, no land could be "donated" to homesteaders, and no one yet had clear title to a claim.

Rachel wrote about Christmas. None of them lost their astonishment at mild weather at winter holidays. "Mama had as Prety a mess of salad on christmas day as ever I saw any time in sumer." She wrote also of her pregnancy: "I have get prety stout again. . . . I had 2 doctors when I was sick. They did not expect me to live. . . . I have a very good girl a staying with me this winter to help me with my work." There was no clear sign of malady, only "billiousness off the stomache," a common enough complaint of pregnant women. But there had been two doctors called, and in Abigail's words, "I thought she almost died." Rachel commented only that Little Charley was "as smart as you pleas." (JANUARY 7, 1855)

Susan wrote to her "Honord Sister" in Illinois, "I am now at school whar I learn to Read and spell and study Arithmetic and write & we air very lonesome since Pa dide. . . . Thank god mother is spard." And then, with a child's quick interest in excitement, she added, "a man kild a kougar [and] an officer off the artillery rigament shot a large catamount [cougar or lynx]." Life near the fort was full of surprises, and certainly it was better than chores at home. (FEBRUARY 7, 1855)

John Biles reported:

> Mother has been appointed Administratrix on Fathers Estate. There is not one person out of a hndred that has left an estate in a better condition than our Departed parent. The inventory has been made out and in the course of two days will have the personal estate appraised. Our Executive & Administrator Law is remarkably Liberal to the widow, Gives to her one yoke of oxen or Horses, two cows, & one cow to every two in the family two hogs. All House hold Furnature, Beds, Bedding, waring apparral, All farming implements & 6 Months provisions for herself & family and one half of the remaining property. (FEBRUARY 18, 1855)

In due time Biles was appointed guardian of "persons & property of Shindle, Jane & Susan. So you see the settling up & the taking care of the minors property are in the hands of the family and you may be sure it will be done correct." If John Biles had not been part of the family, the court could have appointed a male member of the community—a stranger—as guardian for the younger children. They were lucky Biles was there. At twenty-seven, he was the titular head of the Malick family in Washington Territory.

Abigail instinctively turned toward what gave her strength—the land. The passionate renewal of life did not escape her eyes. She wrote about the spring, "The young leaves Are Aputing out now And the goos burye leaves Are All out, As large As any i have sene." On the sixth of March 1855, Abigail notes, "This is my birth Day and I am 54 years old this day. Oho I wish that you Could have Bin here this day. We have gust eat Dinner and . . . the girles Cooket it. And they Woried Me very Mutch that they Must Cook Me A birth day Dinner so they got At it and Cooked A splended Dinner for my birth day. It is the first Birth Day Dinner that I ever had Cooct for Me on My Birth Day." It was the first dinner that she had sat down to as a guest in her home: "My Children All respect me very Mutch since Fathers Death and they Are All very good to Me Accept [Shindel]. He will not Mind Me Atall. I do not know what to do with Him." (MARCH 6, 1855)

There was so much to do on the farm. The girls did what they could, but it was Shin she needed, and he would not mind her. That was that.

Jane and Susan dutifully wrote to the Albrights in April, and Rachel described a late spring storm where "the hail . . . knocked off a great many peach blossoms." She wrote that "Charley is a fine Boy," but her letter was shorter, less buoyant than usual. (APRIL 1, 1855)

Abigail wrote a long, newsy letter in June, full of her usual gossip. The schoolhouse had been completed, she reported: "It is a butiful school house And I had to help to build It. It was built by the District. I had to pay 10 dollars And A quarter for my share. It Cost 3 hundred dollars." Next to a church a schoolhouse was the most perfect image of home the settlers carried in their minds, and emigrants reproduced the New England schoolhouse clear across the nation. It signified a stable community, a safe place to make a home.

"To Morrow I send the two Little Girls to Mr. Silus Curtis. He is to be the teacher, the first that teaches in the new school house. The [girls] Are hile [highly] delighted." The old teacher was not popular, and Abigail wrote that she was glad the community decided not to rehire him. Shindel flatly refused to go to school no matter who presided. "He thinks it woud be to Confining for him," wrote Abigail. "He would rather lounge About And not work. . . . I have told him that I would not Cloath him enney If he will not work or go to school." (JUNE 10, 1855)

The Indians in the region had begun to threaten emigrants, and soldiers were patrolling the roads. "There are Agreat Menney soldiers gone out on the emagrant Road to protect the emagrants to this countrey from the States. . . . The Indians . . . say no More people [shall] Cros there

Country enney More And that if there is [more who] wil come to orregon and washington they will kill All the Bostons—that is Al the Americans." The governor went out to make a treaty with the Snake tribe, but, Abigail wrote, "if they will not treate with him they will have war" and then the Americans would "kill them All [the Indians] so that they cannot kill No More Americans As they travel to this Country. And that would be the best way."

In the meantime, "Rachel Henrietta is here now. She has something Like the Aigue but I think that After she getes over her other trouble she wil get rite well. She has a terebel time . . . this time this far but I hop she will be better soon." (JUNE 10, 1855)

Rachel was often sick, feverish, attended intermittently by doctors, by Abigail, relieved of her household chores by the young girl who had come to live with her. But pregnancy was too commonplace to rouse concern. Abigail took charge of Little Charley, who helped her feed the chickens and was with her "nearly all the time."

Then suddenly, like lightning in a summer storm, Rachel died trying to deliver twins in breech position. John wrote the letter:

> It almost kills me to think how she suffered before she died. No one but God knows how intense was her suffering. Pen Cannot describe my grief. . . . No one but God could relieve my Dear Rachel from her pain. It was beyond man on this earth to do it. Everything was done that could be done. The doctors could do no more. She told me . . . about six or seven hours before she died, She put her armes around my neck and drawed me close to her bosom and told me she could not live long and said oh, Biles, my mother, my boy, my sisters, my Brother. . . . She was quite well about Sundown. She says Biles I think I will be sick to night. I then went after two neighbour women and they came. I then went after the doctor who came and was with her until she was gone, about eleven oclock Sunday night.
>
> She was taken with severe pain in her stomach and vomited. . . . The pain . . . threw her into convulsions oh dear such suffering. She had some twenty of these convulsions one right after the other and went to her home in heaven in one of the fits. . . . I would have loved to see the Child or children. They all say she bore twins, but the doctors told me that they were dead after the first convulsion. . . . The doctor said it was not a natural Birth, that it was a cross birth. . . . [She was] not 20 years old yet, and what was worse than all, Mother was too feeble to come over and see Rachel when she wanted to see her so bad. When Mama was able to come Rachel was insensible.
>
> (JUNE 20, 1855)

The doctor who tried unsuccessfully to deliver the infants refused to show the bodies to the distraught young husband. Poor Rachel, dead at nineteen, crying for her mother.

It was seven years since the Malicks had come to Washington Territory. Along with hundreds of others, they had been filled with hope, willing to work hard to homestead "free land." But amid prosperity and mild winters and burgeoning crops, Hiram and Charles and George had died. And now Rachel, in the bloom of life, was dead too. "Rachel was interred yesterday by the side of her dear father," wrote Abigail. "My eyes are so weak and ful of tears I cannot see to write much more and I feel so bad & weary that I cannot Write." (JUNE 20, 1855)

There was no pattern in all that had happened to the Malick family. Hiram might have drowned at home; accidents occurred wherever one might be. And as for Charles, young men were at high risk during the gold rush. George could have had a stroke in Illinois or in Pennsylvania as well as in the Northwest territories. Rachel's death seemed the most extravagant blow. Yet childbirth was a universal risk. The risk of death in childbirth at midcentury was so high one can only wonder how young women saw the marriage bed.

It was the frontier itself, so untamed and dangerous, that seemed to threaten them. Even John Biles, careful, prudent, strong, almost capsized on the river in a heavy rainstorm. Every day brought new encounters with their own fragility. In the first few years of settlement, the Malicks seem not so much brave builders and pioneers as grieving exiles, far from the protection and the healing of home.

All around them, the land bloomed. Oregon Territory set up its provisional government, built up its trade, and would move from first settlement to statehood in only a decade. Abigail wrote home to Illinois, "We are All well. All that are left of us." (AUGUST 5, 1855)

III. Coming Apart, *1855–1858*

With Rachel's death, there were so many ghosts in this "new" country. All the older children were gone. John Biles moved into Abigail's house and gave Little Charley over to Abigail's tending. He wrote to Mary Ann, "I enclose a pair of ear rings . . . that was Rachels. I bought them for her some time ago . . . and Rachel often said she would send them to [you] and wished you had them. So to comply with her wish I send them to you. It is a poor gift but it is something that Rachel once

Unidentified woman, Oregon Territory. Keeping the family together by letter writing lessened the isolation of frontier life and somehow made the loneliness bearable.

wore that makes them valuable." (JULY 5, 1855) He was suffering. "I am so very lonesom since my poor [Rachel] Henrietta died. The fact is no man knows how to appriciate a wife until she is gone from him forever." (AUGUST 12, 1855)

In her confusion and bitterness, Abigail turned against Biles; he was alive and Rachel wasn't.

> I have Biles And little Charles A living with me. Poor fellow he could not have staid At home, he would have fretted him self to death if he had had to. I Let him build him A littl bed room Atached to our house. And so he now lives with us but [I] Do not know how long he will stay with us. I gues not Long for I expect he will soon marrye Again. He said he will not but I do not believe him for he is young And is very fond of girls Compeney. He is only a fu Monthes older than Charles would have been if he had lived. . . . I think he wont stay long with us. Sometimes he said he will leave And go some place elce And then he said he never will leve Me as long As I live. . . . [Meanwhile] I wash for him And it Costs him nothing And take Care of the child. . . . And if he is not satisfied with that he must go. . . . I cannot help it.
>
> (AUGUST 5, 1855)

There was news of sickness from Illinois too. Michael wrote that Mary Ann had been very sick. That news "scard Me very Mutch," wrote Abigail. (AUGUST 12, 1855)

Each new grief made the hope of reunion more tenuous, a fairy tale told to while away the years of separation.

It had taken Abigail a year and a half before she could write about Hiram's death. Now she did not write about Rachel's death at all. There was too much pain for words.

Outside the household, gold was discovered to the north of them, and that was all the excuse Shindel needed to get away from the sadness of home. Even John Biles wrote about the news.

> I must tell you about the Gold Mines. . . . They are about two hundred and fifty miles from here. . . . They are very rich. I have seen several hundred dollars worth of the specimens. It is of a superior quality. The general impression is that another Eldorado has been found. (AUGUST 12, 1855)

Young men and old men who heard word of gold "of superior quality" ran off to catch the new wheel of fortune. To find a rich vein, a quick road to wealth, that was the dream that fired the cold mornings of homesteading.

As if life were uninterrupted by tragedy, Abigail had pictures taken of her family.

> My beedes look like A string Around My neck A hanging down. . . . My gold rings shows very well on My fingers. . . . You Can sea A little of my Cap on the top of My head. It is A black Crape trimed with black ribband. My dres Was silk and My sack was silk. . . . The children Looks Just lik them And it shows every thing they had on. . . . Susan had A handful of flours in one hand . . . And Jane had A little Book. (AUGUST 12, 1855)

But in reality, the photographs *were* related to the deaths. They were efforts to secure their images against time and loss.

> I wish that we Coud have had Fathers taken, but . . . he did not believe in sutch thinges. I was at him to have ours taken but he would not. After you requested it he told Me to hold My toung so I did not say enney More to him About it. . . . I hated to have Mine taken [alone] but they ware for My Children And they would excuse me. (AUGUST 12, 1855)

Abigail posed in her silks and her beads and her gold rings, the picture of prosperity and stability in her black crape bonnet with its long strings, her estate evident in her children's dresses and jewelry. She did not mention that Rachel was not there. She wrote to Mary Ann and Michael, "Oho I would giv half oregon if I Could sea [my grandchildren]." (AUGUST 12, 1855)

Through it all—through sickness and death, through floods and Indian wars—Abigail worked her land. But she worked it alone: "Shindl is never At home to help Me enney. I have the Cattel And every thing to do Myself. O the hogs Are A holoing now for fead. I must go And feed them And it is Araning As hard as it can." (DECEMBER 8, 1855) "If it was not for Jane and susan I could not get Along Attal. But they Are sutch good girles that I still Make out. Oh if Shindel was half As good A boy As they Are girles I Could get Along very Well." (JANUARY 12, 1856) Shin's defection put in jeopardy her ability to keep the land. But he had no use for the life of a farmer, or for his mother's appeals.

Little Charley, who looked like Rachel, was Abigail's pleasure. Time with him was untroubled and peaceful. The child redeemed her life and all her effort.

> I kissed little Charley And I think it was the sweetest kiss that I ever gave the Little fellow in My Life for he had sutch A nice Clean face. At the time I had Jest bin reading your part of the Letter with My Eyes ful of teares. And he Came A runing out of the kitchin saying mama what is the matter that you Cri so Mutch. I kissed the Letter And then I kissed him. Are you A crying About Me? I Am Alwais A good boy Aint I Mama, Mama? . . . I said no My Dear I Was onley A Crying About Aunt Mary Ann And uncle Michael. They Are so far off and Have had so mutch sickness. . . . [Charley] knows that I Am his grand Mother for his Mother Alwais teached him to say grand Mother. But he now lives with us And it semes to hard for to mak him say. Other wise he is guest like my own Child. (JANUARY 12, 1856)

As winter turned to spring in 1856 John Biles wrote to Illinois to say the Rogue River Indians had "declared war against the Americans and . . . much Blood has been spilt." News that "some fifty whites have fell at the hands of the unmerciful Savages" inflamed the settlers, who went out and killed 250 Indians. "There is now about one thousand whites in the field Against some four or five thousand Indians in all, and within Seventy miles of this place volunteers are being raised every day." John Biles was as determined as his compatriots that "nothing less than a total extermination of the redskins will appease the Americans. The Indians have brought the war on and the Yankees are bound to see it out. . . . I have been elected first Lieut . . . in a company of volunteers. . . . The military post is within a quarter of a mile of our house."

The settlers were moved into town, some of them unwillingly, "especially mother, as her stock etc. are running on the commons and likely to stray off, and other property going to waste for the want of care." (NOVEMBER 9, 1855)

Abigail's account of the Indian wars captured the nervous anxiety of daily life as Indians and settlers were pitted against each other.

> The Indians sent word that they were a coming to distroy [the] whole [of] Washington and Oregon and Burn All that the Bostons [Americans] had and Murder All And Scelpe them. So the people had All to Leave there Homes and go to the nearest towns for to protect themselves. . . . [Some] people volenteard And went And brought in All the friendly Indians. They Were Scard As bad As the white people. They said they ware so glad that the white people Came for them they did not know what to do. They said they did not think that white Men Cared About Indians. But it was not that they Cared enney thing About them. They [whites] ware Afraid that they would turn

traiters And Murder us All. . . . And now they have [the Indians] at the Fourt and Keep A strong guard over them. . . . We staid thre weeks up with Biles, but I found it Cost Me too Mutch. . . . Now we had to Come home to fatten our hogs. I have nine A fatning. . . . The Indians say that they will fight the Americans As long as they have provisions. And [when there is nothing to eat] they will eat there Wifes And Children And fight the [Americans]. . . . Shindl is never At home to help Me enney. I have the Cattel And every thing to do Myself. O the hogs Are holoing now for fead. I must go And feed them. And it is Araning as hard as it can pore. . . . I have Little Charley with Me all the time. . . . The little Motherless child, Al most Father Less, for it semes to me [Biles] does not Care Mutch about him. (DECEMBER 8, 1855)

Accompanying Abigail's description of Indians and soldiers and battles was a swatch of calico from the new dresses she was sewing for Jane and Susan. One way or another, life went on.

In April 1856 families were evacuated again to Vancouver "on A Count of the Indians. We are Not Safe here one moment." But even so, Abigail was careful to distinguish between the local tribes who were friendly and the tribes to the north, who were not.

The governor held council with the Indian tribes—the Yakima, the Cayuse, the Walla Walla, the Nez Percé, the Spokanes—and concluded treaties whereby the Indians exchanged land for monies and an agreement to live on reservations. But sentiment against negotiation ran high on both sides. Lieutenant John Biles thought the governor too tenderhearted for treating with "villains after they have murdered hundreds of men, women & children and laid waste to thousands of dollars worth of property." (MAY 30, 1856) And the Indian tribes, for their part, contained dissidents enough who refused to accept the terms of the new treaties. Hostilities broke out every month.

Abigail continued to make her garden, even as she was interrupted by fighting close by. "I was Down here one day Amaking [my] garden And All at once I heard greate firing of guns. And I started rite for the fourt As hard As I could run."

Everyone had bad colds because they spent so much time "Aruning To the Fourt And then home earley In the Morning throu the rain And wet. . . . We do not know What Moment we May be Attacked By those Auful Saviges. . . . There Are So mutch thik timber that [the Indians] might [be] here unbenonest to us And Murder us be fore we know it." (APRIL 27, 1856) Settlers took refuge in the fort, and the Indians laid siege.

They have taken the town of Caskades and burnt it All Acept the Block house and one store which was saved by there Braking open pork Barrels and yousing the Brine in place of water. The Indians would heat Irons red hot And throw them on the houses And set them A fire. The people whoo ware not kiled went to the block house for protection. And It being so early in the Morning When the Atact was Made that the women and Children were not half dresed, nearley All in there night Cloathes. And they ware in there five Days with out one drop of water, onley what An Indian, A friendly one brought them with a two Quart bucket, so I am Told, And One Barrel of water At the Block House where the people had rensed salmon in be Fore the Atack. And as the people ran to the Block house A great menney Men, Women and Children [were] shot down and scalped And Cut And Slashed to pieces. And one Woman ran with her littl child in her Armes And As she ran A ball struck her and kild her dead And brake . . . the childs leg. And A man pict up the child And saved it. And the Child is About to get wel. And A man, A Neighbor of ours that was up there to work at the time, had A ball shot thru his arm. I saw him this morning Be fore I came home And Asked him how his Arme was And he said it was Mending sloly. (APRIL 16, 1856)

In her intrepid fashion, Abigail told her children in Illinois, "If you should not get enney Letter from us for six Months you can think that we Are All kild by those bludey saviges." (APRIL 27, 1856)

The blockhouse remained under siege until a handsome young lieutenant named William Henry Pearson led an assault and freed those trapped inside. He was every inch a local hero.

W.H. pearson was the first Man to re Lieve the People out of the Block house At the Caskades. And the people told us those that Came down that sutch screeming for joy . . . was never known before. They slaped there hands for joy And screemed hurow For Lieutenant Pearson. Are We rescused at Last? Are We safe to Come out? He Answerd And said yes you Are safe. Come out. (APRIL 16, 1856)

The Indians, desperate and daring, attacked steamships carrying fresh recruits to the region. The ships managed to escape and spread word of the attack, bringing Lieutenant Philip Sheridan of later Civil War fame and forty dragoons from Fort Vancouver.[12] Abigail wrote:

I saw . . . A steemboat And they ware A firing gunes All the time. The steem boat had Ben to the Caskades whare the Indians had distroid the town And they would not let them Land. The boat was laden with volunteears, but they Could not do enney good for they Could not land. So they ware fourst to go back. And then the shang hais [soldiers] Came And . . . blowed there Bugals And then the Indians scaterd And ran And the shang hies Foloed them And drove them away. . . . Mr. Pearson is Now gone to [carry] the express from the governer to that place and the Dalles. He will Comeback perhapes this After noon And perhaps not until thursday. And perhapes never he May be kiled. Because he understandes the Indians very well, so there Is not So Mutch danger About him. . . . I hope he will not be kild for he is sutch A nice young Man. It would be thousandes of pity. (APRIL 27, 1856)

Abigail was astonished by her own loquaciousness. "I write greate riteing. Dont I write guest As if you ware here And I was A talking to you."

But Abigail had special reasons for sharing the details of the battle, and her reasons centered on Henry Pearson's connections with her family. He was someone they knew. In fact, he had been an intimate of the household for some time past.

Now I must tel you that Mr Wiliam Henry pearson Was here yester day And took dinner with us. And Abigail jane And Him Went A riding in the four noon. And A nother Thing, they Are Ingaged to be Married. They thought To Be Married in the fall, but I told Mr. pearson that Jane was to young . . . to Marry And that If he respected her And her people that he Must wate until she was old enough or elce he Could not have her. Well he said he was Wiling to wate eighteen Monthes then. He is A butiful young Man And A very nice genteel fellow And very goodhartid And very tender. (APRIL 16, 1856)

There it was, that piece of astonishing news. Jane and Pearson—"they Are Ingaged to be Married. . . . We have bin very well A quainted with [Pearson] Now for A year or More And he is Avery true and uprite young Man And is well be loved by All who knows him."

Abigail wrote that Pearson was

almost to old for Jane. He is twenty five And Jane is sixteen onley. But he said that she is the first young Lady that he ever kept Compeney With in his Life. Aint that straing. And he Alwais Liked to walk And talk with jane. He would last winter A year ago when her and Susan ware A coming home from schol. he would get of his horse And walk Along with them So I heard. And I told Jane not to have nothing to do with him. I did not think that was nice of A straing young man to Be galanting school girls home and I told her not

> to bring him here Again. So it ended for A while [but] at last I saw that his hool hart hung on her for when he would go Away as soon as he would come back he would come rite to our house to se us. (APRIL 16, 1856)

"Last winter a year ago" when the girls were walking home from school—Abigail was confusing the facts. Henry Pearson had been Jane's ardent beau since she was thirteen!

Once the story of Jane's romance with Henry Pearson began to come out, Abigail could hardly stop. She had been hiding everything for years, through Pa's death and through Rachel's death. The Albrights, who may have thought they were privy to the most intimate details of Abigail's household, suddenly learned that Jane was engaged.

> I will give you the hool histrey of this A fare. Last winter when [Pearson] Came back from Carying the express to governor Stevens, Stevens sent him Immediatley to port land And he would have had to [have] staid All night. . . . [But] he had not sene Jane yet so he hired a horse As soon As he done the bisness for the governer And got on the hors And rode to Vancouver . . . And Came rite down to our house As soon as he Could. . . . He came be fore he had got one Mouth ful to eate. . . . *And after that he would be down every two or three days And then every other day.* And one evening he Asked Me if his frequent visites was not rather Intruding. I told him no, not as long As he behaved himself genteely And yoused no bad language. And he said he was never to Mis be have be fore enneyone, espesheley before ladys And that he would never mis be have. (APRIL 16, 1856; EMPHASIS ADDED)

As proof of Pearson's qualifications as a gentleman and an officer, Abigail added:

> He is very wel off And has Made it All him self. He has the richist Cloathes And A great menney of them and a deal of Monney and fifteen horses. O yes he is A greate rider. And jane Can wride So well, that pleases him. . . . He sais that he never Saw Sutch Abutiful rider As jane for A lady in his Life. (APRIL 16, 1856)

Why had the affair been so secret? For one thing, Biles, who was the court-appointed guardian of the minor children, did not approve. Abigail deliberately hid the romance from him. As she had hidden Biles's engagement to Rachel from her husband, she now hid Jane's engagement from Biles. "He does not know enney thing about [it]. There is only thre that knowes it: Pearson and Jane and me."

Abigail's feeling for Biles had changed since Rachel's death. She wrote now that Biles "is very Jealous" and saw himself as a possible suitor for Jane.

> He sais to jane, oh, give up pearson And have me. Jane sais why Ant you A shamed to talk so to me. . . . In deed Jane would not have Biles for he never Was to good to Rachel poor thing. She sofferd A meney A time with his Abuses And for want or would of if it had not bin for us. He would go of some times And be gone for three or four Months and Leve her A very Scantey supply of food. But when I would find that out I would have her to Come home whare she Could get A plentey. I was not A going to have A child of Mine to starve or half starve When I had enough. (APRIL 16, 1856)

And then Abigail's caution: "do not write enney thing to Me About [these matters] for [Biles] Alwais wants to se All the Letters that you write to me fore he thinkes A great deal of both of you."

But Abigail was uneasy about Pearson and his attentions to Jane. How could she tell if a finely dressed young man like Henry Pearson, an officer with money in his pockets, how could she tell if he were a good man or a wastrel? Had she been wrong in her judgment about Biles, whose political star was rising in the community? Biles, who was educated and forbearing and well-spoken, had he been a poor provider for Rachel when he was away on his long visits to the territorial capital where he was busy making laws and being a politician? Was Henry Pearson a better-hearted man? Was he more in love with Jane? Was love itself a reliable guide to marriage? It was certainly what young women wanted, but her daughters were hardly more than children, given to flirtations and infatuations. Young men on the frontier were without family, without loyalties, without clear prospects. It was hard to set them into place, to read them clearly. Who could know what they would do or become. Abigail wanted to be a good parent, but she had hidden Jane's affair from everyone for two years' time—torn between her indulgence of her daughter and her mistrust of the premature courtship.

> One day he proposed A ride with jane And susan. He Asked Jane if she could ride And she told him that she that she thought there was not Menney that beat her. And for fear of some one having something to say About her A going

> out A riding he thought it best to get some other ones to go with [them]. . . . So he Asked Me if the girles Could go. I told him it was A cording to What Compeney they ware to go in. And he said the peopel war nice Compeney. Well they All went Ariding And jane and Pearson wrode together. And one of the Ladyes said that she thought jane made herself to bold with him. He thought that every man should take Care of there own partner but this lady was gelous because he did not Atend more to her. So he said when him And jane would go A riding A gain they would go Alone next time. . . . He alwais comes And Askes me if I have eney objections to her Agoing out to wride. They ware out Ariding yesterday and now he has become a daly visiter.
> (APRIL 16, 1856)

The community saw Jane as too forward, and there was gossip that the romance was too brazen. Abigail defended her own judgment and tried to impose standards of acceptable behavior upon the couple. She insisted that Henry Pearson use no foul language, that there be chaperones when he and Jane went riding—at least at first—and that he "behave" himself. And Pearson gave assurances of his great respect for Jane, and seemed so forbearing in waiting to marry her. But somehow, the propriety of the match was unconvincing. No matter how Abigail tried to tell herself Jane and Pearson were a respectable couple, the affair did not really seem so.

Abigail brushed her uncertainties aside and wrote about her peach trees and her apples and her lettuce. Jane prepared dinner, and in the midst of war, they had "fried ham and fried potatoes and Bread and butter And Custard and oister soup And stued peaches and Apples and rice and tea." (APRIL 27, 1856)

The war with the Rogue River Indians wore on, and John Biles took care of Abigail and her household. John "Made Me A Nice Box to put Milk In. . . . The box holds twelve large pans of Milk At once. It is As Nice As A springhouse. . . . The box is Made of thick sound plank plained As nice As a Chist and Two nice Covers And two Locks and Kees to it so that I Can Lock them up so nothing Can get at them And I can have My milk so no dust nor fly Can get in it." (JUNE 6, 1856) But Biles was restless. He thought of going to Illinois, and he wrote to Mary Ann asking her to survey all the "pretty girls in Tazewell County for me when I come." He thought of going back to his own people in Pennsylvania. He was not certain any longer where his home might be.

The nation, too, was losing its center. Debates over slavery pulled parties and sections and states this way and that. In 1856 a new political alliance was forged out of an uncertain coalition of Whigs, Free-Soilers, and Know-Nothings who agreed only on their opposition to slavery. The newly formed Republican party looked for support to the western states and territories with their strong free-soil sentiment. But Biles worried about the rising tides of passion. He wrote Mary Ann and Michael Albright, "There is only about half doz 'kinky heads' in this Territory. The Atmosphere is not healthy for them." Knowing the Albright's strong antislavery views, he quickly added, "don't take offence to any thing that I have said." (MAY 30, 1856) The Republicans nominated a westerner, John C. Fremont, to the presidency, but Biles, the frontiersman, voted for the conservative Buchanan "notwithstanding I am strenuously opposed to the extension of slavery." Above all he feared that the

> finatics of the north have acted in the matter very injudiciously and had they not agitated the abolishing entirely of slavery in the south, that slavery would in the course of time [have] died out without bloodshed. As it is the north is only riveting the chains of slavery tighter & I fear the consequences will be a protracted civil war. (NOVEMBER 8, 1856)

The divisions in the nation that Biles foresaw were real enough, and real too were the divisions in his own heart and mind. In July he went with Abigail to have his son baptized; then he resigned his commission in the volunteers, sold his business, closed his office, and headed back to Pennsylvania.[13] His journey had all the appearance of flight—from memories of Rachel's death, from Abigail's resentment. But Biles gave the Albrights—whom he had never met—a different explanation for his leaving. Congress had eliminated payments for territorial officers, and as county clerk, Biles said he was going east to sue for back wages.

> It is the fault of Congress. The Law granting me the salary was plain And I had recd my emoluments up to last Dec, at which time our wise Congress passed a law repealing the clause or section giving clerks salary and allowed nine months to pass by without giving me a shadow of notice. . . . Let us compare the act curtailing clerks of US courts in Territorys with the act passed granting $30.00 per day to each member of Congress. The former takes the Bread out of their mouths whilst the latter loads the pockets of the others.
> (NOVEMBER 8, 1856)

He spent six hundred dollars to cross the country, but he thought of his expenditure as a means to secure a legacy for Little Charley. "I am soly actuated with that desire. . . . you know a Father must or ought to do all this for his own child."

However he explained his departure, he was repeating the pattern of separations that marked all of their lives. John Biles's parents had not seen him for seven years, and Biles would not see his own son for two years more. Little Charley learned to call Abigail "mother," and she to look on him as one of her own children.

The family broke into a grand triangle. Biles would be in Pennsylvania and Delaware; the Albrights were in Illinois where they had always been. Abigail held on to her claim in Washington Territory. Shindel was seldom in his mother's house, and Jane was moving away from it. But with Biles's departure, the dynamics of the family changed; the frontier household contained only women and children. Jane was sixteen, Susan eleven, Charley two, and that was all of them left. The Albrights were the geographic center—and they were becoming the emotional center as well. Abigail was losing hold of her family.

In widowhood Abigail found no lessening of her burdens. If anything, life was more demanding. With George dead and Shin and Biles away, she did a double load or paid hired men to do it for her. She hated to part with money, but she wanted to hold on to her land.

On the other hand, for the very first time Abigail was in charge of her own house. They could all come and go as they pleased. Jane felt her new freedom and wrote to Illinois that she had gone "over to Portland yesterday on the steamer (Eagle) and I had quite a good time. . . . We are all well and Injoying our selves verry well." (UNDATED) With Biles gone, Jane could pour out all the high-spirited news of her betrothal to Henry Pearson. There was no more need to keep secrets; Abigail did not have to caution Mary Ann to mention nothing for fear that John Biles would read their letters. And Abigail decided to give her blessing to the romance in the hope that the proprieties would follow.

Jane wrote that Henry Pearson was no longer in the army but a civilian. He has a "good Education and is a verry smart active Fellow." Jane was full of inarticulate whoops of pride in her suitor's "spunk," his handsome good looks, and his fast horses. It was a frontier romance, nothing like the slow courting and letter-writing of John Biles and Rachel.

We had a good time on the 4th of July this year. I must say that mr. P does not chew the wead, drinks but little and smokes a cigar once in a while. Now letts all Hurrah for Mr. Pearson. Hurrah! hurrah! hurrah! He is the most respectable young man in this Terri tory known of and is heighly honord here and at the capital of this territory. So hurrah for him, WHP. I have got his miniature. . . . Oh he is so good looking . . . . If henry and I married this winter we are going across the plains and we will come [to Illinois] sure in the spring. . . . Oyes and you know you might as well glory in my spunk now. Oh I wish you could se Henry then youd glory in his spunk. Oh he is a splended rider. He has got such a nice horse that I ride. . . . Good bye good bye. Let us heer. Give 3 cheers for Henry Pearson. Hurrah! Hurrah! Hurrah!

Jane Malick
(JULY 10, 1856)

Jane's romance poured through the letter. Abigail told how

in '53 he Came to this Countrey With Governor Stevens A Crost the plaines And Shortley got acquainted with us And Alwais Stuck to Jane ever since until he had her. He tryed to Come here Every way before I would Countane him. . . . I thought that he had no business to notice a little school girl but He must Cal every now & then. . . . At last I found there was no other Way . . . and I saw that Jane thought So very Mutch of him & He of her That I was obileaged to sub Mit. . . . I concluded that they Loved each other very Mutch And that [she] Could do no better perhaps in All her life. And I found that his hol hart hung on her And no one elce And so I thought They Might As well get Married now As eney Time. (UNDATED, 1856)

Abigail bowed to the inevitable fact that they would do as they pleased whether or not she approved. It was better to get them married than to oppose them.

On December 21, 1856, the Reverend James McCarty, First Episcopal Minister of Vancouver, noted in his own journal that he had "solemnized the marriage of Wm. H. Pearson at this place to Abigail [Jane] Malick, daugher of said Abigail. Persons present, the mother of the bride, John Mahony, Mary McPaden & others."[14]

In her account of the wedding Abigail wrote:

Janes Brides Made Is A Judges Daughter And Mr. Pearsons grooms Man Is a Stour keeper. Mr Pearsons grooms Mans Name Is John May han And Janes Brides Mades Name Is Mary Mcfaden. She goes to the Same Academe that

> Jane goes to. Jane is Agoing to the Academe three Monthes that I pay for And then Mr. Pearson sais that he will send her As long As She Can go After that for they do not want to keep hous yet. . . . I do not know how he would do if he was Master of the Place as I Am but what I know of him he is a Very good young Man. . . . In May [Jane] will be seventeen. . . . Oho I hope that they will do Better than poor Rachel and Biles. (UNDATED, 1856)

She described a proper wedding ceremony, an event in its ideal form. But the details included an unmistakable picture of Jane as a schoolgirl. After the wedding, Abigail was to pay for three months school, and then Pearson would send her for "As long As She Can go After that." Schoolgirl or not, in all likelihood Jane was some three months pregnant. "Inclosed you find some of sister janes Bridal Cake."

In January Abigail wrote, "Mr. Pearson has Bought A very nice house in Vancouver And gave seven Hundred dollars for it And they will Move up there shortley." (JANUARY 28, 1857) She sent a piece of Jane's wedding dress, a small cutting of blue silk.

Maybe the marriage would work out.

In February Abigail thought of giving up the claim and going "home" to Illinois.

> I Am not Well and Afraid That I never shal be A gain In this world. And if I live I think that I shal get readey And Come to you As I am A getting old And cannot Carey on farming enney Longer. . . . I shal sell out And take susan And Come right A way, that is, If I can stay With you—susan And me. But if there Would be enney Ob Jections then write And tel Me. Then I Will not Come . . . I will go to Pensylvania. . . . Jane Is A going with her husband to California or to texas, so I have no one enney More. And It Is not Worth My While to Carey on Farming enney more And . . . have to depend Altogether on other people. It Costes Me More than I Can Make. . . . I am not Able to Wait on farmers And Milk eight or ten Cows And do All the Cooking And Washing And A Menney A time I Am left to feed All the Cattle and hogs My self And A Menny Atime to Chop Wood My self. And I Cannot stand it Longer. And some times there Is not A Man to Be had To do eny thing for one. This winter I had to go And Chop wood My self When the snow Was three Feat deep for I Could not get A Man to do it.

Her account of her frontier neighbors provides a caustic view of their "pioneer" virtues.

> The people Are so lasey And so Inde pendant that if they Are A Mind to do enney thing they Will do it And if not they Will not. They have Alwais had Indians for survantes, And now they Have sent them All off for fear on a reserv[ation] so they think them selves A Bove Mutch Work now the Indians are gone. (FEBRUARY 11, 1857)

Shindel, like his "lasey" neighbors, was away from the farm most of the time. He wrote to Mary Ann and Michael, telling them that come spring, he would go back to the mines, or perhaps carry the express "through Indian country." He was nineteen and "wanted to get maride [but] the girl that I went to see did not prove to be the person she said she was." Maybe he would come back to Illinois to find a good "country girl." "So Mary Ann you pick me out one [and] I will come back perhaps A bout one year from this time." (JANUARY 27, 1857)

Almost the very same day, Abigail was complaining to Mary Ann and Michael that Shin "Makes Me the Most trouble [and] whare he Aught to be A Comfourt to Me he is a trouble. . . . I have to depend A pon Straingers for All the help."

> When I think of poor Hiram I have to Burst out A Criang so that I scarseley Can se. . . . To think of His Awfil death And the diferance of the two Boys shin and him. (JANUARY 28, 1857)

Abigail would never, in all her life, forgive Shin for leaving her alone on the farm, for abandoning her after his father and brothers were dead. "Shin does not live at home any More And he does not Care enney thing about me enney More and he does not do enney thing for Me enney More." (FEBRUARY 11, 1857)

> He will not work, but when I have enney person A living with Me he tries to hender them from the Work. . . . In the spring he went off to work for the government. I thought he Could farm the place but he took Another notion And went. . . . I thought he would do now something for himself but Alass in About three Weakes he Came Home and had not one Cent of Money to help Him self with. He had spent All he had A gambling And had not got him self one bit of Cloathes And has loiterd Around ever since. Well he Could get five dollars A cord for Wood if he would Cut it but he is to lazy to Cut And hall it for him self. I told him . . . he Might have the oxen to hall All he

> was A mind to If he would And he Could sell All he Could Cut to government And get the Cash in hand. But [he lives] on My expence And wastes All that he Can get his handes on And will not even help to Milk the Cowes unless I drive him to it. And then he wont do It, onley if he pleses. He will start up town And gamble All night. . . . All the good I Can say of him [is] that he is honest. He does not steel. But in spite of Me he will Brake the Sabath, he will not go to school nor to sunday school. I have oferd him Almost everything to go to school but he will not And he cannot hardley read one Bit. . . . I am A get Ing very old now And you know that I have had Agreate Deal of trouble. (JULY 13, 1856)

She wrote of growing old and pictured herself at the end of her rope. But that was only another fiction. Letters had become fictions of sorts, untruths that satisfied a need for propriety or obligation or the fulfillment of wishes. Or maybe letters were the testing ground for directions one might take—or might not. The fact was that, although Abigail was growing older and was more frail, she clung to her claim with tenacity. She was tough, and it would take more than the death of her husband and sons, more than Indian wars, more than floods and headstrong children to pull her off this land that was, for the first time, her very own. "I hate to leave this country." (FEBRUARY 11, 1857)

Almost three months after the wedding, Abigail wrote to John Biles to give him the news of Jane's marriage, and John answered—in that grand style of his—"I was not a little surprised to learn that Jane was Married. . . . It is an agreeable Surprise, for Mr. Pearson is a gentleman. . . . His character is far above reproach and I am only too happy to think that Jane had made the Selection. Jane is worthy of any man & I join in with all in wishing them Success and a Long life of Happiness." (MARCH 16, 1857)

Biles's language, with its school rhetoric, represented the values and the social class Abigail clung to, and however she might rail against him, his approval was important to her. She wrote to Mary Ann and Michael, reassuring them that John Biles approved the marriage. She admitted, however, that Pearson was a strange young man. "You would think him A very Quear fellow . . . but I tel you that he is A nice Man And as pretey As a picture. . . . But farming he knowes nothing About. He Cannot work on A farm. . . . He is now Carrying the express from the Dolls [The Dalles] of the Columbia to Fourt Walla Walla And Jane Is stil At home. He getes three hundred dollars A Month for Carrying It And he wrote to jane that he would Be home next week. . . . Jane wantes to sea Him so very Mutch. Her hool thoughts Is About him . . . but he has Bin gone now two months." (APRIL 5, 1857)

Jane went to live with Pearson in April, and Abigail created another of her fictions—a description of Jane's life as she wanted to know it:

> Mr. Pearson Has A butiful Clame [at The Dalles]—so he sais, I have never seen It—And has A House on It with three Roomes to It. He has had men Building it all this Spring And onley Came for Her Last Monday. He is very Proud to have everything nice Be fore he would take her there. He bought A Captains furniture that Is A going Back to the States. He sais that It Is the grandest furniture that he has sean since He Left Baltimore. . . . He said that he would rather that Jane would stay at home until he Could get the house Cloathed and paperd so that . . . she would not have Mutch to do, but there was no perswasion. She Must go With him for he had Bin gone Nearley two Monthes And she did not want to be Away from him eney Longer.
>
> (APRIL 27, 1857)

But The Dalles was a rough place for a bride of barely seventeen; it was a rough place to leave any young woman alone for many days at a time. It was not a town but a military outpost, a jumble of log cabins and cheap shacks, ninety miles from Vancouver. The site had been an Indian fishery. Old French traders called the place "la Dalle," the trough of the Columbia. "La Grande Dalle de la Columbia" marked the rapids. Emigrants on the last lap of the overland journey built rafts and had the Indians take them through the swirling waters. The U.S. government sent a company of soldiers there to protect the settlers, but by 1851 there was only a single civilian house to be seen. In 1857 it was still a raw settlement.[15]

Through the spring Abigail's problems increased. Before he died, George Malick had begun a lawsuit against a Frenchman named Preaux, whose land bordered his. Preaux held title to his claim through the Hudson's Bay Company, and those rights would not be extinguished until the end of the decade. In the meantime, Preaux was cutting timber on land that George Malick considered his own. When the court made Abigail the administratrix of George's estate, she inherited the lawsuit. Preaux was "a hudson Bay Man And [had] no friends here." But legal expenses were piling up. "It Cost me seven dollars and A half." Abigail, who liked things clear and settled, was drawn into lengthy litigation over land title. Biles wrote to the Albrights that the surveyor for Hudson's Bay issued judgments that were "wild and evasive." Abigail's claim, he wrote, was based on so much "sacrifice—almost of life itself" that she has the sympathy of "all the American neighbours. . . . If the settlement of the case was submitted to an american jury we do not fear the result." (NOVEMBER 8, 1856)

The case came to be viewed as an affair of Americans exorcising the last evidences of the British-owned Hudson's Bay Company. Abigail's lawyer presented Preaux and his witnesses as foreigners who did not have the same rights as American settlers. At one point Abigail wrote that a witness for Preaux was so drunk he "fel off the Bentch And went to Sleep And no one noticed it until the Judge saw him li there. And so sais the Judge, hoo is that liing there? Take him out. And the loyer turned round And looked And said oho that Is a hudson Bay Man." (APRIL 27, 1857)

Clear across the country she rebuked Biles for telling the Albrights about the lawsuit, for troubling them with such problems, for mixing in her affairs. Biles, for his part, promised the Albrights, "I shall keep you posted from time to time as the cause progresses." (MARCH 16, 1857)

All through the winter of 1856–57, Abigail battled with the court. And she punished John Biles in the way she knew best—she refused to send him word about Little Charley. "I have not recd a word from mother or any one of the family there as yet," wrote Biles. "Notwithstanding I have written them several times. . . . Not a word have I had concerning my Dear Boy and I feel very uneasy in consequence. . . . I do not rightly understand it." (DECEMBER 9, 1856)

Abigail clung to Rachel's child. "He has lived so long with us that he seames so natural As one of the familey." (FEBRUARY 11, 1857) She worried about Charley and watched over him. "We are Alwais Afraid He might get in the Lake and dround." The child was the apple of her eye. Tranquil moments came when she and her grandson were alone.

> One day Him And Me Ware A Sitting In the Doar And He said Mama Aint I your own Child. . . . I love you Dearley I love you as Mutch As A ship Load of people. . . . When I get Big enough I will Cut All your wood and Milk All the cows And do All the Work And then you Will not have to Work so hard. . . . I told him that Rachel was his Mother. . . . But Rachel Is dead. . . . O I Almost Alwais had him since he was Born. (AUGUST 9, 1857)

Except for Charley, Abigail's frontier home meant only wayward children, lawsuits, early deaths, backbreaking work, and the winds of change.

But the more she clung to the child the more she worried that Biles would come and take him away. "Biles writes every Mail ever since he has bin gone." She did not say that she answered him.

Biles, for his part, that stable and responsible young man, had become a straw in the wind, looking for a new direction. Maybe he would "go to Illinois & there take a wife and become a citizen of that State (A Democratic one)." Maybe he would go back to the Northwest Territory. Maybe he would stay a little longer in the East. Biles was thirty years old, "studying architecture [and] working at House Joining." He confided to Mary Ann and Michael that he had gone to an astrologer to help him see into the future.

> [I] went to consult Mrs. Vauliou the Astrologist. . . . She said that my boy was very sick. She was telling [me] that I never would raise him.

Biles was tormented by the woman's predictions about his son.

> She showed me [Charley's] sweet Likeness through an instrument. I could see him as plane as life & pale as death. . . . I almost dread the coming of the next mail.

He was so worried that he rushed out and "consulted another Lady of the same profession who told me precisely the same things."

The astrologer also seemed to tell him about Abigail's lawsuit. She said "that I had relations far off that was in difficulty about some property which worried them a great deal." True to form, the astrologer forecast that his own life would improve very soon:

> She also told me I was going to travel [and] said I would marry again but that I was not in a Hurry. And when I did marry it would be a wealthy person. That most of my troubles was over & my best days [were] to come.
>
> (JULY 12, 1857)

Interest in spiritualism began in the 1830s and continued to grow through the period of the Civil War. From New England to the Midwest, distinguished men and women—Abraham and Mary Todd Lincoln, Harriet Beecher Stowe—as well as ordinary people were drawn to promises of health cures and visitations with the dead. To families in which death was the common experience, the occult offered an irresistible promise of happy reunion. Spiritualism embraced a variety of practitioners, from believers in "animal magnetism" to phrenologists, mesmerists, "spirit-rapping" holders of seances, and mediums.

John Biles, along with other middle-class men and women, searched for truths that lay between religion and science, trying to find comfort out of the uncertainties that afflicted their lives. Biles, who journeyed from the Atlantic to the Pacific and back to the Atlantic again, was a young man without moorings, looking for a new place to call home.

On the other side of the continent Abigail was also buffeted by indecisions and impossibilities. She was offered four thousand dollars for half of her claim, but she could not sell until the land was surveyed. "As soon As I get My pattent I think I shal Come [to Illinois] If I live And Am Able to stand the Journey." In the meantime, the Columbia River had risen and was threatening the crops. "We have bin working our selves nearly to death to keep the harvest out of the Water." The "we" she spoke of were Susan and herself. Susan "gets up And gets Breckfast for me while I Milk the Cows."

In June, Jane Malick Pearson came home to have her baby.

Abigail made no mention of its birth in her letters home.

Abigail wrote to Illinois only once over the summer, complaining about Shindel. She wanted him home, but she also wanted him to behave like a sober Christian farmer.

Shin's gaming and gambling mocked her careful husbandry and violated her vision of home and order. She and Shin were warring spirits.

> [He] is up At the Caskades At Work. He Will not stay At Home With Me. I suppose it is to Lone som Fore Him. He Cannot Have sutch compeney At home As he Likes. He Cannot have gamblers And Card players At Home As He Can Away from Home. I will not Alow that In My House. And When He Brings sutch Home With Him I Alwais look sour At Them And do not youse them As Well As I do others and that Afrontes the Gentel Men. . . . And then he Gets mad And goes off. I Alwais tel him that I will not Intertain gamblers About My House. (AUGUST 9, 1857)

There were no more letters until October, and then Abigail was overcome with dark memories. She wrote again about the clouded affair of her parting from Mary Ann in 1848.

> When I was the last At your House And I had not Mutch [then], for your father Was not pleased for me to go When I did go. But I Would go and then He Would not give Me no spending Monney to go With. But As It hapend I Had Enough of My own And Hiram poor fellow had some And He Was determind that I should go to se you. And When We Came Home We got an Awful Scolding for Staing So Long. And I knowed that was the reason that I Had not Mutch Comfourt At Home. I was Oneasy At the time. But that fear Is All ovr now And if I should come I shall have no fear A bout Enney one. (OCTOBER 18, 1857)

It was the event she had written about in June 1853, and here it was again, four years later. If George disapproved of Mary Ann's marriage to Michael Albright, then the reunion of the families in the northwest country was doomed at the start. After all the years of letter writing, after almost a decade of time and separation, Abigail kept reliving the same bitter memory, wondering if that was why the Albrights had never come to join them.

Tucked into the letter was a fragment of paper, a scrap of another letter, saying that Jane was home again.

> She rises every Morning be for day And Cooks Breckfast be for I Am up. And she does All the Washing, so I have no nead to wash enney if I aint A Mind to. (OCTOBER 27, 1857)

Nothing about Jane's baby. Abigail would not admit to its premature arrival; she did not give his name. There were long months when she sent no word. When she wrote again at Christmastime, it was a strange letter, detached and distant. She wrote about her garden, not her children.

> The grass is A Groing fine. . . . I have A plentey of Feed for our Cattel. . . . I think I have hay that is half oats . . . and that Makes Splended hay. It is nearley As green Looking As it Was be fore It Was Cut. . . . We have Butcherd And Made A plentey Sausages. We Butcherd six Butiful Fat Hogs and A Beef, So you May think that We Will not Starve. . . . [I have] A good Meny Squashes and Cabag And . . . Beanes. . . . The Sun is shining So Nice. . . .

> O We have had the Nicest Christ mass that I Ever Saw. . . . The flours Are A blooming in the garden like in Sommer.
>
> (DECEMBER 27, 1857–JANUARY 5, 1858)

Like a disease that begins with a slight fever at the cheeks, Abigail's frontier household was stricken. Shindel, always a thorn in her side, was gone. He was twenty. Abigail hardly knew at any given moment where he might be. He could be in the mining towns, Colville or Boise, Idaho. He could be at the military posts at the Cascades or The Dalles. Or he could be in town, working in a store. Susan was fourteen, and she boarded in Vancouver over the winter months when she went to school. She was almost old enough to get married. The only persons in Abigail's house were Little Charley Biles and, from time to time, the shadowy presence of Jane and her infant.

Abigail presided over a house that was almost empty.

But not empty yet.

It was not until April 1858, two years after the marriage of Pearson and Jane, that Abigail told Mary Ann and Michael more of Jane's life and misfortunes:

> Your sister Jane is now At Home At present And is Agoing to stay At Home this sommr As her Husband is gone to Utah on An Expedision or As Guide for the government So that she Could not stay At the Dolls Alone. Poor Jane Has Had very Bad Luck. She Had A butiful Littl Boy And It took The Lung Fever And they got scard And They Both Came Down to Me to se if I could not do Something for It. But o Alas It was to Late. It died the Same night they Came down. They Thought It was better. But As soon As I Saw It I thought It was struck with death. But I did not say Enney thing to them. O He was A butiful Boy. He had Blue Eyes Like his Father. (APRIL 18, 1858)

Jane's baby was born in the summer of 1857, and it died in January 1858. The Reverend McCarty noted the burial in his journal. He was the only person who ever called the baby by name:

> On the 14 of jany 1858 attended the funeral of Thom jefferson, infant son of W. H. Pierson & Abigail [Jane] his wife, aged 5 months.[16]

If Abigail refused to acknowledge the baby's birth, she felt obligated to tell of its death. But all she told of its identity was to say that the baby had blue eyes, "like his father." The baby's name—Thomas Jefferson Pearson—drew the thread of Pearson's southern (Baltimore and then Texas) antecedents through the family's northern sympathies. From the beginning, Henry Pearson was an outsider.

After the baby died, Pearson left his wife and went to Utah. He gave Jane an Indian boy to help on the farm.

> Jane Has Like Wies An Indian boy that Henry Bought for a survent With her At our house. He Is A very good Boy. He Milks All of My Cows for Me And is Abl to cut the Wood on the wood pile. (APRIL 18, 1858)[17]

Finding it difficult to write about Jane, Abigail changed the subject. She wrote instead of relatives in Sunbury, Pennsylvania, and of Preaux, who was still "cuting And Selling Wood of our Clame. He has the Wood ready Corded up for sale now." Abigail tried to have the court issue an injunction but, she said, she couldn't get the injunction to "work Write." It was only effective, she was told, "if He sels or re Moves that wood." In the meantime, Abigail had no recourse but to keep close watch on Preaux's corded wood. Jane's Indian boy cut enough wood for the house, but not enough for sale. Abigail wrote, "I Cannot do Hardley Eny Hard Work Eny More."

She was offered $13,000 for the whole of her claim, more than three times the $4,000 she had been offered the preceding year for only half. But the children would have to agree to sell their shares, and the territory still waited to be surveyed.

Abigail noted there was no letter from John Biles in three arrivals of the mail steamer. But if Biles was no longer writing to Abigail, he was writing to Mary Ann and Michael, bemoaning his situation as an "old widower" with "no wholesome diversions for Idle Hours." He sent an ambrotype portrait of himself to his young nieces and nephews so that they would know what he looked like—he had become a man who "wore eyebrows under his nose." (FEBRUARY 8, 1858) One way or another, he maintained his ties with Rachel's people. Brushing aside Abigail's prickly scolding, Biles kept track of her lawsuit against Preaux. He wrote Mary Ann that as soon as the government bought out the rights of the Hudson's

Bay Company, title to the claim would be assigned to Abigail, and she could sell their shares. But that was at least a year away.

In the meantime he was working as a "confidential clerk" in the firm of Bush, Lobdell & Bush Locomotive Foundry in Wilmington, Delaware, and he was unused to working in an office.

It was clear Biles wanted to remarry, and Mary Ann suggested she could play matchmaker for him, even describing a particular widow as a suitable object of his attention. Biles quickly wrote back:

> Now I come to this all important Subject—Matrimony. . . . Let me ask you was you really in earnest when you said that you could get me a wife if I really desired one. . . . Sometimes I think you were only jesting. Then again there is so much matter of fact about your allusion to the matter that I am almost constrained to beleve you are in earnest. (FEBRUARY 8, 1858)

He had been east for almost two years, more than enough time for a young man to have found a wife. But Biles had not married in haste the

John Biles served at different times as county auditor, justice of the peace, commissioned officer, elected member of the territorial legislature in Olympia, and later Speaker of the House.

first time and he was not about to do so now. There were so many things he was uncertain about—he did not know whether he would return to the Northwest, or stay in Wilmington or Philadelphia, or go to Illinois. He was trying to figure out where he could do better. "Have a strong notion of making money fast." And he watched the signs that portended the nation was headed for Civil War.

Abigail took no notice of politics, but she too was wrestling with a kind of civil war. As Jane's life is reconstructed out of the deliberate omissions and half-truths of the letters, it is clear that her marriage was more disastrous than Abigail had ever chosen to tell. Jane and Pearson themselves were at war, and Abigail was drawn into their conflict.

When Jane came home for the birth of her baby in 1857 that homecoming had been traumatic: "When She Came Her Feeat Had Bin Wet All the Way From the Dolls [The Dalles] And She Had A triable Caugh And she never got over It until She Had A Hard spell of sickness [the baby's birth] in May and June."

Jane came home not only because the baby was about to be born, but because Pearson had squandered all of her dowry:

> When They Ware Maried [they] Went to the Dolls to Live. And When They Went A Way He Had Nine Hundred Dollars Besides four yoke of oxen And A Nice Teem of American Horses . . . And A greate Meny Indians Horses And A Butiful Wagn And Plow And Harrow And meny other Things. And When Jane Went A Way She Had Thousand of Cloathes And A Splended Bed. And I gave Her A First Rate cow And A Hefer Calf. And the cow was onley three years old. And I gave her Half the Foules That I Had. She Took Three Chestes Full of Cloathes And A Larg goods Box Full of Blankets and Sheats And Pillow cases And Five pares of Shooes And Stockings, I Do Not know How Many pares. And When She Came Home To me she Had onley Mockones [moccasins] on Her Feet And Not Hardley Eny Cloaths. He sold Nearley [all] Her Cloathes I Expect, For She was Not gone onley Ten Months and All the poor girl Brought Hom [was] her Featherbed And pillows. Her Nice Sheates And Rose Blankets Ware All gone And Bolster And all the dishes, And She Had Enough to Set the Table For A dozen of persons And Every thing Elce suitable For to Set out A Nice Table that I gave her.
>
> (MARCH 24, 1859)

Every single thing Jane lost was something Abigail had worked for—the chests full of clothes, the rose blankets and sheets, the dishes, the calf and the cow. It was Abigail's hard labor, out of her land and her life, and she had given everything to Jane. And now Jane—or Henry Pearson, it hardly mattered which—had thrown it all to the wind. Just as Shindel had done. The frontier children were laying waste to her work and her home.

Jane's Indian boy filled in more of the details of Jane's troubled household:

> There Survent Indian Told Me That There House Was Alwais Ful of Gentle men When He Was At Home And No Ladeys. I Asked Him If No Ladeys Never Come To Se Jane And He [said] Some times, But They did not Stay, Onley until Evening. But the Gentle men Would Stay All night And Drink Brandey and that Way got In Debt. . . . He wasted His propertey [with] Gambling and Runing Horse Races. . . . He Was Sold Out All But one Hors And That Was Janes or It should have been sold two. Her Cow and Nice Heffer Calf And All Was gone And Then he Went A Way. (MARCH 24, 1859)

In the autumn of 1858 Henry Pearson came back from Utah and, with amazing forbearance, Abigail allowed him and Jane to come and live in her house. Maybe she thought she could keep them under control if they lived under her roof; maybe she was tired of an empty house; maybe all she could see was Jane's need. But when Henry left again in the winter of 1859, he left Jane "In A Delicate Situation Without one Dollar to Help Her Self With."

> Now She Will Be on My Hands A gain poor jane. And After I had taken Care of Her day And Night He Never As Mutch As said I Am Obleadged to you . . . Nor Oferd to Pay the Doctor. . . . Poor Jane. She Is Sutch A good girl That I would do eny Thing for her, But Every Thing Is Left on My Expence. (MARCH 24, 1859)

Abigail's language was the language of household economy, but she was telling Mary Ann and Michael that her family was coming apart. Children were supposed to help their parents. Family and farm were a union: indissoluble. She could not survive, the farm would not survive, without their help. The house divided would not survive, not on the frontier.

The "frontier" children were indeed different from the children raised in "the States." Even the girls, to whom Abigail was fiercely loyal, began to think they could go their own way.

> None of [the girls] youses Me None To Well. . . . I cannot help it. They Will Not Mind Me eny. . . . Jane thinks That She Is Married And Can do As she pleases. And Shindel Like wise. And so susan thinks She Must go two. . . . The girls Can stay here or If Not they can go. I Have staid Longer With them than I have staid with you And Schooled them And took Care of them And None of them youses Me None To Well. They go off And Leave Me Alone At home. (MARCH 24, 1859)

Abigail was feeling the farm slip away: "I am tired of Being here and Loosing So Meny of My familey." The work of holding on was almost more than she could handle.

> I have don Nearly All That Men Do. Now I Had To work very Hard To get A Long the First Two years After your Father died For Every Thing Was Left on My Hands And Shin would go of to Town And stay A Way. . . . If I should Have eny one do the Work . . . I would Have to give them Five dollars Aday And I thought I could save that Mutch And so I don it my self.
> (MARCH 24, 1859)

To make matters worse, Shindel married and brought his bride home to his mother! Like a bad penny, Shindel was back.

> I Must Tel you That Shindel Is Married To A young girl By the Name of Sarah Armstrong. She Is very young and Very poor. But I think She Is A very good girl. I have known Her These Three years And I Never New eny Harme of her. [For] one thing, She Is two good For Shin If He Does Not Mend His Wais Which I hope He Will Now. But I Am afraid He Will Not [and she will leave him]. (MARCH 11, 1859)

"When They Marey," wrote Abigail with asperity, *"They Aught to take care of them Selves."*[18]

IV. "Poor Jane's Insainity," *1854*

A decade had passed since the Malicks came into the northwestern territories. The land was as rich as they had been promised, but it was not surveyed. They did not own it and they could not sell it. They were in the midst of wars with the Rogue River Indians. And they were in the midst of rapid shifts of population, first to the gold fields of northern California and then to smaller strikes in Oregon and Idaho. Families that held together over the long journey west were "dis-assembled" on the rich landscape of the new land. An accident or an unplanned errand took a life unexpectedly. The promise of a new fortune could mean that a son or a daughter might wander away. And even when they remained at home, young people fought free of the restraints of parental obligation. There were so many different roads to follow that the circle of home seemed too small and new directions became a way of life.

Little Charley was Abigail's safe harbor in the world that had gone askew. With Charley she escaped the contentious squabbling and wayward adventures of her own children. The aging woman and her grandson were thieves together, stealing peaceful moments in a storm still gathering force.

> Very often Little Charley and Me Are Left A Lone two Miles From Town And no ones for Thre Miles Be low us onley the Indians.
>
> (UNDATED FRAGMENT, 1859)

Little Charley was four years old, and he was Abigail's delight.

> He groes Finley And is A standing By My Side With a Tin Cup And A pipe A Making bubbles And Bloing them up. He Makes them With Soap Sudz And He Can Blow them As Big as his Head And then Throw them up to the upper Floure. O it is fine Fun For him. . . . It is a raning so I supose that Charley And Me Will Hve to Stay A Lone At home. (MARCH 11, 1859)

That's what it all came to—the best of it—Abigail and Charley, sitting in the doorway, blowing bubbles as the silver light of evening came upon them. There in the doorway of this new land, after Hiram's drowning and Charles's disappearance and George's tyranny and Rachel's death, there was Abigail with her grandson, looking out at the orchards, smelling the cool air of early spring.

One day Charley asked where babies come from:

> He said, mama How Does god Make Babeys out of Clay? If I knowed I wuld Be Making Babeys All the Time and sell Them. It is a grat Mistory To Him How Children Comes. Shindel told Hime That When Adam Was made He Was Made out of clay And Sat up A gainst the Fense to dry. And Then When he was dry he Began to walk. . . . And That Was The way people Came. [When] he Asked Me how Babeys came I told him that god Made them out of Clay two. (UNDATED LETTER)

Writing about Little Charley, Abigail was like a young mother sharing the progress of her own youngster, giving shape to the child with the eye of a sculptor, correcting, evaluating, changing an attitude here, altering an aspect there, trying to see better the human relationship. In her letters about her daughter's child, Abigail painted a life as it should have been were all of them in their proper places, safe and alive. Parents, children, and grandchildren. The farm and the children to work the farm. Little Charley was what home was all about.

Abigail knew there would come a day when John Biles would take Charley away. She knew full well "Biles Is Able to take Care of Him." But "the Child Could Not hardley give Me up, For I seem Lik His Mother." And Biles did come back to Washington Territory in August 1858; he did not take Charley away, not yet.

Away or at home, John Biles was their rock of stability, and whether Abigail liked it or not, on his return he set out to put her house in order the only way he knew, by concluding the lawsuit against Preaux.

> I called on Preaux and advised a settlement. . . . We agreed verbally to divide the claim equal and placed it in a Lawyers hands to draw the Decrees & Deeds. . . . In the meantime we have had the claim Surveyed and a division line . . . agreed upon by both parties and all that remains now is to get the Decree from the District Court. . . . The court will set off to the widow her half of the claim. . . . after which she is to Deed to Preaux all her right and

> title [to the remaining half]. . . . Both parties are much disappointed as to the quantity of land, both acting under the Supposition that there was 640 acres. But after the Survey they found out quite different, there being only 397 acres. This is first time it was ever Surveyed. As soon as I have a little spare time I will draw a diagram and forward it to you. It will show you its location from the Columbia river and in what manner the parties were deceived as to the number of acres. . . . [Mother] . . . is determined to sell out and go to Illinois. (JUNE 5, 1859)

Abigail did not thank him. Both parties discovered that their claims were smaller than first supposed and felt cheated. But under all her complaining, Abigail was relieved to have the suit ended.

In October, she wrote that she would go to Vancouver to sign the papers for the division of the land according to the settlement, and after that, she expected the probate court to grant her clear title. Then she would sell the land. "If I Can Get it Settled [I can] sell out And get the Monney, For [then] I Do not have to Work so Hard in My Old Age."

But there were other affairs John Biles could not settle at all. Jane, who was a shadowy presence in Abigail's letters to Illinois, was the center of a separate brewing storm. In the fall of 1859, with no embellishments or evasions or omissions, Abigail wrote that Jane would not come back to Illinois with her:

> And I Would Not Wish to bring Her [because] She distrois All that Come Before Her When She Has Her Crasy Spells on her And Wantes to kill All Derest Frendes And her Little Babe. And . . . I Have Had to Tak her Babe And Not let Her See it for two And thre dayes At A Time And tie her down on the Bed and it took Three of us to do it At that. So you May think I Have Had a hard time of it with her. (OCTOBER 18, 1859)

Jane had "crasy spells," and Abigail could not explain them; they were past her powers of explanation. The baby she wrote about this time was Jane's second child, little Frank Pearson, born during the summer of 1858, a baby with black eyes and white skin, "like his mother." "It took three of us to tie her down on the bed." That would have been Susan and Sarah Armstrong and Abigail.

Jane's insanity came upon the household with overwhelming force. If there had been signs before of her erratic behavior, Abigail had covered them up. Six months earlier, she had used curious language to describe her own feelings:

> I Am Tierd of Being here And Haveing So Mutch Trouble About Every Thing About this Land. And Loosing so Meny of My Familey has put Me Almost Besid My Self. Some Times I Think I Sirtenly Will get Insane.
>
> (MARCH 11, 1859)

Jane's madness set its awful imprint on the household. Jane was nineteen.

Abigail wrote, "I Have so Mutch trouble with [the] children. They Are Not Like children Raised in the States And they have no Father And they Will Not Mind Me."

Jane was an unstable teenager. Her courtship was celebrated by whoops and cheers, by too many suitors from the fort, by horseback riding through the countryside, and by an atmosphere that paid only occasional and ceremonial address to parental restrictions. The shadowy events in her life—the birth and death of her first child, her young husband's gambling and drinking, possibly his physical abuse of her—all came in rapid succession. She ran home to her mother when she was first pregnant ("When She Came Her Feeat Had Bin Wet All the Way From the Dolls And She Had A triable Caugh And she never got over It until She Had A Hard spell of Sickness in May and June"). But she went back to Pearson, and to the wild house at The Dalles. The emotional damage of early pregnancy and marriage, her baby's death, and her abandonment by Pearson took their toll.

In the end the frontier was more powerful than Abigail's cautionary restrictions. The cohort of frontier children made broad swings away from her prescriptions of land and work and home. They rushed headlong toward independence, bloodying themselves to be free of parental restraint, coming home when their wild ways had damaged their lives.

Abigail was angry with them, and she was tied to them. She could not let them go, and she could not accept their ways.

> I think It Is the Best For Me to go And Leave them. They Have Never knowed the Loss of ther Father For I have cept Every thing A going On the Same As if He was A liveing And Alwais cept House So that they Always had A good Home to Come to In Eny circumstance of theres. And they do not Even thank Me For It. And now I have staid with them until they have All Bin Rased And Able to help them selves And schoold them on my one expence

> Fre of Charge And Alwais clothed them. . . . So now I will Go And leve them And see If they Will Mis Me Eny. I suppose they Will. Perhaps they Will have to Work A Little More than they Have Had to do Here to Fore. They think that A fu hindred dollars Will keep them all ther Life time. But depend Apon It It will not kepe them Long In this countrey. So they say they can do with out Me, So now I Will Let them try it now. (OCTOBER 18, 1859)

On December 12, 1859, the probate court for Clarke County finally confirmed Abigail Malick's title to the claim on the banks of the Columbia River. It granted "in all respects a final settlement." By that year, almost a decade after the Donation Act had been passed, only twenty-four claims had been filed in Washington Territory. Forty-four claims were pending under preemption laws. The Federal Census of 1860 for Clarke County, after a decade of settlement, reported only 2,384 persons.[19] Settlement left only a tenuous mark upon the vast expanse of the Northwest region.

Abigail was fifty-eight years old. It had taken eleven years to clear title to her claim, and when title was finally conferred, she was getting ready to leave. Her children had died, or left her, and those who remained at home were not interested in the toilsome life of farming. They had no use for their inheritance and would as soon see it sold or sell it themselves.

But none of them were at the end of the journey yet. Jane's madness was increasing in intensity. On New Year's Eve, 1859, Abigail described more of the startling drama: "The reson that I did not Write For So Long Was on A Count of Poor Janes Insainity."

> Before She came to Her sences she went out to the Well And drew Eighteen Buckets Full of Water and thru Water All ovr her self And striped Her Self down to her Wast And took A black Boll Brush And Some Sand And Scourd her head and Her Cloathes And Her Bodey All Over And scourd the Well And the ground In Frount of the Well. She Washed And rubed it With A stone And A Neighbour Woman come A Long And sais Jane What Are you A douing? Why I Am A scrubing For Mama. Dont you think that is right? The woman sais yes, But you Aught to put on your Clouthes. I will When I get Radey Was her reply. She Washed her Cloathes And scourd them All over With Sand And She Was Wett All over With cold Water For A Bout thre Hours. Then She climed upon the Top of the House And Began to pull the Shingels off the House And Nearley tore the Hool roof All off And then she Tore the top of the chimney down. And then We coaxt her to Come down But she Would not And We did not know How to get her down. It was A geting night By this time so We had to get her down By Cetching Her With

> A rope unbenownest to her. And A young Man tied Her And Him and Me and Helped Her down. And sais I, you Aught to Be Made to Carey All them Bricks And stuff out. The Bricks And Every thing come tumbling downe in the House. And then she commenced to cry And Went to Carying them out. And after that she came to her senses. And Oh how glad I Was When I saw she was coming to her senses a Gane. Oh I have had An Abundance of trouble with Jane. (DECEMBER 31, 1859)

Abigail grew so accustomed to Jane's insanity that she came to write about it as if it were an everyday event. "Since coming down from the roof, Jane has never Had Eny simptoms of it since." As if madness were no more than a common cold. But Jane's condition had deteriorated. For one thing, when they had tied her to her bed in October no one but family knew about her or her threats to kill her baby. But when Jane was up on the roof of Abigail's house, stripped naked to the waist, brought down by a soldier from the nearby fort, it was a matter of public attention. Abigail feared she would be forced to have Jane committed unless she demonstrated she could care for her at home. Explaining why the doctor had been called, Abigail wrote:

> If We Could not of got Him We Shuld Have Had to of sent her to Stockton to the mad House or the Insane Ascilum. And that would Have Bin very hard for Her And us. For They Whip them Every Morning or When they do Eny thing, so I am told, And get hardley Eny thing to Eat. (DECEMBER 31, 1859)

Abigail's knowledge of the "Insane Ascilum" in Stockton is a startling piece of information. There actually were three separate institutions for the care of the insane in the Northwest before 1870, in northern California, at Stockton, and in Oregon, at Salem and Portland. And the Catholic nuns near Vancouver operated an orphanage that may also have housed the insane.[20] Reports of the Insane Asylum of Portland, Oregon, between 1870 and 1890 show a total number of patients that increased from 260 in 1870–72, to 411 in 1876–77, and a grand number of 734 in 1884–86. Of that number the ratio of female to male patients began at one-third and increased over the first decade to one-half.[21]

Emotional breakdown was a frontier "secret," a special hazard spoken of in whispers and shakes of the head. Women brought into mental asylums for depression caused by years of searing isolation were called simply "prairie women." Diaries tell of women in Kansas and Nebraska who would walk ten miles or more just to see human faces on a train that whizzed by. "Down at the edge of the hills a mother of three hung herself." "North of Hay Spring a man killed his brother with an ax." "A neighbor on the south table hanged himself in his well curbing and dangled unnoticed for two days in plain sight of the road, so nearly did his head resemble a windlass [a bucket attached to a rope] swinging."[22]

In the Northwest territories asylums, along with statehouses, jailhouses, churches, and schools, were built with all due speed. The environment bred instability as much as it provided the ground for success. And Abigail's frontier outpost was home to a small boy, an infant, a schoolgirl, and a young woman who suffered periods of madness. It was a strange redemption to the dream of family in the "new country."

V. The House Divided, *1860–1870*

The last months of 1859 were restless and uneasy. Almost on the day Abigail tied Jane to her bed to keep her from killing her baby, John Brown led thirteen white men and five black men in a siege of the arsenal at Harper's Ferry. In a makeshift prison, the "blood-stained fanatic" from Missouri was urged to plead insanity, but Brown said he was content to "die for God's eternal truth on the scaffold as any other way," and he was hung on December 2, 1859. A strange Christmas season was upon them all.[23]

Abraham Lincoln sounded the warning in Illinois. "A house divided against itself," he said, "cannot stand. I do not expect the Union to be dissolved—I do not expect the house to fall—but I do expect it will cease to be divided." Both in the political arena and in the private transactions of family life, a house divided could not endure. The struggle went on a little longer, the nation and the Malicks holding on, digging in, before a cataclysm.

Abigail's frontier children made wider and wider swings from the fixed point of home, and she began to let them go. They could do as they liked. Although she assured Mary Ann that she wanted to come "home" to the States, she was learning to manage the claim on her own.

> I Have A Young Man A Workeing For Me And He Is Busey A geting Supper And A Making Coffee. He is the Best Hand About the House That I Ever Saw. He will get up in the Morning And go And Feed the Horses And cattle And then Com In . . . Befor we know That He is up. . . . I Have Had Him hear A Making Fence and Paling in the Yard. (JANUARY 26, 1860)

She wrote repeatedly of her wish to go back to Illinois where Mary Ann and Michael would care for her, but she could not effect the sale of the land: "I have Ad vertised [the land] For Sail All the Time And the People knowes It And I Cannot Sell It As yet. . . . I wish to Sell It As Mutch As you Wish me to For I Hav to pay Taxes onit And I Have no need of Land Eny How For I Cannot Half take Care of a Farm or Land. . . . If I Can sell I shal pre pare to Come to the states. I Am Detirmind to under take It." (DECEMBER 31, 1859)

But behind her assertions that she meant to leave, she was as determined as ever to stay where she was. She even invented fanciful explanations as to why she could never go back. The overland journey was too arduous, she reasoned, and she would have to go by sea. But if she did, there were perils:

> I should get sea sick And die A Board the Ship And have to Be Throne over Board for the Sharkes to Eat. That Would Be Almost to Bad that they Should have My Boddey After All My Toiles And Troubles of this Life.
>
> (DECEMBER 31, 1859)

Ship passage cost seven hundred dollars. If Abigail were to sail, "I woud Not go Without Being A Caben passanger." And if she were thrown to the sharks, as she feared, she would lose not only her life but her passage money as well!

The truth was that she still clung to the land: "I Have Abutiful teem of Creem colered Horses. . . . One Is A Horse And the other Is A Mare.

And I have A most Butiful Wagon and Butiful Harnice and A good plow and Harrow." (DECEMBER 31, 1859)

She was mistress over a good farm. She had clothing and a house with a porch all around it. She had a wagon and horses, and she had supported all of her children. She had the never-ending blessing of fruit in winter. And she was still needed. She cared for Rachel's child, Charley: "Sweat Little Fellow. . . . He Alwais Calles me [Mother], poor Motherless Child. But He Hardley knows the Difreance Now Wether I Aint His Mother. . . . And I Alwais Treet Him As My own Child." And she cared for Jane's child, Frank Pearson. "He Is Avery Butiful child And grows Fineley." She worried constantly over the two children: Charley was too thin—"He is the slenderst Child I Ever Saw. O such Little Bones and No Flesh on them At all." (JANUARY 26, 1860) And Frank was slow to speak.

Of course, there was Jane herself. Abigail wrote of Jane's condition as if it were an everyday matter. "Jane Has Got over her Insainety And is quite well." (JANUARY 26, 1860)

Abigail was content for the moment that she had no buyers for her farm.

John Biles was back in Washington Territory, trying to take root again. He did not take Charley away yet, and though he wrote less frequently to the Albrights, he did keep in touch. He wrote about the political and economic changes in the region, as it turned from agriculture toward lumbering and mining.

> We are having some little excitement about the gold mines recently discovered in the north part of our Territory about 250 miles from this city. Many are going there and I fear to their sorrow. . . . Nine out of ten [mines] prove to be humbugs. . . . Yet many persons who have suffered by former reported discoveries have again left their usual avocations and departed for these new mines. I hope they are extensive and will prove profitable . . . for I assure you our Territory badly needs something of this kind to help its money market. . . . The people are very extravagant, and unless something turns up our country must be drained of its coin. (MARCH 23, 1860)

Slavery continued to be argued in the territories as passionately as it was in the States. Settlers read the Supreme Court's Dred Scott decision of 1857 that protected a man's property in slaves as contravening the prohibition against slavery that was written into the Northwest Ordinance of 1843 and the establishment of the Oregon Territory in 1848. And as the legislators drafted a constitution to bring Oregon Territory into the Union, they listened closely to the Lincoln-Douglas debates of 1858. When they finished they had devised a curious "solution" to the contradictions that underlay the Civil War. The Oregon state constitution outlawed slavery *and* kept free blacks out of the state. Oregon came into the Union as a "free" state, but one that was also free of all men of color. And then the legislators added a "Bill of Rights" that prohibited Negroes, mulattoes, and Orientals from ever exercising the franchise. Antislavery sentiment was satisfied on the one hand and southern loyalties on the other.[24]

John Biles still hoped against hope that accommodation would prevail and civil war would be avoided.

> I notice by the States papers that Senator Douglass has a hard road to travel, but I hope from the bottom of my heart that at the Charleston Convention he will be proclaimed the Nominee . . . standing upon the platform of People's rights [and] nonintervention. Hurrah for S A Douglass. I wish I had a million of votes to give him I would do so Cheerfully. The principles he inculcates and advocates and boldly proclaims to all the world are wholesome in every respect in my humble estimation. (MARCH 23, 1860)

But he also knew the Albrights were unequivocal antislavery people, Republicans "by a large majority." The Christian church in the neighboring community in Illinois passed resolutions declaring that "Jefferson Davis & Co are the biggest devils among ten thousand." As civil war approached, the Albrights and John Biles were divided not only by geographic distances but by political convictions as well.

In the last paragraph of his letter, John Biles wrote about the family, where the news was also of breaking apart and unrest. Susan had eloped.

> Susan is living in town, will not live with her mother. She came within an inch of getting married two nights ago and that without my knowledge as her Guardian. She never said much about it to me before that time. I cut you a piece out of the newspaper and enclose herewith. The Ed[itor] got hold of this affair some how. Her intended is 18 she 16. The affair [is] terminated. . . . I gave her a good talking to, but I fear all to no purpose. It may delay the union a short time, but I have every reason to believe that the first opportunity that presents itself they will elope. You will perceive in the printed

> article they call me a refractory Old Gentleman & this is done to avoid being too personal. Confound their impudence. (MARCH 23, 1860)

Like her brother and sister, Susan flamboyantly planted the flag of her independence. And with resignation born of years of experience, Abigail would not even mention her daughter's elopement in her letters. She resolutely ignored it.

In Illinois, the Albright children were also embarking on different and dangerous paths. Mary Ann's son Hiram, just a year older than Susan, enlisted in the Thirty-eighth Illinois Regiment and was sent to his first assignment in Missouri.

Abigail wrote only about the Columbia River that flooded her farm.

> This sommer the Columbia [is] A Raising To Anormous Hight, Sweaping every thing Before It, Taking Fences And every Thing Elce. . . . The Water Was In My House About Afoot on the Floore And I Was oblidged to Moove to town, Whare I Still Re Mane. . . . [But] I Expect to Move Back Home To Morrow. . . . I Have My garden All Made Agane And My Orched Fenced In And Pottatoes planted Agane. . . . I With others Lost Nearly All My Cattle. I Lost Eight Hed And Saved onley Nine Head. They did Not Starve, But chilled to Death. Cattel Are Not yust to Cold and snow [any] More Than People Are in this Countrey. (JULY 15, 1860)

There were fewer letters. More than ever, Abigail's accounts of her children's misdirections seemed an observer's:

> Susan and Her Husband Are parted. He Is a Worthless Retch And He Got Mad At Susan, Swore He Would Cut her Throat. And She Said She would Not Live With No sutch A Man, So they parted.
>
> Jane's Husband Was Murderd By the Indians. That Was good For Him, For He Would Rather Be With the Indians than With White People. The reason I Say It Was good For Him, I thught He was the Caus of Her Incainety And the greate trouble that I Had With her And His child. (OCTOBER 31, 1860)

Abigail's capacity to deflect the eccentricities of her children's lives was endless.

She wrote, briefly, about John Biles. He "Is Married Agane And Has Taken Little Charley A Way From Me. And Now I have No one With Me But Jane and the Babe." (OCTOBER 31, 1860) She didn't say who Biles had married. Just the simple fact that she had lost the one person in all the territory that she loved best, a little five-year-old boy who looked like Rachel.

John Biles married Elizabeth Kelly five years after Rachel's death. He was thirty-three and his bride was nineteen. She had come to Vancouver when she was eleven, the daughter of Major William Kelly, stationed at the fort. She may have known the Malicks during her childhood. Like Biles she was a rare find in the territory—a well-educated young woman.[25] She remembered arriving in Vancouver in 1852 by way of the Isthmus of Panama in the company of Ulysses S. Grant. Years later, when Grant visited the Northwest territory after the Civil War, he looked at her closely and said, "This ought to be Lizzie Kelly." "He hadn't seen me for 28 years and I thought it was remarkable that he should remember me."

Elizabeth Kelly had a strong sense of herself when she described her marriage to a respected, notable citizen of Oregon.

> I was married September 3, 1860, to John D. Biles. . . . He was the first American judicial officer to serve north of the Columbia River. . . . Not long after our marriage we moved from Vancouver to Portland, to a house on the corner of Clay and Frontier Streets.

If Abigail wrote little about John Biles's marriage, she had more to tell about Susan:

> Susan Is gone to victory [Vancouver] Island. She Went by Sea. She Is An Actress In A theater Trupe. She will Be gone A Bout three months. I Am very Well A quainted With them All. They Are All very Nic People. They Ware All at our House on A visit Jest Before they went A way. They give Susan Twentey Thre dollars a Weak Clear of Al Expenses And Tak Good Care of Her. She Is very Well. . . . I Will send you som of susans dress peices—I mene of her silk dresses. (OCTOBER 13, 1860)

Just like that! "Susan is an actress." Abigail denied the outrageous by making it fit into the routine of daily life. "I am very Well A quainted With them All. They Are All very Nic People." Susan was wearing silk dresses; swatches of her fashionable wardrobe would be sent back to Illinois. Susan had eloped, married, left her husband, joined a troupe of traveling actors—and she was still only fifteen. She was Abigail's most dramatic frontier child. Certainly she proved that young women could be grandly free agents of their own lives. And there was no one at home to hold her back, not her father, not her brothers, not John Biles, not Abigail.

Theater was a magnet to frontier settlers. Within a decade of first settlement, Portland had a theater of its own—Stewarts Theatre—that seated six hundred and also served as courtroom, church, military headquarters, and town hall. Theatrical companies operated throughout the territories, often calling themselves "families." Mr. and Mrs. W. C. Forbes, J. P. Adams, Mr. and Mrs. Frank Mayo, and the Robinsons led companies, or "families," that played the Northwest territories. Mrs. John Wood formed a company of her own and entertained in San Francisco and Portland. Abigail didn't name the company that Susan joined, but other single young women like Susan were members of touring troupes. Local newspapers and billboards proclaimed Miss Lulu Sweet and Miss Lizzie Gordon Stewart as "stars."[26]

All kinds of theater were popular. Rachel as a young bride had been taken to the circus in 1852—"Mr. Biles took me thursday knight. It was 2 dollars a person." And when Biles was away at the legislature in Olympia and Rachel was a "grass widow," she felt it respectable enough in 1853 to attend the theater in Vancouver without her husband. There was "musick" and the infantry brass band played "every Wednesday knight."

But theater could mean everything from the "ten-cent shows" of vaudeville to mangled declarations of Shakespearean monologues in storefront rooms. And the line between the saloon and the vaudeville show was a fine one. Women in vaudeville sometimes mingled with the customers: "Miss Bell Divine" won fame up and down the northwest coast as a favorite with audiences during—and after—the show.

The men who lived in mining towns made rough audiences, and troupes had to pay well to keep a company intact. Travel was by horseback, canoe, boat, or stagecoach, and actors had to be a hardy lot. Abigail's comment about Susan's wages suggests that the company was not without its risks and dangers.

> She gets twentey thre dollars A Week For Plaing With Them. She Is Well A Quainted With them All And She is With Two Very Nice Ladyes. And they promised to take Good Care of Her And Bring Her Back Safe If she Lived. And if she Died they Would Bring Her Back in Som shape or form.
>
> (APRIL 5, 1861)

Out of habit, Abigail did the best she could with what news she had to tell. She had no more strength to be disturbed by her errant children. She wanted to be let alone and to tend her land. "I Must tell you that I have Had A very good Cropp of Every Thing I Raised this year." (OCTOBER 13, 1860)

As days and lives were blurred by her advancing years, the notorious and the new and the untoward were washed in with tired strokes. "Shindel and His Wife Are Both Well And doing Midling Well And They Will Do Well Enough As Long As They Have his Mother to Back them."

If she chose to make excuses for Susan, she was less charitable with Sarah Armstrong, Shindel's wife. She is "No Wife For A Poor Man. . . . She Does not Like To Work. I Do More yet In one Day Than She Does In three Days. And . . . She Is So Wast Ful. It Costs Shindle Twice As Mutch As it Does Me To Live." (OCTOBER 13, 1860)

Sarah Armstrong was all of fifteen when Shindel married her in 1859. Shin was twenty-two. According to Abigail, Sarah spent most of her time jealously watching the new clothes Abigail bought for Susan and Jane— "When I would Buy For the other girls She Would be jelous And Would say I Did not Care so Mutch for Her As I Did For my own girls." But life came upon these children of the frontier quickly. Only a year after her wedding, Sarah had her first baby, and it died. The Reverend McCarty noted its death: "Attended the funeral of Eugen[i]e Clementine, infant daughter of Peter G [S] Malick, aged 1 month, 8 days." The entry was dated February 9, 1860.[27] Abigail was more careless. She did not mention its death until the summer.

Four infants had died since the family came to the Northwest: Rachel's stillborn twins, Jane's first son, Thomas Jefferson Pearson, and now Shindel's first daughter, Clementine. The family had more dead than living. And the living seemed driven to such volatile paths. Jane had been insane and her husband murdered by Indians. Susan had eloped, returned, married a man who threatened to cut her throat, and now she was an actress with a troupe of traveling players.

All these worrisome young people, they kept coming home with their troubles. Abigail helped them, reproved them, berated them, held few illusions, felt herself growing older, planted and cared for her crops, tried to find a place to rest, and knew she would never find that rest through her children.

She was fifty-nine.

In December 1860, news came from Illinois that Mary Ann Orndorff, Michael's sister, and her two children, Emma and Ulala, nine and seven, were murdered in their own home by a drifter looking for money. The event was so grisly that the entire county focused on the details. It was only the third murder the county had ever known, and an ax murder of a woman and two small girls!

The culprit, one John Ott, was found almost immediately, hiding in the corn in the next county. Newspapers described the murderer as a man "enamoured of a woman who must have had a large amount of the demoniac in her nature for she urged him to set fire to barns, to rob and the like."[28]

When Ott pleaded guilty a mob gathered and there was doubt whether the jail could keep him alive until the hanging. The Peoria National Blues and the Washington Rifles were called out. The Emmett Guards and the German Rifles marched to the courtroom.

> At an early hour Friday morning, people came pouring in from all parts of the country, and by ten o'clock it was estimated that at least five thousand had assembled in the city.

By the time the prisoner was on the scaffold "a dense crowd filled the streets . . . and the tops and windows of many neighboring houses were filled with spectators. The military were drawn up around the scaffold to prevent the crowd from passing the fence."[29]

Just a few weeks later, on April 12, 1861, the nation was engulfed in civil war.

As she had not noticed the eruption of Mount St. Helens in 1852, Abigail hardly noticed the start of the Civil War in 1861. Her vision was all upon the convoluted affairs of her children. "Susan Has got her Devorce From that ugly Fellow and is gone to the Dolls [The Dalles] with the Theatre Troup And Will soon Be Home Agane." (JUNE 9, 1861) A good salary, even from an acting company, was a welcome augury to Abigail. It covered a host of doubts and misgivings.

Susan's career on the stage was short-lived; she left the theater company, but she would not live with Abigail any more. "Susan Has Her devorce From Her Husband and dose Not wish to Marry A Gain very soon." (APRIL 5, 1861) Like Shindel, Susan sowed her wild oats. She was sixteen!

Susan's divorce reflected the rising number of young women who turned to the courts of California and the Northwest territories in marital affairs. "Far from being hostile to women's desires, the divorce court was an effective institution enabling women to start new lives."[30] Although desertion was the most commonly sustained complaint brought by women in the 1850s and '60s, adultery and cruelty were second. In western states and territories, where women were scarce, most did not dally with marriages that did not go well. By 1877, the eight states with the greatest number of divorces in relation to population were Washington, Montana, Colorado, Texas, Oregon, Wyoming, Idaho, and Oklahoma.[31] In Illinois, on the other hand, while divorces were not unknown, they were not common. Sangamon County, not far from Tazewell where the Albrights lived, recorded only three divorces in forty years.[32]

Susan, for her part, set her own directions.

> Susan Is gone to Walla Walla to keep store, A Dry Goods Store, her And A nother Elderly ladey. She Is A very Nice And good Lady And I think that She will take good care of Susan. This Ladey is Also A Pensylvanian. She Is From the City of Philadelphia. She has the Store, Her and Susan. Her husband is A Cabenet Maker to trade And A very Nice Man. (JUNE 9, 1861)

Then, just when Abigail thought she had grown past the snares of her children's lives, Jane, whom she tended and protected throughout her madness, suddenly remarried.

> Jane Is Maryed to A Man By the Name of James Cantwell [Cornwell], A no Manner of A Count. . . . I do not Like Him. I Have Banished Her From Home Apon the A Count And she Is Never to Come Home in My Life time, Nor Him Either. I For Bid Him in the House twice And sent Him word once Not to Dare to Come. . . . But He Would Come When I Was gone. But she is gone With Him now So Let Her go For What she Fetches. And that Wont Be Mutch. We Never Menton Her, But I Am very sorry For Dear Little Frank Pearson. . . . Oho Jane Was spoiled By Marring Pearson And Has never ben Like Her Self since. (JUNE 9, 1861)

A proper young man named Cornelius Austin had courted Jane. He kept an apothecary store and came from Illinois. He went to church and walked the ladies home. He was kind to Jane's little boy and gave her a pair of plum trees. But Jane would not have him. Jane "cares not eny thing

About him. His luck was Blasted and hers two by that Dirtey Meane Cantwell." (APRIL 5, 1861)

Abigail never wrote why James Cornwell was "dirty" or "mean"—and she was so angry she got his name wrong. All that is clear is that Abigail preferred one suitor and Jane another, and that Jane, like her brother and sister, chose for herself. But that was nothing new with the frontier children. *They* had not changed, only Abigail had changed. She had grown less willing to accede to their lives or to their choices. She had stopped putting a decent face on their escapades or on their differences. She "Banished" Jane from her home. "She Is Never to Come Home in My Life time."[33]

At the end she made her peace with John Biles and his new wife.

> Biles and Family Are All Well. I saw His Wife and Little Charley in Church. Biles Is A doing Very Well. He Has Built A very Nice New House And Lives very Nice. [His wife] is very Saving And Avery good girl And very good to Charley. So She Is A good girl After All. (JUNE 9, 1861)

To be kind to Rachel's child was the paramount issue. And they even let Little Charley come to visit her. He "lerns very Well in Saunders new Second Reader And Websters Speling Book."

But Abigail would not be herself without some measure by which the world fell short of her demands.

> [Biles] Has Not As good a House keeper As Rachel Was, Not So Cleanly. . . . She Is of an Irish descent And you know the Irish Are Not very Cleanly Eny how. But She Is of a Good Disposition [and] she is Alwais very good to Me. I think She thinks as Mutch of Me As tho I Was Her Mother In Law. . . . She Alwais Takes My Advice, More than Shindels wife. She Is A Great Deal Better girl than Sarah Is. (JUNE 9, 1861)

Shindel and Sarah Armstrong moved into Abigail's house—or at least into half of it. "It is large Enough for two famileys Like Ours." And in April they helped Abigail celebrate her sixtieth birthday. Sarah was getting supper and the girls had prepared "a Little Partey on My Birth Day. . . . We had Large Radishes [and] lettus . . . As green As Mid sommer."

Sarah was pregnant again. "Shindel's Wife Is Not Very Well To Day. I think There Will Be A Babe A Round Be fore Long If there Is Luck in

Store Fore them." But not even her pregnancy dimmed Abigail's critical eye where Sarah was concerned: "I Can Not Learn Her to Be Saving yet. She Is So Waist Ful, They Never Will Com to Eny Thing No More."

Abigail was as much given to criticism in her old age as George had been. She had become an unforgiving taskmaster who constantly compared the children—the good son and the bad, the wasteful wife and the thrifty, the smart child and the slow speaker. Had she herself forced them out of the house?

She wrote nothing of the birth of a child to Sarah and Shindel. She did not mention that, in August, John Biles's wife gave birth to a daughter, Pansy Elizabeth. She was interested in an ever-smaller circle of people and places. Little Charley came to visit and she made a festive dinner. "We Had Fried Ham And Tea And green Sweet Corn And Bread And Butter And Cheese and green Apple Pie."

Charley was growing up. "Biles was here A Little while A go to se Me And He Is A going to Take Charley Home to Morrow. . . . He Is going to send Him to the A Cademy School. And I support that. I Will Never Have the Little Fellow With me Eny more."

A fragment of a letter, bearing no date or beginning, carried more news of Susan: "I Must tel you that Susan Is Married To A Very Nice Man. . . . They Are Married five Months to day. . . . He Helped to get up all the Rails that Was Floated off By the high water. . . . Oho he has Done A greate Deal For Me." It reassured her that Susan's new husband came from Illinois. "He was Raised in the Sity of Chicago." Abigail promised, "Susan Could Not of got a Better Man than Him If she should have Hunted the two teritors over and He Is Such A Splendid provider. . . . Oyes I Forgot to tel you. . . . His Name Is Levant Molton."

Then she remembered what she had forgotten in September—"Biles's Wife has A Daughter. . . . Charley thinks A great Deal of her and the Baby. It Is A Butiful Littl child."

Abigail was sixty, cantankerous and hard to please, but still worried when letters did not come from Illinois, just as she had been when they first came out west thirteen years earlier: "I Have Not Heard From You For A Long Time. O Why Do you Not Write? Have you Sickness In your Family Or Have you Not Time to Write?" She was feeling her years and feeling her grasp on her affairs grow less secure. "[I] Write very Foolish sometimes. But I Am geting old and hav Had So mutch Trouble It is A Wonder that I Have Eny Sence Atall Eny More. But I Alwais try to keep

My Sences As Well As I Can, But Sometimes I think I Have No Sence Atall." (SEPTEMBER 1, 1861)

But her account of the affairs of the region was as clear and sharp as ever. "The Indians," she wrote, "know of the Troubles In the States And They Want to do something To Make trouble Here." Soldiers from the forts at the Cascades and Vancouver who were not fighting or farming were away mining. Indians north of Vancouver killed three men coming home from the mines. They even bragged "that they Would Come down And kill Awl the people Clear to the Sea." Abigail confessed she was afraid, a sentiment uncommon to her, but she collected herself and reassured Mary Ann and Michael that "part of the Batery Is here Now And three Companeys of Dragoons Are A Comming soon." Besides, "Indians and Squaws Are Afraid of the soldiers As Death." (SEPTEMBER 1, 1861)

And then a strange thing happened. A man came into the territory who seemed to recognize Shindel by his resemblance to his brother Charles, thought dead in the gold rush.

> He sais to [Shindel], How do you do Malick? And said Shindel . . . I do not know you Sir. . . . Aint your Name Malick? sais he. Yes. Then you Must Be a Brother of Charles Malick in California. Sais Shin, I had A Brother in California but he died several years A go. Said the Man, He was Not ded seven months A go. I knowed Charley Just . . . as Well As I knowed My one brother And he keeps Store in Columid [Calumet?] And I yoused to se him Every Day. (UNDATED)

Abigail called the man to her home and immediately wrote to Charles to ask "if he Is Stil A living yet." Whether Abigail was ever in touch with Charles remains unclear. No letters remain to him or from him. If he were alive, he seems to have had little interest in rejoining the family.

Shindel and Sarah did not stay with Abigail. After their baby was born, they moved away and Abigail rented out their half of her house. Except for her tenants, everyone was gone. Only the growing land was unchanged. She had given up the livestock and the heavy crops and even her garden. Her passion, in the last years, was her orchard. She wrote of the fruit trees as if they were her children.

> In About two or thre years More We Will Have An Abundance of chois Fruit. Pears And Apples And plums And Siberian Crab[apples]s And peaches and Cheryes of difrent kindes and Chois Apples Sutch As I Never Saw Eny In

> the states. I paid thirtey Dollars For My Fruit trees and Currentes. There Will Be No End to them And goosburyes And Tame Rasburyes. I have Five difrent plum trees. . . . And four pare trees And I do not know how Meny peach trees And rasing More All the time. And I do not know how Meny Apple trees. I bought a good Menny My Self. I Have got Avery Nice orched. . . . My Neighbour Sais that he Wishes he had sutch A sort [of orchard] as Mine. I got Mine A bout Fortey Miles From here out of the Nursry that Was First planted in this Country. (SEPTEMBER 9, 1861)

"My respects To All frendes And My Love to All the Children and tel them to Write soon. And Michael And Mary Ann Write Soon And Tell Me All the Nues. Your Mother A J Malick"

Then there were no more letters.

At her frontier outpost, near her fruit trees and on her own land, Abigail died. She gave her last instructions to the tenants who rented her house. "She talked to the family that lived in the House with her and told them what to tell her children."

VI. Disappearance

On June 24, 1865, when the Civil War ended, Abigail's life ended too. Shindel wrote the news in a letter addressed, "Dear Neice." He did not write to his sister or brother-in-law, but to their daughter Abbie, telling her that Abigail was dead. "She was Sick only about a half hour. She has had a disease that has ben at work on her for four or five years, which was the palpitation of the heart. The Doctor Says that the Fibers of the Heart bursted and she bled to death inside. [Neither] I nor my Sisters was present to hear her dying Blessing. I was about 12 miles down the River. . . . My sister Jane was up in Oregon on a visit."[34]

Black sheep and ne'er-do-well son, Shindel remembered old wrongs: "I have written to your Father & Mother two or three Letters in the last four or five years but never have received a Scratch of a pen from Either of them. Mother used to talk to me and make me ashamed by my neglegance about Writing to them and I would Sit down and write but I guess they had no feeling for me." Shindel assumed that the Albrights, through all the years of their separation, had accepted Abigail's judgments against him. "Ask your mother if She has forgoten her yongest brother and when She used to nerce him and Sing to him." (JUNE 26, 1865)

Shindel was a grown man, and he had had his own share of grief. Abigail's picture of him as an errant son and wastrel never mentioned his hardships and losses. Two infants and his young girl of a wife, Sarah Armstrong, were dead.

> I have had trouble enough to Set an ordinary man crazy. First loosing my dear Brothers, next my dear Father, next my child, next my dear wife, the companion of my bosom and Heart, next my youngest child, and lastly my dear Kind and beloved mother. Sorow after Sorow. I think I am more to be pittied than Cursed. (JUNE 26, 1865)

Married at fifteen, Sarah Armstrong had borne two children in the four years of her marriage to Shindel. Her epitaph was brief enough—Shin's letter and the Reverend McCarty's journal:

> On the 30 of Dec [1863] attended the funeral of Mrs. Meleck [sic] wife of ______ Maleck aged about 19 years.

The minister did not recall Shindel's first name and he did not recall Sarah's.[35]

Like Rachel, Sarah was dead at nineteen, not strong enough, not tough enough, not lucky enough to survive the frontier. Her babies were dead too.

But Shindel was not one to linger on griefs. If his niece would send her photograph, he would do the same, "for I am Said to be one of the fines looking men in the Territory and that is Quite flattering is it not?"

Shindel did not write solely to share his anger or his grief or his vanity, however. He needed something from Mary Ann and Michael, even though he addressed the request to Abbie Albright: "Ask your mother if She wants me to attend to her property here and mothers Estate."

Abigail was hardly cold in her grave before the quarrelsome children were fighting over the land they would not live on when she was alive.

Jane became the family scribe. Although she had been "banished" for her marriage to Cornwell, she seemed to bear her mother no hard feelings. She had recovered from her madness, or at least experienced no more episodes of violence. And she reframed her life. After a fashion, she re-christened herself, signing her letters after Abigail's death as "Jennie."

> I feel it is my duty to you as a sister to give you an account of the proceedings of our Brother Shindel in conection with the business of the Estate. Perhaps you are aware that shortly after the death of our Dear Mother he took out paper of administration. And he sold all the personal effects. The proceeds of which amounted to some three hundred ($300). After getting this amount he commenced gamboling on the money so obtained [and] acted so unproperly that those who had gone his security withdrew their papers. And in consequence of which a new administrator has been appointed. Every one here interested feels very much pleased that brother no longer has the power to dispose of the Estate.

Abbie Albright Griffin, shown here with her children, Anna, Homer, and Virgil. Abbie took over the writing of family letters from her mother, Mary Ann, as her aunt Jane (Jennie) had taken up the writing from Abigail.

> I inform you of these acts so that you might not blindly give or send him Power of Attorney for the sale of your property herre which I learn he has asked you for. Shindell has had allready an offer for your place (your share of Fathers estate) but the amount offered is far less than its value. Yet shindel has expressed himself to the effect that he will sell on the terms offered.

Shin was dismantling Abigail's property as fast as he could, destroying all she had built and tried to fit his life to.

Jane tried to stop him. She wrote Mary Ann that Shindel "took the liberty of acting as your agent with out proper authority and done with your place as he was of a mind to do." Then Jane recounted the conditions as they existed before Abigail's death, and as they presently existed:

> His brotherinlaw . . . was one of Mother's nearest neighbors and a more detestible! undermining! decetfull! revengefull! and impudent a man never Was in this place. There are several brothers of them and they always was trying to take the advantage of our poor Mother. They would Always impose and tresspass on her rights and take every advantage of her widowhood and loneliness. . . . If we had not stayed on your place and in your house it might of been sold or bargined off long ere this. In fact he has rented this place to his brother-in-law for this Season, but I am glad your letter came in so good season, for now it will all be attended to by J.D.B. [John D. Biles]

Shindel appointed himself administrator and appraiser of his mother's property, and he "deducted three dollars from the bill for half days work." When Jane confronted him "he became very angry with me and said are you doing this business or am I?" "I told him that it suited him but might not the ballance of us and he gave me some pretty harsh words. And I then told him I believed I had a voice in the council my self [because] I was speaking in behalf of the absent ones." "He then told me I had better attend to my own affairs." (APRIL 28, 1866)

Jane repeated her earlier account that Shindel's derelictions were so flagrant that "the heirs here complained on him" and "the Probate Court appointed another [administrator] in his stead." She did not say which of the heirs besides herself lodged the complaint. Shindel, she wrote,

> lives in town on credit and does nothing without it is to gambol and dresses to the top notch and lives high. I guess I have sayed enugh on that degrading subject. . . . If you had sent power of Atty to him your place would have been

> sold . . . to those low lifed persons for five Hundred dollars when I think it can be sold for 800 or one thousand redilly. (APRIL 28, 1866)

Jane intended to go to Portland to see John Biles the following week. Whenever there was trouble, Biles was the one they turned to.

She wrote, "Sister Susan is up at Boise Mines. . . . She has not been here for two years. I suppose you know her husband was killed last June and I have not seen her since. . . . I had a letter from her three days ago. She is well. She has a young daughter some four months old." Jane's news meant that Susan was pregnant when she was widowed. She was twenty-one, and, whatever the reason, she did not come back to Abigail's house.

Jane and Susan, separated for over two years, briefly corresponded as if they too were strangers. Susan sent Jane a photograph of her new daughter and Jane commented with a good deal of her mother's cool appraisal: "It is a beautiful babe, . . . much pretier than mine are when young." She wrote that she had "three interesting children. One boy and two girls. Boy, Six years old, oldest girl 4, and babe two years old. Boy's name [is] Frank E. Pearson, oldest girl's named Hattie Emma Cornwell, and yongest Darsen Cornwell."

Jane and Mary Ann Albright had not seen each other in more than eighteen years, and they exchanged photographs as if they were being introduced for the first time. Jane sent one of herself:

> It is a bad one though. Shin was here to day and said he would not know whose it was if he was not told. . . . When I get some that are better looking I will send one (but I am afraid I shall have to get some good looking girl to sit for me). My clothing I wore when [the picture] was taken was deep black. . . . My Spring hat is white trimmed in velvet and crape, but my last summer's Hat is black with crape trimming. (MAY 7, 1866)

The last daguerreotypes they had were taken in 1855, over a decade earlier. They showed Shindel and Susan and Jane together in happier times. Jane asked Mary Ann to copy that photograph and send it back to her: "I will send the money." She promised to send "Susan and babe's likeness and my ugly ones as soon as I get them taken." But she took pride in her "interesting" children. "My boy is large enough to go to town for me and get anything I send him for and I can rely on what ever he tells me as being correct."

As if writing to Mary Ann opened a floodgate of need, Jane apologized about pouring out so many confidences. "When I do get to talking I can scarcely Stop. I am an awful gossip." But her letter concluded with the confession that Abigail's land "has no charmes for me nor never would, only for My Mother being here." "All my interest After is to go to Portland." (APRIL 28, 1866)

John D. Biles was living in Portland with his new family, and he agreed to serve as agent for the sale of Mary Ann's share of the land, and to dislodge the Armstrongs as trespassers. Biles authorized Jane's husband "to take charge of the place until further diposistion is made of the Property so you can rest easy on that subject for a while and I will endeavor to keep you posted as near as possible." (MAY 7, 1866)

In September 1866, Jane wrote, "You must not expect a long letter this time as I am not able to write yet. I have another young daughter three weeks old." "I am just able to cook the children two meals per day. Frank & Hattie go to school now & My Husband boards in town so you see I have but little to do. . . ." She did not explain why she was alone or why her husband was boarding in town, but she immediately reassured Mary Ann that "I have one of the kindest best Men most indulgent best natured husbands This coast can afford."

Mary Ann asked about the sale of the land. She had been asking about the sale of the land since George Malick died in 1854! There was always a reason the sale could not go forward. Now Jane wrote, "I think Biles will not get a bargin for the place this summer or fall." She doubted, too, they would recover the year's rent from Armstrong. "He will deny all charges prepared against him." The fact of the matter was that "he has Shin on his side & against us all."

But the claim itself was no longer intact. Jane told how it had been chipped away over the years. "Mother sold 22 acres of her land when it was first set off to her in the fall of 1859. She sold 20 acres to one of her neighbors for the sum of $50.00 per acre I think. And in the spring of 1860 she sold two more acres to the vancouver butcher for the purpose of erecting a Slaughter house there. She received $100 per acre for that piece because it was right on the river." (SEPTEMBER 17, 1866)

Shindel was "at those new mines lately discovered . . . and very seldom comes to town. . . . He is with a copperhead crowd I tell you." Political faction followed family dissension; Biles was an old-style Whig, looking for moderation through a time of war; Albright and his people were Lincoln

Republicans, antislavery by conviction since 1828; Shin and his "copperhead" crowd were a splinter wing of the Democratic Party, accused by Republicans of hatching treasonous plots along the border states in order to end the war on any terms. Politics was simply another arena of familial disaffection.

The Malicks and the Albrights made a last effort to keep in touch. Mary Ann and Jennie exchanged photographs of their children, Mary Ann's now grown. "I did not realize that [Homer] was a young man." The years had changed them all.

Shindel continued to write to his "Dear Neice" about a life full of hardship and self-delusion.

> Your Letter . . . found me Sick with the Feaver & Ague . . . in the Cascad Mountains. It Snowed & rained on us for about a week. Our clothes was not drying during the time night nor day & it was allmost impossable to get a fire. We could get warm by camp fire but the longer we would stand by it the weter we got. We made Some very rich discoveries such as gold & Silver Quartz Galeenea . . . & a Large Copper mine that we can get 800 lbs per ton out of which is pure Copper. That is Smelted copper. It also contains gold & silver. We have a chance to Sell the copper Ledge for $50,000 or work it ourselves. . . . We have not decided yet. (OCTOBER 15, 1866)

In a childish hand, Shindel wrote of old hurts and of childhood resentments that were unforgotten:

> When I come back [to Illinois] I shall have plenty of money. . . . I will Steal in on [your parents] Some day Still and Silently when they least expect me, my words will Burst like a thunder cloud on your mother for not writing to me when I was a child. When she lived at Home in my father's House I Loved her as well as I did my Mother if not better. It did not seem hard as long as Mother lived because Mother used to get Letters from your mother and if I was not at home she used to Save them until I would come home & then I could read them. . . . I can feel the hot tears swelling in my Eyes to think that she never gives me one thought or word in my lonliness.
>
> (OCTOBER 15, 1886)

The family hardly had strength any more for letters. Time had played them all out. A second generation tried their hand at letter writing. Abbie Albright took up the task from her mother, Mary Ann. Jane wrote to Abbie, "The mighty columbia twenty steps from our door is coming up booming.

Sister Sue is here but does not live with us. She stayed with us quite a while after she came down from Boise Mines in Dec[ember] but got coaxed away. I guess by Shin, & they both stay at one place now as family in town. Their Politics [are the same]. I will write your mother the particulars." (JUNE 4, 1867)

The last letter from Jane told that she was living in Portland, eighteen miles from Abigail's land. She too thought of returning to visit in Illinois. "I am so home sick to go back. . . . I don't think of any thing else." "Home" was not the West but Illinois, where Michael and Mary Ann were the fixed point of the family. Susan and Shindel were "up in Idaho." "They do not write to me at all." Even John Biles, who lived only six blocks away, was hardly in touch.

> I hope you will write soon & tell me all the news
>
> your Sister A.J. Cornwell
> Portland, Oregon
> JANUARY 3, 1869

The land was sold, the children scattered, the family separated. All the work of Abigail's life was gone. Nothing was handed down, nothing passed on to children or grandchildren, hardly even memory.[36]

VII. The Albrights

When George and Abigail Malick set out for Oregon Territory in March 1848, Mary Ann Albright was expecting her fourth child. The baby was born on April 22, a few weeks after her parents' departure. Abigail told herself her children would follow the next season; it is not at all clear that Mary Ann or Michael ever entertained the thought seriously themselves.

The Albrights, on their side, were part of a close-knit family, two-going-on-three generations, living in close proximity and working harmony. Jacob Albright left Tennessee because he "did not believe in holding slaves." In 1829 he and his wife, Esther Touchstone, and their children arrived in Tazewell County in Hittle Township, Illinois. They were among the first settlers—intelligent farmers, antislavery people, sober Christians, hardworking men and women. Like the Malicks, the Albrights were German Lutherans, and both sides of the family served in Washington's Revolutionary Army.

Jacob and Esther Albright raised eight children, six boys and two girls. Michael was their eldest. He married Mary Ann Malick, an eldest daughter, in 1843, when he was a prudent twenty-three and she twenty-one. They too had eight children, six of whom lived to maturity. Family names echo through the two families, Malicks and Albrights: Ann and Homer, Esther Abigail and Rachel Jane, Charles and George. Although they hardly knew each other, the children carried on the legacies of relatives whose names they recognized from family Bibles.

Tazewell County became an area of "well-built farm structures, neat fences and fields, where *useful* grain has the upper hand." The farmers of Tennessee and the Carolinas who came to Illinois rejected not only slavery but the cavalier culture of tobacco farming, in favor of the sober work of growing wheat and corn.

When he arrived, Jacob Albright bought clear title—to himself and his heirs—to 80 acres of land. In 1830 he bought 240 acres from George and Michael Hittle for $800. In 1837 he added another 80 acres for "$200 in hand." The land was already surveyed; the first land he bought was the "west half of the North west quarter of Section no. Seventeen of Township No. twenty-two North Range No. Two West of Third principal Meridian. Containing 80 acres more or less." Over time, Jacob deeded parcels of his land to his sons for the sum of $1: 95 acres to John; 60 acres to Michael; and 75 acres to Thomas.[37]

In his adult years, Michael Albright owned 240 acres of prime farmland. His brother John F. Albright live on 165 acres close by with his wife and seven children. Michael's sister Sarah Jane married William Martin Shellenberger in 1855, and they too made their home in Tazewell County. The Edward Cornelius who came out west to "look over" Abigail's daughters went back to Illinois, where his brother John married Susan Shellenberger, Michael's sister-in-law. Two of Michael Albright's brothers married sisters—Louisa and Eliza Judy.

Michael's sister Mary Ann, so brutally murdered in 1860, was married to George Orendorff (also Orndorff) whose father came to Tazewell in 1833. Orndorff brought his family from Logan, Kentucky, in 1837, and purchased 270 acres of "choice timber and prairie land." The Orndorffs had eight sons and four daughters. When their father died, five sons and three daughters were living, and all but one resided in Tazewell County. George Orndorff remarried five years after his first wife's death; he left all his real property in the county to his two surviving daughters. His brother Benjamin Orndorff also lived in Tazewell County, had a family of eight sons and four daughters, as had his father and mother, and they lived in neighboring counties.

The intermarried families were politically similar. Southerners who rejected slavery, they voted the Whig ticket until 1856, when they followed Abraham Lincoln into the Republican party.

During the years of the westward migration, these families remained in Illinois. The Albrights, the Judys, the Orndorffs, the Shellenbergers, the Corneliuses—they wove a web of cousins and aunts and uncles. Sons and daughters remained in their parents' home well into their twenties. William Albright helped with his father's farm until he was past twenty; Michael and Mary Ann's home in the 1870 census contained three children aged twenty-two, twenty-one, and fifteen. Michael's brother Thomas was still at home with his father and mother when he was twenty-four.

When Mary Ann died she was surrounded by her family. All of her children except Homer, who farmed in Plymouth, Missouri, attended the funeral: "A slow sad dirge greeted the entrance of the mourners. The pall bearers placed the beautiful casket containing the remains in front of the platform where loving friends with tremulous hands covered it with flowers." Mary Ann's youngest child, Florence, was seventeen and still at home.

The rootedness of the family was borne out in headstones; the cemeteries of neighboring townships held their dead over generations. There were two Albrights buried in Antioch Cemetery; two Albrights buried in Elm Grove Cemetery; eighteen Albrights buried in Oak View Cemetery.

In their living and dying, the Albrights were family over generations, an interlocking of time and people and place. They had found, somehow, a way of tying their separate lives together.

The Malicks uprooted, touched the Pacific shores, cleared the land, grew crops, planted orchards, extended the boundaries of America. As they transformed the "wilderness," they were also transformed by it. Those who did not die were marked by the struggle. They left the circle of the "tribe," and followed their separate ways, each to another road. They would not come together. On the frontier, they learned not to be family, but strangers.

The Albrights declined the great challenge of their time—free land in the West. They live today where they lived then, puzzled a little by the Malicks, whose letters were discovered by chance in an archive on the east coast, sold by a dealer of old books who never knew them. The Albrights chose neither adventure nor new lands. Miraculously, they told themselves that what they had was enough.

Notes

1. *Portraits and Biographical Records of Tazewell and Mason Counties* (1879), p. 383.

2. Even in Illinois the Malicks were restless, settling in Tazewell County in 1836, moving to Kendall County in 1845, before leaving for Oregon Territory in 1848. Ibid.

3. Malick Family Correspondence, 1848–1869, Beinecke Library, Yale University.

4. See John M. Faragher, *Women and Men on the Overland Trail* (New Haven, Conn.: Yale University Press, 1979), pp. 20–25.

5. Deaths by drowning were common accounts in the overland diaries of emigrants. See Lillian Schlissel, *Women's Diaries of the Westward Journey* (New York: Schocken Books, 1982), pp. 15, 92, 103, 153, 204. Also Fred Lockley, *Conversations with Pioneer Women*, ed. Mike Helm (Eugene, Ore.: Rainy Day Press, 1981), pp. 166–67.

6. The Malicks first filed a claim about a mile from the river but they were preempted by a settler who got there before them. They settled then on the banks of the Columbia, 1850. *Washington Territory Donation Land Claims Before 1856* (Seattle, Wash.: Seattle Genealogical Society, 1980), p. 181.

7. Oscar O. Winther, *The Great Northwest: A History*, 2nd ed. (New York: Alfred A. Knopf, 1950), pp. 124, 154.

8. *Federal Population Census for Oregon Territory, 1850* (Washington, D.C.: National Archive Trust Fund Board, 1979).

9. Howard R. Lamar, *The American West: The Readers' Encyclopedia* (New York: Thomas Y. Crowell, 1977), p. 446.

10. Ibid., p. 448.

11. Chinook Jargon was a trading language developed by sailors and settlers in their dealings with the several Indian tribes. It remained in usage long after the frontier days were passed. Gill's *Dictionary of the Chinook Jargon* went into eighteen editions and was still sold in Portland bookstores into the 1920s. See also Edward H. Thomas, *Chinook: A History and Dictionary*, 2nd ed. (Portland, Ore.: Binfords & Mort, 1969). I am indebted to Kenneth Holmes for a copy of the dictionary; see his series of books, *Covered Wagon Women* (Glendale, Calif.: Arthur J. Clarke, 1983), 1:59.

12. Winther, p. 175.

13 Reverend J. McCarty, First Episcopal Minister in Vancouver, Ms. Journal, Clark County Historical Museum, Vancouver. "July 6 baptised Charles Edmund [Esmond], son of John D. & Rachel H. Biles, deceased, born 10 January, 1853, the Father with Miss melick [sic] sponsors," p. 5. In September Abigail also had Susan baptised. "Sep 7th Baptised as an adult Susan Ann daughter of George malick deceased & Abigail his widow, born 13 of Sep 1843 the Mother witness," p. 5

14. Reverend McCarty's Journal, p. 6.

15. Carl Landerholm, *Clark County, Washington, History Told by Contemporaries* (Vancouver, Wash.: Fort Vancouver Regional Library, 1948), pp. 25–26.

16. Reverend McCarty's Journal, p. 7.

17. The letter is unclear as to whether Henry "bought" or "brought" the Indian boy to become Jane's servant. Given the time and Pearson's dealings with the Indian tribes, either reading seems possible.

18. "Peter Shindle Malick m. Sarah Armstrong, March 13, 1859." *Oregon Weekly Times*, March 26, 1859, p. 2. It is interesting that Shindel and Sarah were not married by a minister but by John Biles, as justice of the peace.

19. Winther, p. 171.

20. Stockton Asylum in California was established in 1852. Before that, "California mental patients had no treatment . . . at all. Police were responsible for the detention of those who exhibited suspicious behavior. . . . In 1852, 124 patients were admitted, the number increasing to 160 in 1853, or 59.2 per 100,000 population. By 1854, the number of admissions had grown to 202, or 70.6 per 100,000 population." From Lee Stolmack, "Care and Treatment of the Mentally Disordered in California, 1849–1862," honors project, Department of History, California State University, Sacramento, 1979.

St. Joseph's Hospital, erected in 1855, was used as both "an orphan and lunatic asylum. For many years the hospital at Vancouver was the only one in Washington

Territory." Fred Lockley, "The Story of Vancouver," *Oregon Journal*, May 18, 1930, p. 4 (magazine section). The Sisters of Charity, a Catholic order, also opened a House of Providence in Vancouver in 1856. Charged to serve as "mothers to orphans, physicians for the sick, dispensers of relief for the needy and consolers of every kind of affliction," they may also have cared for the insane. "The West Shore," August 1883, p. 189.

The problem of the insane was a matter of some attention in the region. An editorial in the *Portland Daily Advertiser*, September 10, 1860, p. 2, declared, "It will be imperative upon our legislators to see that some provision is made for the erection of an asylum for the insane, or a law passed compelling every county to take charge of that unfortunate class some of whom are roaming throughout the State, objects of fear and pity to every citizen."

21. Oregon Insane Asylum, Portland, Oregon, *Joint Committee Report*, 1878, p. 16. *Reports of the Physicians*, 1870–72; 1876–78; 1884–86. *Joint Committee Report*, 1878. See also, Norman Dain, *Concepts of Insanity in the United States, 1789–1865* (New Brunswick, N.J.: Rutgers University Press, 1964); Gerald N. Grob, *Mental Institutions in America: Social Policy to 1875* (New York: Free Press, 1973); and Richard Fox, *So Far Disordered in Mind: Insanity in California, 1870–1930* (Berkeley: University of California Press, 1979).

22. Mari Sandoz, *Old Jules* (Lincoln: University of Nebraska Press, 1962), pp. 110ff; p. 166.

23. Samuel E. Morison and Henry S. Commager, *The Growth of the American Republic*, 4th ed. (New York: Oxford University Press, 1951), 1:633.

24. Winther, p. 160.

25. Lockley, *Conversations with Pioneer Women*, pp. 274–80. Elizabeth Kelly Biles says she first met her husband in 1849 when he was justice of the peace. But Biles was elected justice in 1854 and her father was not attached to Fort Vancouver until 1852. She describes Biles as Speaker of the House in the Washington territorial legislature in 1850, but the first territorial assembly was not convened until 1854, which corresponds with Rachel's letters. This kind of irregularity is not unusual in pioneer reminiscences.

26. Eugene C. Elliott, "History of Variety–Vaudeville in Seattle from the Beginning to 1914," *Publications in Drama*, 1 (Seattle: University of Washington, 1944); Bernard Berelson and Howard F. Grant, "The Frontier Theatre in Washington," *Pacific Northwest Quarterly*, 28 (April 1937): 115–36; Alice H. Ernst, "Eugene's Theatres and Shows," *Oregon Historical Quarterly*, 44, 2, 3 (1943): 127–39, 232–48; Fred Lincoln, "Vaudeville in the Northwest," *Washington Magazine*, 1 (1906): 29–30; Lester L. Schilling, Jr., "History of the Theater in Portland, Oregon, 1846–1959," M.A. thesis, University of Washington, 1960. Fred Lincoln mentions "Four Lamont Sisters in Fancy Dancing" and "Nora Norris, the Irish Nightingale" in *Washington Magazine*, above

27. Reverend McCarty's Journal, p. 11.

28. Chapman's *History of Tazewell County, Illinois* (1879), pp. 228–92. Courtesy Tazewell County Genealogical Society.

29. Women who lived on farms were accustomed to long periods of loneliness and isolation. The usual fear was Indians. Rarely were farm women afraid of thieves like John Ott. It hardly crossed the minds of rural populations that robbery or murder might endanger a woman alone. Abigail first thought the murders were the work of a gang of men, and she wrote they "aught to be Hung And Hanging Is to good For them. They Aught to Be Cut And Slashed After Hanging. . . . There Right Arms to Be Cut off and Burnt Befor Ther Eyes And Then Let that Half get Well And then Cut off Ther Other Arm and Cut ther Leges off [too]. . . . That is the sentence that I Would give Them If I was governor of Illinois" (December 17, 1860).

30. Robert L. Griswold, *Family and Divorce in California, 1850–1890* (Albany: State University of New York Press, 1982), p. 79.

31 U. S. Department of Commerce, Bureau of the Census Bulletin no. 96, *Marriage and Divorce 1887–1906*, pp. 15–18.

32. John M. Faragher, *Sugar Creek: Life on the Illinois Prairie* (New Haven, Conn.: Yale University Press, 1986), p. 83.

33. According to an announcement in the *Weekly Oregonian*, November 5, 1859, p. 2, one James M. Cornwell was married to a Miss Mary A. Stott. How that marriage ended, whether it was ended, or even whether it was the same man who married Jane in 1861 is unclear.

34. "Died, Abigail J. Malick, June 24, 1865," *Daily Oregonian*, June 28, 1865, p. 2.

35. Reverend McCarty's Journal, p. 18.

36. The site of the Malick claim is today primarily industrial land with some grain-loading facilities on the riverbank. (My thanks to Professor Stephen Dow Beckman for this and other regional information.)

37. Even families that remained close had disputes. When Jacob Albright died in 1868 his heirs brought legal action in a dispute over land inheritance, with Daniel, William, and John F. Albright complainants and Michael and Mary Ann Albright and Sarah Jane and William Shellenberger defendants. The probate court apparently ordered the disputed land sold at public auction; the sale raised $5,827. Michael A. Albright, Probate Records, Box 334, furnished courtesy Tazewell County Genealogical Society and Mrs. Jackie Roszel.

2. Charles and Maggie Brown in Colorado and New Mexico

1880–1930

I would give 5 years of my life if I had never seen this state.

MAGGIE BROWN

You must not get so discouraged. Things will work out all right yet.

CHARLES BROWN

Behind the Victorian ideal of the well-ordered home, American families were unruly assortments of comings and goings, as men and women tried to fit their lives into a rapidly changing society. Virginia-born and -raised, Charles and Maggie Brown married in 1876 and should have settled into reasonably stable middle-class lives. Charles was a medical doctor and Maggie a young woman with a good education. But the end of the Confederacy erased the lives they expected to live, and the call of quick wealth in the West was hard to resist. To young men who had had enough of southern defeat, the frontier promised to redeem their fortunes and to provide adventure besides. Young women like Maggie soon recognized that they would have to follow their husbands or have no husbands at all.

Searching through Colorado and New Mexico for the strike that would make them rich, the Browns moved twenty-four times in twenty-seven years, and left six grave markers to children they buried in those rocky lands. They moved until moving became a way of life. Looking for a new home, they were homeless; dreaming of wealth, they were penniless. Charles's hope was incorrigible and his optimism consuming. Failure only inflamed his belief that success lay just ahead. In the deserts of western frontiers Charles and Maggie Brown refused to believe they might not succeed.

I. To Strike It Rich, *1880–1881*

At the end of the Civil War, Virginia was a battered landscape. The Yankee militia had devastated fields and farms, and after that, Reconstruction policies were harsh and punishing. Old families that managed to survive the war buckled in the depression of 1872. A humiliated aristocracy tried to steel itself, as the state was saddled with the largest postwar debt of all the southern states. Plantations that before the war would have sold for $100,000 to $150,000 were advertised in the newspapers for $6,000 to $10,000, and Virginians feared seeing their homes bought by "outsiders." The Virginia Bureau of Immigration cautioned prospective buyers of land and plantations that "sluggards and careless, wasteful men living in the illusion that fortunes can be made in a year should go elsewhere."[1] The South was "for sale," but proud Virginians tried to preserve the way of life that lost the war. Newcomers were needed but not welcomed.

Across the continent, however, there was a different call, as Colorado and New Mexico promoters advertised in pamphlets, "Where to Go to Become Rich." Millions of acres were waiting to be turned to agriculture. And more than that. The governor of New Mexico claimed that gold, silver, and copper were in such abundance that "the armies of the world might be turned into these districts without exhausting them in a hundred years."[2] This was a land for wild-eyed speculators, and even Southern gentlemen succumbed to the temptation to join the surge west to restore their fortunes.[3] "Mining loomed larger than life with its possibilities of instant wealth, its lure of new opportunities."[4] Men of the depleted South, who saw devastation all about them, could smell and taste the success that waited on the western frontiers.

Charles Brown was particularly susceptible to the western lure. He inherited a kind of restless, nomadic fever, a craving for romantic adventure, a feeling for "luck" in life. Only two generations before him in 1790 his paternal great-grandfather had migrated from Germany seeking refuge from the draft and from a flagging economy. In Virginia, as a minister of the German Reform Church, he rode a five-hundred-mile circuit ministering to some thirty churches. His maternal grandmother provided a different kind of travel, a library filled with leather-bound volumes of Sir Walter Scott, Charles Dickens, Gustave Flaubert, Miguel de Cervantes—heady daydreams for a young boy. The West offered Charles real-life adventure to explore.

Maggie Keller, the beautiful southern belle Charles fell in love with, was herself descended from a family with many migration patterns. In the late 1700s her great-grandparents on both sides sailed from France and Switzerland and settled in Virginia, proud first families. Her own father had pulled his wife and children through numerous moves across western Virginia during Maggie's childhood, settling finally in a place called West View. Early mobility, rather than preparing Maggie for further upheavals, made her instead cling to the stability of a home. Well-educated for a woman of her day, Maggie graduated with honors from the highly regarded Methodist Seminary for Women. Still, despite her quite substantial education, she was a playful and flirtatious young woman. "She was the beautiful Maggie Keller."[5]

And she won the young doctor Charles Brown, who set up his first medical practice from the house of his cousin Washington Keller, Maggie's father. Almost a decade after the end of the Civil War, they were married.

From the start, the marriage between Martha Magdalene (Maggie) Keller and Dr. Charles Albert Brown broke tradition. It began in a burst of flame. The *Staunton Spectator*, December 26, 1876, reported:

> FUNERAL OF MOTHER AND MARRIAGE OF DAUGHTER It becomes our painful duty to record the death by burning of Mrs. W. J. Keller, of West View in this county, whose maiden name was Amelia Jane Jordan, of Salem, Roanoke county, which occurred under the following circumstances: Her husband, on Thursday last, wishing to take the oil can to Staunton for the purpose of having it replenished, she filled the lamps, and poured the re-

> mainder of the oil in the can into a glass jar which she placed upon the mantel over the cooking stove in which she was baking preparatory to the marriage of her daughter which was appointed to take place on Xmas day.
>
> Observing at dinner that there was a flavor of kerosene oil in the coffee, she suspected that the glass jar into which she had put the oil upon the mantel over the cook stove was leaking and went to examine it, and when she picked up the jar the bottom fell out, the oil fell upon the hot stove beneath, which put it in flame, which ignited the clothing of Mrs. Keller, and burned her breast, face and arms so badly that she died the next morning in spite of all the medical aid which could be rendered by Drs. Wm. L. Walters and Charles Brown. . . . In trying to extinguish the flames her daughter Maggie, aged 21 years, was burned on her right arm and hand but fortunately not very seriously.
>
> The wedding apparel of the daughter, with some bed clothing, was burned.
>
> At 11 o'clock on Saturday morning the remains of Mrs. Keller were taken to the Church where the funeral was preached by Mr. Wilson of the Methodist Church South. Then the remains were taken back to the house of the deceased, where the wedding of the daughter Maggie, to Dr. Charles Brown of that neighborhood, formerly of Bridgewater, took place, in compliance with the expressed wish of the mother on Saturday afternoon instead of on Monday as originally intended. The deceased leaves 4 children all small except the daughter just married.
>
> The bereaved husband is one of our best citizens, and has the sincere sympathy of the whole community.

Maggie left no record of her feelings, standing there beside the open coffin. Later references give fleeting echoes: a Virginia minister turned circuit rider in El Paso reminding Maggie years later of her "dear mother's" dying words: "I'm so glad I have a Jesus"; Maggie's own flush of pleasure at Charles's praise: "You are like your mother." Whatever inner resilience later helped Maggie weather the twenty-four uprootings in twenty-seven years, the deaths of six of seven children, forged itself then beside the coffin and the bridal wreath. Maggie's life would become an interplay of absorbing shock and moving on.

When Maggie and Charles were married, Maggie did not know even the rudiments of cooking: she had "flashing violet eyes and long black hair—54 inches—a real beauty."[6] Maggie had been raised a southern belle, to be a wife with servants to a southern gentleman. But all that was gone. The war ended a way of life, and upon her mother's death, the beautiful Maggie shouldered her responsibilities. She and Charles set up housekeeping next door to her father in West View, Virginia, and Maggie embraced the role of surrogate mother to her sister and brothers, Amelia Jane (age eleven), Dannie (age nine), and Washington James (age three). Even into their teens and twenties, she referred to them as "the children." Her own child, born a year after the marriage, was, in Maggie's eyes, younger sister to the aunt and uncles next door. Kellers and Browns, they were all one family. Maggie was its center.

Her young husband, however, had dramatically different ideas. Frontier fever was burning in Virginia, and Charles Brown, for his part, had more than enough reasons to leave. When the war was over, he faced two giant tasks. He had to follow in the footsteps of an eminently successful and recently deceased father—a noted physician and civic leader—and he was head of a household of women: his mother, two sisters, his wife and baby daughter. Victorian prescriptions were austere; he was expected to be the head of the family, the social and economic guardian of the women under his protection.

Beneath a veneer of etiquette, Charles and his oldest sister Millie were rivals, perhaps even enemies. Millie's posture of deference to Charles scarcely masked her condescending rebukes and her impatience with his lack of business acumen. Certainly part of his escape from Virginia was the need he felt to escape the women in his family and their expectations.

Collecting few fees from his medical practice, nagged by his older sisters and his widowed mother to "make something" of himself, Charles was tinder waiting to be fired by the wild western promises of wealth. Dreamer, intellect, gentleman, Charles Brown skirted shrewd business deals and humdrum tasks. Closer to his romantic heart was the glamour of the West. Out of the ashes of the Civil War, the West spoke to the southerner's code of courage and gallant endeavor. Here was a field upon which honor and fortune could be redeemed.

The claims of the western promotors hooked men from all over the state—the small town of Staunton sent a dozen or so in the late 1870s. Maggie's own father, Washington, one of the first to test the western promise, worked for six months for a cousin in Larned, Kansas. His accounts must have tantalized his eager son-in-law:

> You have no idea of how this country impresses itself on one who has never seen a treeless, fenceless & in many instances houseless country. Not a shade tree to be seen. I thought I could not stay a week. I could see no prospect & there seemed a want of everything & in fact there is a lack of everything

except land. There is plenty of fine land & if any person will get a lot of this land & then go to work & put all the labor that is necessary to make a home for a human being on it in the course of 9 or 10 years he will have one of the finest most productive farms in America. (NO MONTH, 1879)

A respected physician under whom Charles had interned prodded him:

Your determination to go west is the best conclusion you ever arrived at; Virginia is no place now for a young man. The advice given to young men to stick to the old state is all fudge. You have ere this found out that—in our profession at least—neither the amount of labor you do, nor your degree of success, nor the fidelity with which you stick to your business will guarantee you a livelihood.

In the West it is different; there the chance to get into business is better, and you are sure to get what you earn. There is a code in existence amongst these people to pay what they owe—they are the most reliable and responsible set of people that I have ever met with. . . . I stick to it that a majority of the people in this country [Virginia] are totally unmindful of their obligations; and that a Virginia thief is the worst thief in the earth. When you go west, I would advise you to go far west. (NO MONTH, 1874)

Another spur to head west came from a friend, Joseph Dinkle, a member of an old Virginia family, who wrote Charles from his mining camp in Colorado, where several hometown men were seeking quick wealth.

If you come you will find that I have not told you the half to use the language of the queen of Sheba, as to myself and what I am doing. Jim and I are mining. We have the half interest in a Silver mine, our prospects are very faltering at present but mining is a very risky business. When you write to me you direct Alma Park County, Colorado Try. Our mine is there and we will be there at the time this summer. We are going to move up to the mountain Wednesday and procede to open the mine. Hoping to here from you in due course of time.

I will close for the
present
Your most
cinsere
friend
Jos H. Dinkle

Remember me to all inquiring friends. (NO MONTH, 1880)

When Charles approached Maggie with a serious proposal that he go west, he angled for her sympathies. While neither then nor later did he suffer any problems other than bronchitis and constipation, he argued his health necessitated the move. ("You said 'I would not ask it but for my health's sake.' " [MAGGIE TO CHARLES, STAUNTON, NOVEMBER 7, 1880]) Railroad promoters advertised the West as a panacea for all physical ills: rheumatism, gout, stiff joints, Bright's disease, St. Vitus's dance, sterility, syphilis, alcoholism.[7] Furthermore, the influx of health-seekers, Charles argued, would create rich openings for doctors. Miners, too, in their unsanitary camps, would require physicians; and because in such camps physicians were a sought-after breed, they could charge exorbitant rates—five dollars to ten dollars a visit. Finally, confusing mining and farming country as one and the same, Charles directed Maggie's hopes to the fine land in the West, cheap and available since the Homestead Act of 1862.

To his credit Charles did not make a peremptory decision. Maggie stressed later: "I let you try this." The two agreed finally that Charles would go West to explore possibilities. If fortune looked good, he would amass wealth as fast as he could and return "with his tail up" or he would send for Maggie to make their home in Colorado. But the projected "few weeks" of separation stretched to a year and a half.

When Charles left Virginia for Colorado, he left behind him a young wife and a small daughter, Mattie. While he was gone—"for a few weeks"—Maggie and her baby were to "board around." Charles made no provision for them. He and Maggie both expected that family and friends would extend "hospitality" while he was gone. But the day-to-day realities of Maggie's life without Charles made her a boarder, a visitor, sometimes embarrassingly contributing to the chores to earn her keep. It was a far cry from the life of a southern lady.

Anxiety tumbled through her letters to Charles. Despite his disclaimers, Maggie's mind populated the Colorado mining camps with unkempt men, boisterous saloons, and loose women.

> Ben Myers writes very different from what you do. There is very little money out there and a great many going around with their "knap sacks and frying pans" not having a shelter. And Tom Keller saw Will Wynant in West Crawford [Virginia] and he said that the young men that went from there wrote very

> discouragingly. How is this? Be carefull or you will have to retract some you have said. Write me what you clear every month—*be sure* now, for I am afraid you are so sanguine. *Don't go in debt! don't go in debt!!* I beg you. Please write me about your business. You said you were going to buy a team—did you? Have you a riding horse of your own? Have you bought any cloaths yet? Have you taken up a claim? Have you kissed any one since you did me? *I tell you you had better not.* Now answer *all* my questions. (JUNE 6, 1880)

The thousand miles separating the boomtown of Kerber Creek, Colorado, from the genteel region of Cumberland, Virginia, stretched like an uncharted wilderness in Maggie's imagination. Across that vast distance she could not project the ritual etiquette that defined her southern culture. Charles, she feared, might become a stranger to her.

> Do you read your bible? I feel so sad today. I am afraid you don't give me the true state of things. . . . My dear write me the true state of things and for *mercy's sake* do not deceive me. . . . If I do go [to Colorado] and the people I come in contact with are wicked and regardless of their maker it will kill me outright. In your first *Dear* letters you allways said "God bless" you or something of that kind. But now you do not. Oh! where is my *darling good* husband! . . . My own darling, will I ever behold that *dear dear* face again? Why is it I am so sorrifull? (JUNE 6, 1880)

Trapped in a panic, Maggie scrutinized the words of Charles's letters—believing, disbelieving his reassurances.

> You may read the other page to our friends if you wish. This page is for you alone. My darling I never knew how much I loved you untill since I left you, and I am sorry that I have left you, but I hope my love that we will be with each other soon. (APRIL 19, 1880)

Specters of prostitutes, liquor, and gambling haunted her. A mining camp connoted saloons, sex, and crime. How could Maggie know? Nothing Charles could protest stilled her concern.

> You need not be uneasy about me not being true to you, would rather die than be false to my darling, but I think I trust you more fully than you do me. (DECEMBER 30, 1880)

> Thus far I have seen no prostitutes in Bonanza, but I understand there will be some soon as they are looking for them every day. Wish they would not come for they are the curse of the camps. They are so many of them diseased that they set the men afire and many young men that come to this country with good health go back perfect wrecks to remain so for life. You need never fear me having anything to do with them for if I were single even, I should avoid them. (JANUARY 1, 1881)

> You are always asking if I drink. No, I do not, but if I want a glass of beer I go and take it. But that is very seldom. Nothing more. We have a miners committee here to protect each other from what is called "the gang." In other words, bar keepers, swindlers, pickpockets. They all clog together to rob any and everyone. We will not have a drunkard or anyone that hangs around a saloon or anyone that is intimate with saloon keepers. So you see, that if I was drinking, they would not have anything to do with me.
> (JANUARY 10, 1881)

> You need not fear that you will have a drunken husband or one that runs after other women, for I love my wife too dearly for that, and am too hard up to gamble if I wished. (FEBRUARY 13, 1881)

Lawless society, however, concerned Maggie less than her fear of an instability in Charles himself. She knew his naive readiness to dash into fine-sounding projects. She also knew his pressing need to prove himself to his Virginia family. He had angled away from the scrutiny of his mother, sisters, and wife. Behind his western screen he portrayed an image of success that the women could not test.

To some extent, Maggie's fears were well-founded. Charles's first months in Hayden Creek were helter-skelter.

> The practice is small here but there is a good chance of its getting good. It is good now as far as pay in comparison with West View [Virginia] is concerned, but I mean a big practice. . . . You had better sell the feather bed and try to bring all the bed clothes you can for . . . next summer we wish to start a boarding house for invalids and will need all the covers that we can get. . . . If the times turn out well here, as they must do from indications, and a good population comes, I will get a big practice, for I am getting a very good reputation. . . . There is about two or three hundred mines in these mountains & some of them must turn out well. One was 60% silver and some part gold which will make about $175 per ton. (AUGUST 4, 1880)

Yet, while some men in the camps may have struck it rich, Charles lost money. His medical practice made little, for the camp was small and his patients the "boys" who begged off payment until their mining luck turned. Charles, with the southern gentleman's noblesse oblige, never pressed for money. Justifying himself, he explained to Maggie:

> I ask no man for credit and credit none except those who have nothing and you know that I am obliged to do some of that kind of practice.
>
> (JUNE 6, 1880)

> There is plenty to do here and everyone has money—unless they have been sick . . . and there are some that come from the east that have nothing, like I did, and it takes all they can make to get a start. . . . Did not do much practice last month because there was not much sickness, but I got more money than I ever did in Va.—and when I get you here and my vegetables all in it will not cost so much to live. I lost my account book last month and can't tell exactly what I make, but I think about $25 dollars. Have got a new one, and can keep it strate now. . . . Don't intend to go in debt.
>
> (JUNE 18, 1880)

The obscure "if" quality of Charles's letters characterized his western posture: *if* some intangible materialized, *then* a bonanza would bless his life. Indefatigable optimism coursed through his letters, each glum reality bolstered by a shining dream. Maggie, in Virginia, focused on Charles's empty coffers and on her own waiting. First with one relative, then with another, she bedded herself down with little Mattie, did chores to pay for her keep, and watched the mails for word from Charles that she could join him in Colorado. But Charles's letters only announced fresh new scheme after scheme.

His family haunted him. If he had thought that the West would lessen their cloying pressure, he was mistaken. His glowing descriptions to them of the West had the unexpected effect of sparking in his mother and sisters a desire to join him. Charles's mother was writing to say she would follow her son to Colorado. Rather than tell them no, Charles created smoke screens, and when they pressed, he set up an obstacle course.

> I have written to those at home, if they were so anxious to come out here, they should raise twenty five hundred dollars, and I would buy the Hayden

> ranch, which has about three hundred & twenty acres in it with good improvements and is considered one of the best ranches in this country & I think it is cheap at the price, and if they raise [the money] there is some first rate places for us to put a house there. . . . (JUNE 24, 1880)

Having set the Hayden Ranch project in motion and raised his family's hopes, Charles then dallied in the bargaining, making an inch of progress to a mile of error, while his Virginia family waxed eager.

> Rece'd a letter from home telling me to make some arraingements about buying the Hayden Ranch. They say that they can raise the money within two months. (JULY 26, 1880)

Maggie herself balked at having Charles's family as her neighbors in the West. Even in Virginia she eschewed their company, her attitude ranging from cool reserve to fierce resentment. The little drama of family hostilities—in this case the hostilities of women—was being played out over a distance of a thousand miles! The Browns were of a better class than the Kellers and may have insinuated that Charles married below his station. Misunderstanding existed about the Browns' financial situation too. When her husband died in 1857, Charles's mother, Mary Rice Brown, assumed responsibility for the family finances. Forced to sell their impressive Greek-columned home in Bridgewater, Virginia, after the war, Mary entrusted the eight thousand dollars from the sale to a family friend to invest. When the gentleman died soon after receiving the money, his family refused to honor the transaction because there had been no legal contract signed. The southern code of honor was breached when hard cash was at stake. Again it was a case of women fighting women, each scratching the dirt of hard times to protect her own brood. Although Charles's sisters, Millie and Ella, took teaching jobs and, with their mother, opened a boardinghouse to support themselves, they deliberately hid the extent of their poverty from the community. For years, Maggie believed them to be not poor but miserly.

And surely the Browns' attitude to Charles fueled her dislike of them. While Mary Brown doted on Charles, she also lectured him in petulant, martyred tones about his inattention, his irresponsibility. Maggie articulated some of the anger Charles held inside himself. To his family Charles assumed a polite agreement to their coming west. Only to Maggie did he confess his reservation.

> If I do get the ranch we will not live with the rest of the family, for we could not get along, and I will not have any thing to do with it if I cant hold the purse strings. Old Mrs. H[ayden] says she does not want the old man to sell because she is tired of running around. I have written to the old man, but have not heard from him. (JULY 26, 1880)

That admission soothed Maggie, and her response bubbled with good spirits:

> I have just received your *dear* letter. . . . I have been feeling jolly all evening. I told Cousin Jake I expected to get something sweet in the mail and I did. God bless my darling. How I love you. Write often. . . . Am going to bed now and dream of thee. I have been so blue for the last few days, but feel better now. A sweet Goodnight loved one, the best and dearest of husbands. Be sure I will keep just as good for *you* and *you only*. (AUGUST 1880)

Bolstered perhaps by Maggie's distaste for the Browns' moving west, Charles increased his oblique resistance to the project.

> Rece'd another letter from Millie and she seems to think that they [Charles's family] are all anxious to come out here, but I have not been able to hear from Old Mr. Hayden. (AUGUST 12, 1880)

Finally, Charles piled together enough excuses to blame the scheme's failure on circumstances beyond his control.

> Am going to write to Ma this eve that I could not buy the H[ayden] place. He will not sell it now, and I am not sorry—the man has lost nearly all his crops by hail and water, something they say does not often occur here.
> (AUGUST 22, 1880)

The same letter unveiled his gloom over the collapse of mining prospects in Hayden Creek:

> The country around here is somewhat on the decline and there will be a large number of people that will leave here this fall for southern Arizona. The mines are not putting up much yet, it costs too much to open them up fast & I don't

> think there will be any pay ore gotten out this fall. Some of them have enough to ship a car load, but it has cost them more than it is worth to get it. . . . Nearly all of the talk here is mines and mining. (AUGUST 22, 1880)

The letter then took a curious twist. Charles may have felt he had to entice Maggie with future hopes lest she become another of the nagging women at his back and insist he abandon the bleak situation he had just described.

> I have never known how much I loved you, untill we have been separated. Oh how I long to see you, I think some times if I could just see you for two hours & hug and kiss you that long that I could feel contented for a while, but never mind love we will meet after a while and be happy. . . . God bless my darling and protect her is always my prayer— (AUGUST 22, 1880)

Charles had thrown his lot in with a sorry group of men. The lone miners in the Colorado of the 1880s were already a futile lot, even as they continued flocking to a dead region.

> It is astonishing what a vast number of people are still rushing to Leadville; yet we were told by reliable men from there that there were perhaps ten thousand idle men in that city, many of them without money or means of subsistence, depending upon "luck" for a square meal, and on their blankets for lodging. . . . Leadville has had its "boom" and is doomed. . . . Yet the daily reports that some poor prospector has "struck it rich," will still attract fools enough to keep up the "boom" a while longer.[8]

Yet Charles saw himself on the upward surge of the mining fortunes. For him the playing out of one region only meant fortune calling in another. He had little sense that the dominoes were all falling, that the day of the lone prospector striking it rich was being sucked into night. Thus, when the Hayden Creek Camp died (in his seventh month away from home), Charles prepared, not to quit, but to strike out for fresh terrain.

> Well I am satisfied that the practice here will not pay enough to pay me to stay and I will have to leave. There is a friend of mine that wishes me to go up to southern Arizona with him, and offers to pay my way if I will go with him. He is one of the smart men of this community, and has an invalid wife and a family of small children. His name is Rogers, he is from N[orth] C[arolina]. He will have some money and I think he wants me to clerk in some sort of business for him. I will go with him. . . . From the reports of

various men that have been there the country is a good one, far better than this. (OCTOBER 10, 1880)

And when the tide of excitement switched suddenly from Arizona back to Colorado, Charles switched his plans accordingly:

My darling Wife
Darling just please let me have a chance at Kerber [Colorado]. I have great cause to believe that we can do well there. I have given up all idea of going to Arizona. There is as much excitement about that place [Kerber Creek] as there ever was about Leadville and better mines. All the miners want me to go there. Come my darling cheer up. If I hesitate about coming back [to Virginia] it is because I dread to come back untill I know that I cant do any better here than I can there. Write me and tell me to stay a while longer.
(OCTOBER 21, 1880)

A second letter the same day reeled with Charles's excitement about the potential of the new Kerber Creek mines, particularly about the Bonanza section to which he was moving.

Men are flocking there and a city is being built. By next summer there will be ten thousand people there. . . . All the men are anxious that I should come. . . . Oh, but I'm anxious to see you all, my loved ones, but God will help us in due time. Be patient, love, and don't give way under this blow. It is hard but we have no other chance but to bear it. Write to me soon, love, for I need comfort from my dear wife. (OCTOBER 21, 1880)

The letters between Charles and Maggie during the 1880–81 winter of their separation catch in snarl after snarl. Charles was an enigmatic person. The hyperbole of the western expanse infused his personality. The heady illusion of ownership of the vast stretches of land was an adolescent dream of power. Decisions were made in bursts of excitement. Little wonder, then, that the waiting Maggie (nearing her eighth month of "waiting") bristled at his random speculations and demanded that he send her money to join him. She wanted definition for their life, parameters to their relationship, a focus for their future. It was not a fear of venturing into uncharted territories that fueled Maggie's protests; it was her sense that the mining venture was a mindless darting after fool's gold.

Charles and Maggie, like other men and women of their age, lived out of separate fictions. If what Maggie wanted from Charles was a man who supported her, thrilled to her, comforted her, listened to her, provided for her future, she was discovering in Charles only traces of those characteristics. In his words he was the man of her ideals; in his behavior, he was not.

> They all seem anxious for me to stay and if they can make it pay me enough I will but if not why then I will work hard and get enough to come home on and leave for home. . . . I am so anxious to see you that if things don't look well soon I shall come back. You don't feel our separation any more than I do, but oh! how much I dread poverty all my life—but I love my wife better. And if I don't make some thing soon—I shall come back to my loved ones. This place is destined to go ahead of Leadville, but money will not compensate me for the separation. Everything seems to be alive here. I can hardly write now because there are two or three carpenters at work in the house and they shake me so. Take comfort dear wife, don't give way, for you will see me soon either here or in Va.
>
> Write me here via Villa Grove—and if you say come home I will work hard and get money to come home on. (OCTOBER 28, 1880)

Charles's insistence that he longed for Maggie, laced with his keen excitement over the new mining camp, created a wily ambiguity. He moved toward her and then away like a shadow.

> I have just gotten me a lot that will cost me no money at all. The town company wants some one who will take care of their books and have given me a nice lot. . . . The lot will be worth from three to five hundred dollars next summer. Will not rest until I can get one or two more. My board is costing me nothing and I am making some money but I have not received any yet.
>
> (NOVEMBER 5, 1880)

Trying to catch and hold the elusive man she had married, to pin him to some definitive course of action, frustrated Maggie.

> Have written three letters to Bonanza, but have received a reply to none. Hope to get them soon though. I was dreaming about you all last night, do so often. . . . I would like to come with Mrs Eskridge who is going some time between now and Christmas. So if you find it will pay you to stay and can make us comfortable I would like to come for I do wish to see you so much. Dear send me a lock of your hair and whiskers in the reply to this soon—*don't forget*

> *it.* I have on the dress Fannie Wynant gave me. Can I use calico in winter there? Is there any danger of Indians there? Aunt Mary has taken Mattie and gone to a neighbors. All is very quiet. She is the light and life of any house I go to. Sometimes I think if you could just see her. When I came here the middle of May she measured 28 in, now she is 31 in tall, Nov. 9.
>
> (NOVEMBER 9, 1880)

Before she completed the letter, Maggie received word from Charles that he had entered into a fresh enterprise with a Virginia cousin who was to underwrite a newly patented gold machine. Reaching over the miles to plead restraint, Maggie wrote:

> This morning my dear Charlie [Shuff] and I received your letter of the first last eve. C. says he will write to you and see what he can do, but he can't see any money in it now. Dear, of course that man will tell you there is money in it *he* wants to sell. Now Dear I don't object to you seeing about it but *please* dont spend any money if you have any. I would rather keep it and add to it by degrees than run such a risk now. I say no more, expect I have incurred your displeasure, but cant *help it.*
>
> You said "Just let me go, I would not ask it but for my health's sake" . . . [but] you have been there 7 months the 5th of this month and what have you to show for it? I will let you do as you please. We will never be any better off until you settle some place, but when oh when will that be? Do not spend the last hundred dollars in that machine, if you do no one will help you.
>
> Virginia gold is at the point of the plow share. This is not Colorado. I don't know when Charlie [Shuff] will write. He is not so easily duped or taken in by every excitement. Do not get mad for I love you and don't want you to go *blind.* (NOVEMBER 7, 1880)

As fall became winter, ignoring Charles's warning about the intense cold, Maggie increased her pressure to join him. To shore up her case, she wrote Charles's aunt living in Colorado Springs, a fairly recent settlement founded to attract rich health seekers. Though Aunt Betsy Coyner sympathized with Maggie's urge to be with Charles, she counseled Maggie to wait in Virginia until the spring thaw.

> I was very much surprised to get a letter from you: you want to know if it would be prudent for you to come out hear in winter with a little child. I will tell you just what I think. I will not advise any one to come out hear in winter;

> we have had the coldest wether hear that I ever felt. I dont remember that I ever saw so much ice in all my long life in November.
>
> I have not heard from Charlie Brown since he left Hayden Creek. I thought he was there yet. I sopoes he is froze up: if I were you I would wait until spring. . . . This time of the year it is not pleasent to be out for such a long trip. . . . I think if you have a warm house and kind friends to stay with this winter you had better stay until spring. (DECEMBER 6, 1880)

As if to further dissuade Maggie, Aunt Betsy reflected on the numerous deaths of children. While Maggie might risk the cold for herself, she must pause before risking the three-year-old Mattie.

> We have a great many deaths hear now among children. Just while I am writing they are carrying a little child by our house to the Semetery. The carriages are going in front of our house. Diphthearie is very fatal hear: tis true this is a City but it is nevertheless distressing to see the Hearse so often, all most evry day we see it sometimes twise a day. We have a great many Doctors hear and some good ones too, but they cant keep people from dieing when ther time comes. (DECEMBER 6, 1880)

What could she do but acquiesce and ready herself for a bleak Virginia winter? Charles, initially relieved of Maggie's pressure, soon felt his own bleak winter—snowed in, womanless. Mining camps, unsightly in good weather, were full of filth and disorder in bad. Inside their scrappy tents or log houses, the men were trapped in a mess of rough bunk beds covered with loose hay, rough blankets, the stench of unwashed bodies and unwashed clothes. Outside they sloshed through muddy passageways where piles of manure and trash accumulated, garbage rotted, and cesspools stank—a dismal setting, especially for a Virginia gentleman.

Charles's letters reflected the gloom of the camp. In the cold isolation, memory of Maggie's warm presence haunted him. He and the other men, with mining fever abated, shifted their passions to women.

> Nothing has happened of any interest since I last wrote except that I showed your picture to two or three men the other night and one of the men remarked, that that was enough to keep any man stripped.

Then, perhaps fearing that Maggie would think he talked of such things in a saloon, he added:

> It is a common thing for men to drink here and they think it is strange that I don't. (DECEMBER 8, 1880)

The banks of snow slowed life to a tedious pace, letters from home perhaps the only relief. Charles watched the mails:

> Why have I not gotten any picture of my loved ones? The snow is about eight inches deep here and will remain all winter. . . . There is very little game, the cold has driven them all out.
>
> Now my love write to me soon and tell me all the news that you can think of & send me a county paper some times. (DECEMBER 8, 1880)

Snowed in and lonesome, Charles dreamed of building a house for Maggie:

> I do so long to be with you and look into those dear eyes. I know there is plenty of love there for me and I so long to see you once more under our own roof. Would you be content under an old log cabin for a while? You shall have a better one if I can build it by spring but I can't wait longer than then. The life that I am leading is a very rough one and I do not enjoy it at all. . . . You have been a good, patient wife and you deserve all the love that man can give, but some of these days, with God's permission, I can show you all the love I feel this moment.

His rush of sentiment faltered, though, as Charles remembered, too, the original lure of the West:

> But money is what I want, and must have, and as soon as I can get enough, I am going back to old Virginia, and buy me a good home, and remain there as long as I live. (DECEMBER 22, 1880)

Dreams of Maggie and money fired his winter sleep:

> My loved one, I begin to see where I will make some money in the spring and I don't think I'd be fooled. I have a place for the *Maggie Brown* [Charles's proposed mine] now not far from my cabin. I intend to dig it forty feet more for half of it. That will leave me one-fourth. From the indications I think we will strike mineral in fifteen feet and it is in close proximity to four or five of the best mines in the camp. Some of them stand at from eighty (80) to an hundred (100) thousand dollars. That, you see, will make our mine sell well

and if I can get enough to start on in Virginia I will come back. But not until I do. . . . You need not be uneasy about me not being true to you, would rather die than be false to my darling, but I think I trust you more fully than you do me.

Have not commenced the house yet, can't get lumber. Will as soon as I get it. . . . Give my love to all the family and kiss my babies for me [Charles's "babies" were Maggie and Mattie]. And remember that I love my babies better than anything else in the world. And that I neither drink or run after other women. (DECEMBER 30, 1880)

But separation fed suspicions, and Charles defended himself against what must have been Maggie's words of distrust:

We work hard all day and sit up and talk until ten or eleven, or go out to see some of the other boys. . . . If I had my loved ones I would be happy. But sometimes I lay awake from two to three oclock thinking of you.

(JANUARY 10, 1881)

You don't know how much I long to see my loved ones or how anxiously I look forward to the time when I can go home or have them brought out to me. . . . If I make a raise here I shall not do as the rest do, stay here and spend it trying to make more. I shall go to Virginia and lay it out in a home for my loved ones. And then for two or three more babies. Don't you think so? (JANUARY 17, 1881)

You seem to think that I don't love you. Why, I can't tell. When you see how poverty has compelled me to live you will then know how much I have loved my darling, for nothing in the world would I live like this but for my dear wife. And the prayer of my soul is that I might soon have her with me. (FEBRUARY 3, 1881)

Some letters were full of sexual innuendo and longing.

Write to me soon and write me all the love in your soul for I do so long to hear it poured out, there is nothing in the world that I appreciate more than I do it. I feel as if it was all that I had in this world, altho, I love my babe [Mattie], yet my love for her is nothing in comparison to my love for the mother of it. Oh! how I wish that I had her [Maggie] in my arms at this time and I think that I'll soon have her there. Ahh wont it be bliss to be together once more? Then nothing but death will part us. I feel that I could kiss that little "tater hole" if it would do any good, to have it back with me. And I think I will kiss the other when I get to, for its so sweet.

Charles concluded that letter with a disclaimer of gossip circulated about him in Virginia:

> It does not hurt me for them [the community in Virginia] to talk about me if you don't believe it, for there is no truth in any of it, and I don't care who thinks it is so, just so you trust me. (FEBRUARY 16, 1881)

But the real or imagined exploits of Charles Brown fed the hometown appetite for scandal. A professor at the University of Virginia who had escorted Maggie to a social confessed to Charles:

> I did hear that you were a drunkard, and a gambler, but, of course I got it from a quarter that everything must not be believed, and I doubted the story when I heard it. I heard some thing about your dear wife from the same quarter. I did not believe when I heard it, let alone after I met her. I dont believe everything I hear, . . . when you hear a tale it all depends upon who tells it. You are a long way from home. . . . When ever you do return I should be glad to meet you, hoping you may be successful in the far West, and make money enough to buy a nice house, then return, take your dear wife & child in your barrow to part no more. (FEBRUARY 22, 1881)

When the muddy spring thaw began, Charles still lacked money for Maggie's ticket or logs for her cabin. Feeling doomed, Maggie wrote:

> I will be so glad when this is all over. . . . I just feel like crying out, My darling, my darling, if I could only see you. How are you getting along with the house? My love, when will you send the money to come out on? When will that be? I will go with you hereafter through thick and thin, then let come what will. (SPRING 1881)

Maggie added a vignette about little Mattie, who probably picked up her mother's impatience (after a solid year of "waiting") to leave for the West:

> Mattie often starts to "Colonadie" [Colorado], gets Fannie's shoes on and off she goes. (SPRING 1881)

Charles did not seem to understand the depth of Maggie's anxiety. In his mind, he was handling matters as fast as the curious mining environment allowed. That he missed her physically seems true; the desire pressed him at night, but left him in the day.

> I don't think my love that you could stand it here in this dredful cold before the first of May, but oh I am so anxious for you to come then, and I pray God that we will meet by that time. Darling I am beginning to think that I have nothing like the passion that I used to have, altho every night, I have that old pain, but in the morning there is none of it left, it seems strange to me, the fact that it is there at night, and gone in the morning. (MARCH 14, 1881)

Maggie quipped:

> So you have not gotten out of the old way of "wanting it" at night. Never mind you wont have to suffer much longer, will you? (MARCH 23, 1881)

Perhaps Maggie said more to Charles on the subject of unsatisfied passion, suggesting that maybe he eased his urges with some of the camp's loose women. For some reason, Charles felt he had to explain to Maggie how he released his pent-up sexuality:

> My virtue is all right and I think that it will remain so for I do not care to meddle with any of the women that I see here but I look forward to something nice soon. I know that it will be the best in the world, so I am satisfied to think of how nice it will be and go and jack off. Now don't blame me for I do get awful hard up some times. (APRIL 16, 1881)

A dilemma of the nineteenth-century woman then came to issue—how to balance sex and birth control. With few options at her disposal, Maggie, like her contemporaries, gambled on the uncertain rhythm method—plotting the monthly course of ovulation/menstruation and limiting sexual intercourse to the supposed "safe period" from the sixteenth day after the end of menstruation to the twenty-fifth day. Even after they had been apart for a year, Maggie and Charles were still concerned to synchronize the date Charles would send the long-waited-for ticket money with a date on which Maggie would be "safe."

> Send the money you have & I will come right on. Send it as soon as you get this. . . . I was taken sick [began menstruation] this morn' so see, I must hurry up. (APRIL 24, 1881)

Letter writing itself became an expression of the ambiguities of Charles's nature. Several times he brought Maggie to the point of departure only to write that she must wait still another month.

> My own darling
>
> I am so sorry to say that I failed to get the money to send for you but do not think it will be long. It discourages me so much, the house is all right, all but the carpet and chairs, and that will be very easy, money is dreadfully scarce here at this time. The mines are not being worked at this time and no one seems to have money. . . . There are men going off every day that are owing me money and I cant get it, but darling you may depend upon it as soon as I can get the money you will get it. (JUNE 5, 1881)

Drawing her into his own dreamy vision of their future together, Charles described her Colorado cabin:

> Our house is sixteen by twenty feet square, with two windows in front and one door between and one door at the end to the left as you enter the front door; the windows will require curtains two by five feet. Will put a cloth partition on the right for a bedroom but will do that when you come & will get a tent to put in the rear for a kitchen; have a first rate cook stove and a nice little heating stove for the sitting room; you may think the heating stove is useless but the nights are always cool. The house is on a hill over looking the town of Bonanza and the only objection that I have to the place is that I will have to have all the water hauled. . . .

In the western euphemism, rough board shanties and makeshift lean-tos became suburbs:

> It is going to be the place for private residences; there are some here now. (JUNE 5, 1881)

As the anticipated July departure neared, Charles emphasized his eagerness and his concern that Maggie arrive in Colorado during her "safe" period.

> When you get to Kas [Kansas] City your ticket should take you via the Santa fe road to Pueblo and not by Denver, and then you would touch Cincinnati, St. Louis, Kansas City, Pueblo, Canon City and South Arkansas and Bonanza where you will find one of the most loving pair of arms to meet you that you

ever saw and they will always remain so, for I think that you are one of the sweetest little wives that ever lived, and when you come I can swear *that I have been true.* . . . Try and get here by the twentieth of next month and I will be ready for you then, and I think that you will be ready for me by that time. (JUNE 23, 1881)

Hopes and fears poured from Maggie. She was concerned that her physical charm would still allure Charles. Her anticipation of being with Charles stayed strong, even to the point of her considering another pregnancy.

I want to see you *so so* much. I do think if you wanted to see me near as badly as I do you you would, I wont say it for I know you do *nearly*. I am *almost* willing to have a boy for you, but if I start Monday I will be clear of all & I don't want to get in "that way" at once. (JUNE 26, 1881)

But fate then halted the exodus for Colorado. What had seemed only a passing sickness for little Mattie suddenly escalated into a potentially fatal illness. Nineteenth-century women raising small children lived close to such sudden disaster. Panicked, Maggie wrote Charles twice in a single day: she feared Mattie's death and could scarcely bear the thought. For the long year and a half of waiting, Mattie had become the center of life for Maggie. It seemed impossible that the pinched, thin figure on the sickbed, discharging pus and blood, was the frolicking child who had been packing trunks with Maggie only a few days before.

My own darling:

I wrote to you today telling of our babe's sickness but I must write to you again for I feel that if you are not here or we there we can be some comfort to each other. I fear that we will soon be alone, & no babe. Oh! the thought chokes me. She is my companion as well as child but, dear, the omniscient one may take her to save her from future trouble. Now, if she dies, she is safe. She was rational a while this morning but looked so pinched and thin when the fever was off that it distressed me so I just exclaimed, "Darling, are you going to leave your mama?" She looked up & said, "No, me leave you—be back in a little while." About sundown last eve she commenced passing blood and slime. Now, this is 1 o'clock the next day and the discharge is like that of a rotten boil. Uncle H[enry] thought I ought to have her baptized so I did. . . . Do not give up for I will not leave a stone unturned to save our babe, & if she has to go I will fly to my only love with all speed. . . . Darling, bare up, I have good kind friends to support me. I will pray for you. I tell you this so you may be prepared for anything that may come. I am trying to become resigned but it is only trying, I fear.

The Dr. says the symptoms are against her recovery.

Your loving and clinging wife

(JULY 4, 1881)

The fever did, however, break. And Maggie's next letter to Charles was flooded with pent-up emotion at the unfairness of their two lives: his, free from responsibility; hers pressed with frantic concern.

I received your invitation & card last eve'. It just showed how far off you were, the difference in our feeling on the 4th. You no doubt were having a nice time (I don't blame you if you did) & I was sitting over the cradle of our darling all that day thinking what a short time I would have her with me & seeing her lying there sitting in pain & so perfectly helpless to relieve her. The Dr. had dispaired of her. Oh! how could I give her up? It would not be so hard with you, for you have not watched the growth & development like I have. She is so lively, so affectionate & so smart—[she] can say one verse of "Twinkle little star." She is the image of my darling husband, more especially since she has been sick. Her eyes & brow & mouth are true to yours.

(JULY 9, 1881)

The impact of Mattie's illness jarred Charles. Yet he continued to read both Maggie's and his plights as veiled harbingers of good things to come: "The darkest hour is always just before day." (JULY 19, 1881) Though he still had no money for their tickets, though his mines had failed to produce and his patients failed to pay, Charles's words rang with unshakable optimism:

There is no money to send to you, but it must come after a little, and we will live in hope if we die in dispair. No. I have not had the money to go into partnership in the P.O. Drug Store, but I have a fourth interest in fifty town lots, and have three in my own name, and a fourth interest in two good prospect holes; one of them has a tunnel thirty feet long and the other has a shaft thirty feet deep and I consider them both good, but I don't think any thing of those that I dug on last winter and it will cost me two dollars and fifty cents per foot for every foot that we sink on the two that we have, but I have eighteen months to do that in, and if I don't sell out by that time I think that I will be able to do my best on it with perfect ease. (JULY 19, 1881)

Almost like a miracle, little Mattie recovered.

Through the long winter of waiting and anxiety, Maggie played the role of loyal wife. Southern women were raised to defer to male authority and "to stifle in themselves alien thought, cynicism."[9] A wife was expected to follow her husband as a docile subordinate. Maggie's feelings of loneliness and humiliation in being a "poor relative" in the family are all apparent in her letters, yet she managed as best she could so that in her manner she softly complied with Charles's wishes.

And then, after more than a year of their tug-of-war in letters, Maggie had word that she and Mattie could start. Charles had somehow, miraculously, scraped together the money for their long-awaited tickets to Colorado. They were on their way.

II. Reunion, *1881–1884*

The year-and-a-half delay ironically gave Maggie a great enthusiasm for the West. Her initial suspicions of the godless, uncouth society diminished with her eagerness to be with Charles. When she finally journeyed into the Rockies, she managed to view the towering mountains as welcoming gateways to Charles. Despite harrowing moments en route, a gentle delight colored her first letter home to Virginia:

> My <u>dear</u> pa & family
> I am at home at last. Arrived here Saturday eve, after many trials, at least after I reached Pueblo, where a tellegram was received that 5 bridges were washed out from that place to Leadville. So we laid over there a day & started at 6 o'clock Friday eve for Canon City, where I had to have my baggage checked & get another ticket to South Arkansas. But there was a very kind conductor on & as it was raining so hard & so dark he attended to it for me.

So after a few moments we started on & got about a mile & a half, when the train came to a stop. They said it would have to go back to Canon City, as there was a large bolder & land slide on the road. So we did, and they went up with an engine & chains to drag it off, but it was so large it had to be blasted off. Well after three hours we started on & I was in such perfect dread all the time it realy made me sick & the Conductor saw it & told me not to be uneasy, that they had road walkers every two miles with lanterns to signal if there was any danger. Well at 4½ o'clock we got to South Arkansas, when at six I took the train for Mears Station, & there found a mail wagon without any cover (but it was all to be had) so took my seat for a 40 mile ride in a constant drizzel & rain for Bonanza, but pa I did not mind that for all the lovely country I ever saw I saw that day. These are called Rocky mountains. The tops may be Rocky but I could not see them that day for the clouds. . . . [After riding fourteen miles] we started up this gulch on the each side of which Bonanza is situated & my house is up above all overlooking the town which is a goodeal larger than Bridgewater [Virginia]. Now we drove in about 5 o'clock and at the post office in front of about 15 or 20 men there stood Dr. B. not knowing us until we came to a dead stop. He took M[attie] & told the driver to drive to Mrs. Rose's, where we were real kindly treated, & staid until Sunday morn when he brought us up home, which is just a little bird cage of an affair. Nice new stove, carpet on the floor, nice new dishes better than we ever had in West View, set of chairs one a rocker & high chair bed sted with mattress & spring wash stand with drawers & drop handles & other little things. I am nice fixed. I am nicer fixed than I have ever been. I will be real happy if you write to me often for Dr. B. is doing very well.

Don't let the children forget me. (AUGUST 1881)

Charles, the Rocky Mountain grandeur, the crisp climate, and the new culture kept Maggie in good spirits through her first year in Colorado. A sightseer rather than a settler, she detailed to her Virginia family the curiosities of "this strange country": burros packed with great bundles far larger than themselves; the climate that froze water left by the embers overnight, yet that warmed so pleasantly in the daytime that by early afternoon Maggie could sit on her front porch with Mattie playing on the floor at her feet; January earth so frozen that it had to be blasted to make a grave; fierce winds that drove them some nights to take shelter in a sod house; the eight-thousand-foot elevation that made her pot of beans take three hours instead of one to cook. She mailed home cactus plants and buffalo teeth.

Charles was appreciative of the sacrifice Maggie had made for his speculative venture. In addition to the "nice" house furnishings, he purchased several lots in her name, giving her "complete control" over what revenue they might bring. The initial excitement buoyed her so much that for almost six months Maggie was able to project onto Colorado enough cheer to stave off facing the radical differences between the eastern and western life-styles. In the first months, she thought she found in Bonanza the cultural values of Bridgewater.

> Dr. B. came home for dinner & I had to get it ready then go to Sunday School which is half past two. Dr. B. has the bible class & I have a class of boys. I have had company every day since. I am invited out to tea tomorrow. (JANUARY 22, 1882)

For those first months, Charles, too, viewed the family's stay in Colorado as temporary; at least, that was what he wrote to Pa:

> You may not be surprised to see us back there [Virginia] by fall if things look up here this spring as everyone expects. I shall sell out and come back. I have property enough if I can sell for anything like their value. I can get me a very nice little home back there. Times are very dull here, but I can always get more money here than I could back home, but I can't say that I like it here. There is too much yankee about the people, and then we have everything to buy; can raise nothing here. (JANUARY 30, 1882)

With spring, however, Charles changed his mind. Instead of pulling up for Virginia, he battened down to stay in Colorado. By that time, the glow of the new adventure was fading for Maggie. There were times when she put energy into western enterprise.

> Today a week ago, I went in partnership with a lady friend to start a boarding house, but only run 5 days and found we were about to come out "the little end of the horn," so we closed. I bought me a sewing machine last week. Hope to make something on it. (MARCH 1, 1882)

She was beginning to suspect that if she were to stay married to Charles in the frontier west she must work for a living or see their small family starve. This was where her marriage to a Virginia gentleman, a doctor, had brought her. The reality of her new situation began to fill her thoughts. Charles's boundless, groundless optimism, close at hand, with the impact of each day's reality to set it into sharp contrast, was infuriating.

> Dr. B. always has some new project on hand, but as he has no money to put in anything he does not lose any thing but "chin music" & you know that is cheap with him. He has a hospital scheme on hand. Now he is talking of building a house down on our other lot & running one there, but I fear this is only talk or he will be undermined by some other physician. There are some awful mean people here. Will do *any* thing for money, & you know how Dr. B. talks about his plans to any body.

Her wry comment on the mining economy was: "That is the way with this country—one day flourishing & the next just the reverse." (MARCH 1, 1882)

Life in Bonanza soured for Maggie. She could no longer pretend that she and Charles would return to Virginia rich. And while she had imagined that she had said good-bye to Virginia, in reality, she had only wrapped her southern culture around her and traveled west more as a tourist than as a settler. By March 1882, she had to admit that Charles had no intention of returning home. Failure only sparked fresh speculation in him. Even in the dust of the dry land, he saw the West as consummate possibility, a land so rich that the law of probability made ultimate success certain.

The more Charles dug in, the more Maggie tied her hopes to returning to the Old Dominion, the country of her birth. Fourteen out of fifteen of Maggie's letters from Bonanza outlined projects for returning to Virginia. Symbols of the community she had left played on her imagination; she held on to them as the folklore of home. The family fireplace, the company parlor, the scenic bay window, the fruit trees, the mild weather—she dwelt on these in her letters. In the cold mountains such images filled her thoughts.

Maggie had reasons other than homesickness to be disenchanted with Bonanza. The big mines were playing out; the poverty-stricken area was becoming a ghost town.

> There is no money in the bank & so very little in town. I saw in the paper tonight that "It was reported that there was a man in town today with fifty ct [cents] in currency" but, the editor said, "I don't believe it." Oh! Pa, what are we to do? (SEPTEMBER 9, 1882)

Charles moved the family to the mining town of Poncha Springs, a change that broke Maggie's rash of ill humor. She saw beauty and civic virtue. Mountain streams ran through the town, rushing with fresh abundance from the rocky heights. Local leaders in Poncha Springs had held out for sobriety laws within the town limits, making Poncha Springs the rare mining camp in which the major trade was not in liquor.

For a brief moment, Maggie thought Charles might, indeed, have found his place of fortune. He replaced a physician who had been netting between four and five thousand dollars a year. Until that time, Charles, at his best, had cleared no more than thirty-five dollars a month. But although Charles had had a steady practice, he could never press patients to pay their fees. Maggie had begun to suspect—must have known—that Charles had no genuine interest in becoming rich as a doctor. He could have been a simple physician in Virginia. That was not why he had risked everything to come west. It was easier for her to sympathize with him as a poor businessman than as an inveterate speculator. Subtle changes were taking place in the balance of their marriage.

Charles frequently rode horseback the forty miles between Poncha Springs and Bonanza to check his claims. At other times he traveled for days to minister to patients. Maggie never adjusted to those absences or to the precarious economics of their new life. Moving to the frontier was downward mobility for Maggie, who was charged with making a home. It was downward for Charles too, but it was also freedom from old responsibilities to his mother and sisters and even from the routine existence of being a doctor in old Virginia.

Life for Maggie was not only a downward move; it was also uncertain and dangerous. The forgotten but still-smoldering coals of a campfire could catch anew from a gust of wind and suddenly blaze up, igniting blocks of the tinderbox shacks. Once Maggie marked a photograph of the town to mail to Pa, but before she got the pictures off, fire had destroyed most of the structures she had labeled.

•

> Last eve' about 3 o'clock I was standing in the door looking for Dr. B. when a volume of smoke came from a building on the opposite side of the street & I screamed fire. Within 20 minutes seventeen (17) buildings were in ashes. The best part of & center of the town it was. With the greatest exertion our house was saved. The street is about 40 ft wide, but fortunately the wind came up & took the blaze the other way. But then the heat was so great as

> to blister the varnish on the wash stand through the window & it sat 3 ft from the window. (NOVEMBER 22, 1882)

Disastrous fires were like epidemics to mining-camp towns. Only a few weeks later, Maggie again wrote Pa:

> There was another fire this morning, burnt up a dwelling & stable. A young man was sleeping in the house & got up and made a fire & went back to bed & asleep & when he woke up the whole ceiling was on fire. He barely got on his pants & out, the hair on his head nearly all burnt off. This is four fires since the last of Sept. I am uneasy all the time. . . . If the whole town burns up I don't know what will become of us. (DECEMBER 10, 1882)

When Maggie wrote "uneasy," she must have felt terror. The flames that engulfed her mother's body were keen in her memory. In actuality, fire did kill the town. By the end of 1883, ashes and skeletal cabins were all that remained of Poncha Springs.

And Maggie had other terrors than fire. Avalanches thundered down mountainsides, burying men alive—traveling men, like Charles. "One man leaves a family—and is under 100 feet of snow." Violence was a part of daily life. Maggie wrote Pa of the man who came to Charles with an "awful-looking bleeding hand," a pistol wound. And with "frontier justice," there were hangings, bodies left dangling in the wind.

Maggie was physically drained and feeling increasing resentment that Charles continued undaunted along his path of failure.

> Since I started this letter I have had two teeth extracted & took ether. It took a half pound to get me under the influence of it . . . but one tooth pulled so hard & tore up the gum so, I have not been able to eat anything solid since. Oh, pa, I am so homesick or rather V[irginia] sick, but Dr. B. will *not* come back. . . . He has too much pride to come back & have people taunt him. It will be 3 years in March since he came & we are really no better off than in Va. I don't say half I feel to him for I know it will do no good.
>
> (DECEMBER 10, 1882)

Christmas, 1882, was spare, with not even money to purchase stamps for a letter to Virginia; furious, Maggie wrote that she was ready to steal:

> I have received two letters from you since I wrote one. I hate to give my reason for not writing but will be frank with you. I wanted to write last Sunday but Dr. B. said wait until we get some stamps. So I waited & no stamps yet so I will write & get one if I have to steal it. No, we have not had enough money in the last month to get a stamp. (DECEMBER 25, 1882)

There was no way to survive unless Maggie were to *do* something herself to stem the family losses.

> If I could take in washing to help along I would do it, but if I did Dr. B would not get any practice, for people are so suspicious any way for fear they will employ a quack or some one that is not any account. (JANUARY 21, 1883)

It was not so much the deprivation that rankled Maggie; it was confronting the fact that Charles was a bungling provider.

> He is such a poor collector and we can get along on *just so* much & he don't try to get out of that, maybe if I was away he would have to "russel" more & send me some. (FEBRUARY 11, 1883)

Charles, the Virginia gentleman, forgave his debtors, yet attended scrupulously to his own debts. He trusted people and lost his best mining claim to a slick move by a "friend," then he sank money into new prospect holes while the family struggled just to buy food.

To escape the haunting terrors of fire, avalanche, violence, and poverty, Maggie remembered Virginia, her dreams linking her to childhood, to a paradise of fruit and flowers. When she wrote of being "Virginia sick," she begged for her symbols of Virginia: apples, chestnuts, persimmons, "chinkpins," peaches, melons, snapbeans, black-eyed peas, ginger cakes—requests that sang like the refrain of a melancholy folk ballad. *Home* was back with Pa in Virginia; she had not been raised for Colorado shanty towns.

Charles, for his part, entertained no thought of returning to the "Old Dominion." When Poncha Springs failed to recover after the 1882 fires, his dreams wandered farther west: Utah, Idaho, Montana, Oregon, Washington. However, he merely shifted the family from the burnt-out Poncha Springs to Villa Grove, another Colorado town. More of a farming than a mining area, Villa Grove housed a friendly community where people had requested Charles as their physician. The town's proximity to Bonanza (about ten miles) allowed Charles to continue to check his mines, which he was still certain would make him rich.

At first Villa Grove improved conditions for the Browns, especially Maggie. There was an actual church building and an organized Sunday school. Charles was invited to be assistant and superintendent and Maggie, secretary and teacher. It was a pattern reminiscent of her South. With delight she wrote Pa that she had left her breakfast dishes unwashed "to join a neighbor for a walk and dinner and a chat." (APRIL 9, 1883) She could write then of "good kind friends."

Villa Grove, however, did not change Charles's habits of behavior. Despite his insistence that he had come west to get rich and that he was "determined to do so"—a chorus quite typical of improvident frontier husbands—he continued to be unproductive. Busy with a continual flow of patients, he seldom collected his fees.

Instead, Charles sank what money he did touch into his Bonanza mines in fevered tries for quick wealth. Never was his dream steady income; always it was a lucky "strike." By September 1883, Charles had lost every one of his Bonanza claims because he could not afford the yearly assessments. The Colorado mining code demanded annual proof of labor on all mining claims, and the amount of improvement (only twelve dollars for mines the size of Charles's) had to be officially recorded in a sworn affidavit. Failure to comply with the regulation resulted in the mine's being reclassified as public territory. Although the required amount was small, Charles could not afford even that. By late fall he was shingling the Methodist church at $2.50 a day. Maggie, then five months pregnant, was rising early to assist a neighbor in cooking for a team of brickmakers in exchange for the family's board.

It was a dramatic crisis: Maggie, in the course of a difficult pregnancy, dragging herself to knead and bake loaves of bread, Charles hammering shingles—community projects that could have raised their spirits, but instead sank them into a sense of melancholy failure. Maggie wrote Pa:

> I don't see any likelihood of times ever being any better. I feel if I do stay here two years longer I will be lost body and soul. . . . I would give 5 years of my life if I had never seen this state. Now we have been married 7 years nearly & getting worse off every year instead of better. (SEPTEMBER 1883)

Maggie's feelings about her pregnancy must have been ambivalent, wanting the child, resenting Charles, who would be no more of a provider for the new infant than he was being for Mattie, resisting, too, giving birth in a land so raw and different from Virginia culture. A weary sadness trailed through her letters:

> Suppose you are at home now with the family, & having a nice time. I almost envy you all the pleasant times you have together. I think it is so hard to be out here and going through with all kinds of hardships & not have a friend to turn to. Being deprived of seeing our friends is the hardest of all. . . . If I can't write more cheerfully I had better close. I know you would rather not get any letter than one of this kind. (SEPTEMBER 2, 1883)

In mid-November, Maggie experienced a sudden onset of hard labor pains. After twenty-four hours, her infant was stillborn. Then she hemorrhaged and, in the bleeding, almost died. Charles seems to have been the only person assisting her in the ordeal. As he held his lifeless infant, one might wonder what emotions stirred. Did he link his uncompromising determination to stay west with the tiny body's failed life?

Maggie's account to Pa was listless, more indifferent than sad or angry. She referred to herself as "your own child." How helpless she must have felt.

> I am sitting up but very weak & so poor you would not know your own child now & pa some times I think my lungs are going to be weakened by this. I am stooped & it hurts me to straighten up. I doubt if you can read what I have written, so I will close & write more when I get stronger. I wish you would send me some persimmons for Xmas. (NOVEMBER 25, 1883)

For weeks she lay listless in bed. She mentioned no one other than Charles who cared for her during her recovery. If the "good kind friends" came, she seemed unaware of their help.

By Christmas Maggie was mending, but they had no income at all: "Not a cake or nut did we have & not a cent of money." (JANUARY 5, 1884) Though by January Maggie began breadmaking for the public, she was a faint image of the feisty young woman who had traveled three years before from Virginia to set up housekeeping in Bonanza. A gently playful response from Pa suggests the bleak description of herself that Maggie, only twenty-eight, must have sent him:

> Sorry you have grown so old . . . to think I have a daughter so much older than I am. I suppose from your letter that you must be some 65 or 75 years old by now. Why don't you & the Dr. have your likenesses taken & let us judge for ourselves. (FEBRUARY 24, 1884)

Maggie was changing; she saw herself becoming an old woman with a thin face, sunken eyes, and prematurely wrinkled skin. Her youth and beauty were being snatched away by her husband's golden West.

Martha Magdalene (Maggie) Keller Brown, 1884. The "beautiful Maggie Keller," raised and educated in Virginia, was hardly prepared to be the wife of a prospector in the dingy mining camps of Colorado and New Mexico.

III. Another Try, *1884–1886*

Charles's response to Maggie's bout with death was true to form: he searched out the places where the newest mining excitement was rising. The railroad had just connected New Mexico, that mysterious country, with the rest of the United States, and the legends of gold that had lured the Spanish began calling the Anglos.

When an old mining "buddy" from Bonanza days offered partnership in a pharmacy in Rincon (at the southwest corner of New Mexico), Charles gambled that he could find his fortune there in mining, ranching, and medicine. With little discussion, he orchestrated a family move into that terra incognita.

For Charles, his train ride down to prepare a place for Maggie and Mattie opened treasures of myth and folklore. Charles wrote about stories he heard: Starvation Peak, where "the Indians ran an hundred and fifty Mexicans on the top and starved them to death"; tall, spare crosses that marked the truth of the story; the ruins of the old church in which Montezuma took refuge from the Spaniards 450 years ago; the beacon fire burning since his death.[10] The letters Charles sent to Maggie carried adventure rather than concern for family stability. The habit of moving was, after all, the hallmark of the westering experience.

Whatever it was, Charles's sense of New Mexico was not Maggie's. If her isolation from Virginia was acute in Colorado, it was compounded in New Mexico. Houses in Rincon were scattered like dice tossed over the bare earth. Each was a small one-story adobe rectangle, scarcely two or three rooms with only slits for windows. Barbed-wire fencing surrounded some of the houses, enclosing yards that were flat bare patches of earth dotted with scraggly desert sage or tumbleweed. It was a sharp, painful contrast to home in Bridgewater, Virginia, to its stately two-story antebellum structure, with its white columns, a wide veranda shaded by spreading oak trees, cultivated flower gardens, and bordering wrought-iron fences.

In Rincon the craggy, barren earth was beaten by sun and whipped into fine, sandy dust by the ever-present gusting of dry, hot wind. The Rio

Grande, which snaked along but a mile or so from Rincon, created a ribbon of fertility, but it was unreliable, given as much to muddy flooding as to encouraging farming.

There were difficult adjustments to be made. The Pueblo, Apache, and Navajo Indians, the Spanish, the Mexicans, and the newly come Anglos formed a complicated sociology. Anglos themselves were divided into warring factions—miners (boisterous and often criminal), farmers, cattlemen, investors, and eastern "barons."

Although the Indians were "conquered" and the Hispanic element subdued, New Mexico was still a foreign culture. Language, foods, art, religion, social institutions, and even world view resisted the imprint of the American way. The land itself represented a hostile, resistant element, strange and sometimes inimicable in its ways. To Americans used to the bounty of forests and rivers and rich prairies, the desert could prove an implacable foe.

A set of lawyers, politicians, and businessmen called the Sante Fe Ring exploited the region, controlling ranching, mining, and railroad development.[11] The territorial governor resigned in 1881, contending that he had no real power to act. Even religious orders fought in the desert. Protestants and Roman Catholics clashed over a range of policies. And in the center of the territory, Lincoln County, a vigilante legal system (with Billy the Kid and his cohorts) effected "justice" through violence and murder. This was where Charles and Maggie, with their ways of the Old South, had come to make a home.

Pa claimed he could not find them on any map, while Dannie teased that they might as well go on to China where things were also "opening up."

The first years in Rincon bit hard into Maggie. "The sun," she wrote, "never shown on a worse set of people than Rincon contains." (FEBRUARY 1, 1885) While Charles trafficked with a variety of men in Rincon, Deming, and Silver City, Maggie lived housebound. Writing to Pa repeatedly of homesickness, Maggie imagined Virginia as the only civilized place on earth. She feared that six-year-old Mattie would grow up wild and western. In place of dolls and proper Protestant-American playmates, Mattie was playing with rabbits, horned toads, ponies, and goats and speaking Spanish with Roman Catholic Mexican playmates.

To both Maggie and Charles, New Mexico was a world of many new "languages," demanding countless new survival skills. Critical among these was the adjustment to a concept of water wholly different from that held by Virginians. Promotional pamphlets of the 1880s did, indeed, mention, in asides, that the advertised "greatest garden spot with the richest alluvial soil in America if not in the world"[12] would depend totally on a complex system of irrigation. But eastern farmers like Charles, from a land "where the early and the latter rains rarely fail to come"[13] and where fields were amply watered by running springs, had little concept of the problems of desert farming. Surely, they were hardly prepared for the gigantic responsibilities of diverting water from mean rivers.

In New Mexico the system of water rights and waterways, begun as early as the Pueblo settlements in the thirteenth century, increased in complexity with each new wave of settlers. The springs, streams, and rivers belonged officially to all the people of New Mexico—a situation opposite that of Virginia, where water belonged to the person over whose property it flowed. In New Mexico anyone had the right to tap into a body of water. But over the years a series of controls developed to establish rights of priority. Though by 1883 a legal formula designated who along a waterway had such priority, court challenges abounded. A parallel issue involved right-of-way across a property in direct line to water, an issue ripe for endless dispute and violence. In addition to all these points of altercation, there was always argument about who was responsible for upkeep of connecting ditches.

The unruly Rio Grande itself posed a problem, alternating between flood and drought. When Charles wrote that "if properly irrigated," the land they were on could be the most productive farm country a person could ask for, he simply had no idea of what "proper irrigation" in that desert land meant.

Moreover, Charles still had mining fever. From his earliest years in Rincon, he speculated and made mining connections with "boys" exploring the nearby mining regions of White Oaks, Black Range, Organ, and Silver City. The mines fed his hopes and reinforced his resolve to stay in Rincon against all odds.

To Maggie, however, Rincon was the ash heap of her dreams. The wild environment threatened her on all sides.

In that grisly atmosphere of the Southwest, Maggie's new neighbors, the Mexicans, seemed to her part of an unknown and frightening world. Though reputedly "quiet, orderly, law-abiding, frugal people,"[14] they were suspect to the class-conscious Maggie. They spoke a different language, ate different foods, and practiced a different religion. They lived in adobe homes with floors of earth bound with sheep's blood.

In her letters to Pa, Maggie seldom mentioned the drama surrounding her—range shoot-outs, the political coups, the Mexican-Anglo tensions—except to note that Rincon was a "hard place." She and Charles wrote Pa about the curious new country, as if they were gentle naturalists observing a new and somewhat exotic land they were visiting. Charles sent his own brand of written Spanish to Pa (as Pa had requested): "No mass, a mass poko tempo." (APRIL 12, 1884)

Charles liked the hot seasonings: "By the way, you ought to see us eat red pepper. I eat about 6 or 8 pods at a meal and don't think anything of it, am very fond of it." (MAY 25, 1885)

Maggie, with the same curiosity she had shown in Colorado about the bizarre West, acquainted her eastern family with the incongruities she discovered: "I send you an egg of olive wood made in Jerusalem & brought by me from an Arab. We have quite a mixture of people here, a Chinaman is doing my washing." (APRIL 23, 1884) (Numerous Chinese had labored laying the railroad tracks and—since they could not go home—remained in the area after the lines were completed.) Among other things, Maggie mailed to Virginia a denizen of the area: a live "horned frog"; "You put the Frog in a box with dry earth in it and set it in the hottest sun you can find." (MAY 9, 1884) Horned toads so overran the Rincon area that folks nicknamed that section of railroad line the "Horny Toad Division."

Both Charles and Maggie bragged about Mattie's Spanish. Charles wrote:

> Mattie has a little Mexican boy that she plays with and is learning Spanish very fast. (MAY 25, 1885)

And then Maggie:

> Mattie is learning to talk Spanish real fast. If we don't know what they say I just call Mattie up & she can nearly always tell me & when she is playing with the little boy she talks it all together. (JUNE 22, 1885)

The Mexicans were better, Maggie wrote, than the Virginia blacks whom she feared; still, for Maggie the Mexicans were not potential friends. The fact that Mattie played with Mexican children was no indication of frontier egalitarianism. In Virginia, white children regularly played with black children. Segregation began with puberty.

Maggie admitted that the Mexicans' respect for the Sabbath observance hallowed the atmosphere as the secular climate of Colorado had not. And Charles doctored the Mexican community. In the collection of letters there is a faded note in an elegant penmanship from a Señor Alizandro, with enough of the penciled Spanish clear to decipher it as a thank you to the doctor for restored health. Charles may even have been the first to bring smallpox vaccination to the Mexican population in that area. Mary Gose (not yet born in these first Rincon days) wrote of her father years later:

> When my father first started practicing in New Mexico, smallpox raged among the Mexicans. They felt it was a scourge from God and they were not supposed to do anything about it. When my father learned why they would not be vaccinated, he went to the priest and explained to him what he wanted. "And you'll do it for twenty-five cents a patient?" asked the priest astounded. Father answered, "yes." "*Well*, come back Monday morning and you will have all you can take care of." Father started out Monday morning and they stood in line. He vaccinated all day long, the next day, and the next day.[15]

But life in New Mexico depressed Maggie. When a photograph of Maggie arrived in Virginia, a shocked Amelia Jane wrote Pa:

> So pleas write for sister Maggie and little Mattie to come home. I believe she will die out there. Aunt B and I both think she looks nearly as old as Ma did when she died. (AUGUST 1, 1884)

Barely two weeks later Amelia Jane wrote frantically to Pa:

> We received another letter from sister Maggie. . . . I will try to tell you the most important part. She said if she came home could she live with you. Cousin Charley is getting so wicked that she cant stant it. Every thing she says nearly he just telles her to go to the D—l. She says she is liveing on fat middling meat and irish potatoes. She says she is so bound up she don't know what to do and [when] she asked him to get her a little fruit all she got was a cussing. She says if she don't come home she will go elsewhere for she don't believe she can live six months the way she is living. She works as hard as she can. She said if he had remained the man she married she would have been another sort of woman but as it is she is as much broken as an old

> woman and she is not middle aged and he cares nothing for her since she has broken so. She says she can take in sewing to support her and Mattie and she knowes she will not have to work any harder any where then she does there.
>
> Pa do please write for her to come home. I am afraid she will die if she does not come home. (AUGUST 17, 1884)

Maggie's anger underscored her frustration at the swift changes in her physical beauty. Within three years she had lost two teeth; the wind, sun, and low humidity had wrinkled her skin prematurely. Since the stillbirth, she walked stooped. Fear of new pregnancy may have halted her sexual relations with Charles. Their earlier intimacy eroded.

Renewed efforts by Charles's mother and sisters to join Charles in the West also fueled Maggie's anger. Two months prior to Maggie's furious letter to Pa, Charles's mother had sent him eight hundred dollars to build her and the Virginia family a house in Rincon. With scorn, Maggie wrote Pa about the Browns' proposal. By September, though, Charles's mother, in exasperation with Charles herself, canceled the enterprise:

> I have not written before because I was too much concerned about what to do for ourselves and because I could not determine what is best to be done about sending more money to New Mexico. I can see now that it was a rash thing sending the money to have the house put up. Now I do not think one rash act ought to be followed by another. . . . We think it would be a safer thing to lose the eight hundred. It seems to me if you would bring a little business talent to bear upon it you would be able to do something. If the eight hundred is lost, it would be easier for us to lose that than fourteen hundred. . . . Now try to be reasonable and consider well this matter. There is too much risk in hastening to be rich. (SEPTEMBER 15, 1885)

Even without her in-laws, Maggie's life was bleak. Once Charles was called in the middle of the night by a Mexican saying, "Pete shoot Harry." When Charles reached the saloon, Harry was dead, "shot in cold blood," the sheriff standing casually by. Maggie recounted, too, about "rollers," men who lurked in the night shadows just waiting for someone with money to pass so they could "roll" him over and rob him. Maggie summarized Rincon: "There is 3 grocery stores, 1 dry goods store & 5 saloons, [and Rincon is] the vilest place on earth." (SEPTEMBER 3, 1884)

Maggie's only solace seemed to be six-year-old Mattie: "My every thought for the future is connected with her. I feel if it was God's will to take my babe all that is sweet to me on this earth would be gone." (MARCH 11, 1885)

While Christmas 1884 had found Maggie and Charles as in Colorado, without money even for a cake or nuts, by March fortune turned a mite. Maggie began to work for herself raising chickens; by April she had over one hundred. Charles set out four thousand grape slips in addition to acres of corn, peas, and melons, projecting a fertile harvest for fall. Yet by May the sun and wind defeated the Virginia farmers. A sprinkle of rain wet the ground scarcely half an inch, and they could not afford two hundred fifty dollars for an irrigating windmill that could have brought water to the parched crops.

In June 1885, as if there were not already enough calamities, a band of ninety Apaches made a fierce, desperate run for the Sierra Madre mountains of Mexico, leaving a wake of panic. Maggie wrote Pa:

> We have had quite an Indian scare. The Apache Indians got off of their reservations & did a good deal of murdering but never got across the river or within 20 miles of us but we put adobes in the windows & were fixed for them. One night we watched all night with pistols rifel and shot gun.
>
> (JUNE 9, 1885)

Summer brought more played-out hopes. In debt and still looking to the skies instead of to the ground for water, Maggie and Charles hoped for rain as the sun charred their planted fields.

> We have no money at all. Dr. Brown is in debt for what we had to get to eat. He is almost in rags & I am no better. I think our corn will die. There has been no rain for more than six weeks. . . . For the last 10 days there has been a hot dry wind blowing that was so hard on the corn. Friday & Saturday the thermometer here at the house stood at 110° from 10 o'clock in the morning until 3 & 4. If our corn fails I can't tell what we will do this winter. There is *so* little practice. Dr. B. is painting a roof for the man we owe.
>
> (JUNE 5, 1885)

Charles put the ranch up for sale in July 1885, but there was no buyer. The whole region had been hit by drought. Not only had rainfall been minimal, but the river itself had changed its course. There was wholesale movement out of the area. The ranch with its wasted fields symbolized, at least for Maggie, their barren western dream.

Incredibly, the parched crops barely scorched Charles's faith in the West. Admitting that without sophisticated irrigation he could not reactivate the farming potential of their fields, and that his practice brought no income, the West was still his El Dorado. The crop disaster merely pushed him to look for a place to start again. And that place for him seemed the new Atchison, Topeka & Santa Fe Needles Run between Albuquerque and Mojave, California. The railroad was hiring scores of new employees. Charles applied for and received an eight-hundred-dollar-a-year job as mail clerk.

The Virginia doctor, come west to strike it rich, had in the past five years been miner, carpenter, housepainter, farmer, circuit physician, and now mail clerk. It was the checkered career of the typical "westerner." Maggie, Virginia belle and young wife, had come to the West to raise chickens, take in washing, bake bread.

Abruptly, in November 1885, the couple split apart and went separate ways: Charles to his Albuquerque-based railroad run and Maggie with Mattie home to Virginia.

A melee of emotions must have churned inside Maggie. For one thing, she was returning without Charles. How did she explain to the inquiring friends? While she probably parted from him with resentment and anger at his casual uprooting to Albuquerque, to the Virginia public she still presented a proud, defensive front. They would have pressed to know his fortunes, his gold strikes. How did Maggie mask her own smoldering wrath at the four giftless Christmases, four years of moving from one shanty town to the next, four years of debts and losses? How did she exonerate Charles's naive enchantment with adolescent adventure, his improvidence?

Yet for a time she may have been able to squelch the anger in the sheer thrill of going home. In one sense, Maggie never left Virginia. Unlike the Overland Trail emigrants earlier in the century who viewed the wagon trail as a journey without return, Maggie had never envisioned settling for life in the West. They were Virginians seeking fortune with which to return to Virginia. So far she had not strained to transplant her Virginia culture to the West, nor had she opened herself to new social possibilities of the frontier. In most respects she was a tourist. Her roots were in the East.[16]

Going back to Virginia was returning to civilization, to the social structures that had defined her life. After her years of poverty and dislocation, to be in Virginia would restore her again. The West had been exhausting, stifling. The worlds of exploration, mining, politics were closed to her. When she did not have the ready-made network of church and female companions she could only be a ladylike recluse. The frontiers of the West had been her prison, more binding than the South had ever been., Returning to Virginia was to open a door into a larger world, to have for herself suddenly the mobility and the friends she had known as a young woman.

In addition, Maggie expected that being back in Virginia would somehow transform her again into the beautiful Maggie Brown of 1876. The stooped shoulders, the wrinkles, the haggard look would vanish as she was whisked back in time. Such hopes thrive in the unconscious. And when they are not realized, they create the shadows of strange bitterness.

Maggie's return to Virginia was filled with ambiguity. At first she seemed to flourish. One of her first acts was to enroll Mattie in a proper school. Whatever glow brightened the start of the visit, however, soon dimmed. Maggie developed a painful inflammation in her heel, making it uncomfortable to walk and restricting her the whole time she was in Virginia. She wrote to Charles, two thousand miles away, accusing him of not caring about her pain.

Few letters remain of Maggie's Virginia visit. What she must have written has to be read from Charles's responses to her; rather than answers to excited accounts of friends, family gatherings, and parties, they reflect complaints, aimed particularly at Charles, provoking responses such as:

> You must not get so discouraged, things will work out all right yet.
> (JANUARY 29, 1886)

> Hope by this time that you have gotten your shoes and your heel is much better. No it is no laughing matter to me. Hope that your head aches are much better, and that you will be in better health when you come back. (FEBRUARY 28, 1886)

Behind Maggie's poor health was the slow realization that the Virginia she envisioned was no more: the sister and brothers she continued to call "the children" were all in their teens, the two boys taller than Maggie. And the flesh-and-blood Pa was not the same man as the one who lived in her memory. Pa was happy to see her again, but more than five years had intervened since they had last seen each other, and there were issues he and Maggie now disagreed on. He resented her advice about household affairs and the discipline of the young people.

By the end of her second month, Maggie, who had planned to stay for six months in Virginia, began writing Charles to send her money to return to New Mexico. As he had done during her "waiting" to join him in Colorado, Charles kept her again several months expecting any minute the tickets and the travel money.

While he scraped up the needed money, Charles wrote Maggie descriptions of the California desert:

> Well I have been out to Mojave and I think the country the most desolate that I ever saw. From Needles to Mojave there is nothing but desert, not a living thing to be seen except at the section houses and they are few and far between. There is two extinct volcanoes that is interesting. One of them about two miles from the road with miles and miles of lava all around. It impresses one with awe to see it standing there amidst the great desolation that it has produced, grand black and ugly. (DECEMBER 8, 1885)

Separated from Maggie, Charles felt strangely disenchanted with his western adventure.

> I did not write you since I came in this time because my bowels have been troubling me and I was too nervous to do so. (DECEMBER 31, 1885)

> Am sick of this separation and life is "*too* short" to stand it. (MARCH 9, 1886)

Charles negotiated a new position with the railroad, one that would put him on a run between Rincon and Silver City. When he finally got the job, he wired Maggie ticket money to return home. He wanted no more distance between them.

Maggie and Mattie started from Virginia May 18, 1886, and arrived in Rincon in late May. By that time Charles was making the regular train runs on the new route, but his schedule kept him away for long stretches. During the first weeks Maggie and Mattie were back, he came home for only an hour and a half in the midday. He and Maggie had no nights together.

The absences depressed Maggie. The empty ranch house echoed her inner emptiness. Virginia had, for all purposes, failed her. After that visit, Maggie could no longer fantasize about a home she could return to. Rincon was her only home. Her present had to be her only reality. Yet Rincon, especially without Charles's presence, was still only the dry, windswept desert of "mud houses" and tumbleweed. There seemed nothing there to center her life.

Her only company was seven-and-a-half-year-old Mattie. The June weather that year was blazing, almost 102° daily. Mattie cried in the heat, so every evening Maggie let her run out to the pump and splash in the cool water before getting ready for bed. Maggie watched Mattie with sad affection, the little girl who had been privy to much of Maggie's adult heartache. If Maggie had motive for trying to build a life in New Mexico, it was for Mattie. And if Maggie had relief from the loneliness of the stretching sands, the relief was Mattie.

Mattie's sudden illness then, in mid-June, first panicked Maggie and then pitched her into heartsick despair. Something warned her that the illness would be fatal. With Charles unable to be released from his railroad schedule, Maggie became doctor and nurse night and day. At 2 A.M. June 16, Maggie wrote Pa a melancholy letter:

> While keeping a lonely vigil over my darling I will write to you for I cannot sleep. Our darling has taken sick Sunday (13th) afternoon. She said "mama my throat is so sore I can hardly swallow," I called her to me & looked in her throat which was very much inflamed & swollen, then in a few minutes a high fever came on & an eruption down her back looking something like measles. By nine oclock she complained of pain in her stumac & throwing up everything I gave her to operate on her bowels. Well up to this time we have been unable to brake the fever & she is broken out thick. Dr. B. thinks it scarlet fever & if it is it is in a most malignant form. She has not been rational since noon yesterday. Dr. B. can only be home about one ½ hours in the middle of the day. He has asked for a lay off. I have my house hold duties & her to attend to but if God just spares her is all I ask but I have my fears she is so much reduced, not a mouthfull of anything has been [in] her stumack since Sunday.
>
> I can't write more now. Pray for me if I should lose her I will need them [prayers]. (JUNE 16, 1886)

Through telegraph messages Maggie signaled for Charles to rush home. His own child was dying while he whipped along on a train, more duty-bound to it than to her. Finally, Charles did get to the ranch, but only to be present in Mattie's last struggling hours. The child died around 10 P.M., Thursday, June 17, 1886. Her funeral was June 18, one month exactly after Maggie and Mattie had left Virginia. The desert had taken its toll. The West was burying their hopes.

Only between the lines can one read the stark grief that gripped Maggie. Too overwhelming to express, the devastation packed itself down, numbed her. Almost as if she had no emotion at all, Maggie wrote Pa of preparing Mattie's body for burial:

> The flowers A[melia] J[ane] sent in her first letter after I came out, I pinned on our darling's breast with the little breast pin her Cousin Mattie C. gave her. She was dressed to look as natural as possible, lying a little on one side with her doll Aunt Mary gave her in her arms just as when she went to sleep Sunday night. She would have me undress her doll & give it to her when she went to bed. I can't fully realize I won't see her here any more. I suppose it is better so too. (JULY 3, 1886)

In one sense, through Mattie's many illnesses, Maggie had anticipated that this child would never reach adulthood. The fear of losing a child was not, for a nineteenth-century mother, idle or morbid. Child mortality was

Charles and Maggie's first-born daughter, Mattie, who died in Rincon, New Mexico, June 17, 1886.

common. Maggie's own mother had lost six children; Charles's mother had lost four. Yet the fact of commonality did not dilute the terrible fact of Mattie's obituary:

> Died—At Rincon New Mexico of scarlatina, Martha A. only daughter of Dr. and Mrs. C. A. Brown June 17, 1886, age 7 years, 10 months and 26 days.

Death's presence shadowed women every day. It was almost life's major event. Children's literature, for example, was often a pulpit for beliefs about death. Stories emphasized particularly the idea that all lives were guided by God, who is eternal love and wisdom. Even death was seen as a result of His fatherly concern. Every tragedy hid a blessing. The death of a young person was a removal to heaven.

The fact that most people in the 1880s still died in their homes surrounded by relatives made the process of dying a vivid part of daily life. The happy death of a good Christian was something that occurred in the bosom of the family. In rural communities of the time, such as the one Maggie and Charles had come from in Virginia, relatives, neighbors, friends all attended the funerals of any of the townspeople. The frontier disrupted communal mourning. But the distance did not halt the impulse, and letters from Virginia poured in to Maggie and Charles after little Mattie's death.

The letters show how the community came to terms with death. Emphatically and repeatedly the fact of death was stressed—without euphemism. No softening adjectives buffered the reality. It was "an unbearable pain," a pain "too great for a mortal person to endure." The letters talked of Maggie's "empty arms," her "crushed and bleeding arms." Mattie was gone. Her beauty and loveliness, her bright ways, her delicate, affectionate, sensitive nature—all these Maggie and Charles would have with them no more.

Along with the undiluted painting of grief, however, each letter moved on to a ritual outpouring of solace. In a chorus of biblical cadences, the letters spelled out reasons not only for resignation but for hope. The essential doctrine was what the middle-class religions of the era preached: God is good. As a tender, loving Father, a good Shepherd, he did nothing that was not for the best. He loved Mattie and because she was, indeed, so special, He wanted her prematurely for His own loving arms. The transparent parodies of biblical phrases increased the measure of comfort, the tie with a sacred Scripture binding the persons together in shared belief.

> I have been where the very *billions* of sorrow *over-whelmed* me but God was with me all the time though I could not see it then—now I know it and *believe* and *feel* that *everything* God does is *right* and *well.* (JUNE 23, 1886)

> Our lives are not in our own hands. They are as grass in the morn, it flurish and groeth up and in the eve it is cut down and dies. (JUNE 25, 1886)

> Mattie has gown to that home of hers in heaven to live for ever whar thir is no sorrow nor trouble thire. (JUNE 28, 1886)

> All that was mortal is changed now, and clouded forever. But how great is your comfort in the well-grounded assurance that the good Shepherd who, "Careth for his flock"—has taken the gentle Lamb into his fold. Your darling child has gone to him who said Suffer little children to come unto me. And we know not, when how soon our hour may come. . . . Oh, that we may all meet in that brighter and happier world, where sorrow and sin and suffering are alike unknown. (JUNE 29, 1886)

The letters counseled Maggie to talk or write about the whole gamut of her grief and to seek comfort in the presence of friends—even friends a thousand miles away. Maggie wrote Pa a refrain of what had been so many times written her:

> Pa dear, I am not rebellious, but feel thankful we had her the time we did have her with us. She has escaped much, for this world is full of unforeseen troubles. Now they are all over with her. She has only gone before. (JULY 1886)

Maggie sent mementos of Mattie home to Virginia. In quiet, small gestures of pained movement, Maggie resumed her life. Nothing the West had taken was in any way as total as having her child snatched from her. The pain Charles had caused her, separation from her Virginia community—these had tangible causes. Mattie's death came from life itself, and Maggie's response, as with the stillbirth and with the death of her mother, was to bend to the blow. After Mattie's death, Maggie almost never mentioned returning to Virginia. Facing life as it came to her, stark in the West, Maggie stopped buffering herself with illusions of escape to the East and began at long last, like a battered tree at last rooted, to craft a western reality for herself and Charles.

IV. On The Move Again, *1886–1889*

During the period between September 1886, and November 1889, the Browns' ranch in Rincon slowly, in infinitely small ways, began to flourish. Charles brought in a steady income from the railroad job, supplemented by increased medical practice. With Charles on his railroad run, away from home for longer periods than he was at home, two things transpired: Maggie took on the day-to-day running of the house and the farm; and she initiated money-making enterprises. Selling small amounts of milk and butter to regular customers in Rincon (one and a half miles from the ranch), Maggie wrote about milking *her* cows and about extending *her* sale of dairy products. From her own income she hired a Mexican farmhand to help her with deliveries, and she invented a saddle pack for the milk containers. With part of her profits, she invested in several pigs that she intended to fatten up, slaughter, and sell. She even encouraged a female friend in Virginia to move to Rincon to join her in a large-scale dairy enterprise.

The business contacts with residents of Rincon improved Maggie's opinion of them. In fact, in response to a Virginia letter that criticized New Mexicans, Maggie composed a spirited defense:

> I beg leave to inform [you] we are not living among savages & the Mexicans are better although they speak a different language from ours & the white people with whom I visit are more intelligent than it was my fortune to meet

while in Va: There is one *great* difference in this country & that people have to comply with their promises or they are not thought well of.

(APRIL 14, 1888)

As the ranch flourished it gave a warm hearth to the neighbors Maggie was viewing with new eyes. There in the West Maggie and Charles were modifying their dreams of the Virginia plantation, re-creating their brand of southern hospitality in the rocky canyons and deserts of New Mexico.

The small adobe house in no way resembled the antebellum home of Charles's youth—no trees, no green lawns or cultivated flowers. The house had no curtained bay windows—only slits covered by stretched material. The mud roof, in the occasional times of rain, dissolved and had to be reinforced with more dirt. Yet Charles enjoyed trimming the large cactus surrounding the house and felt proud as he killed a large wildcat at his own front door. The gentlemanly sport of hunting came to him there.

For Maggie and Charles, New Mexico was becoming an acceptable echo of Virginia motifs. Even when money was scarce, Maggie planned her meals so that anyone around could be welcome and well fed at their

The Rincon post office in New Mexico reflects the bleak terrain.

table. On his days off, Charles lived much as a southern gentleman: he entertained, hunted and fished, socialized on neighboring ranches, participated in local and national politics. And Maggie agreed with him about the people in Rincon: "I had no idea they had such nice people there." (JANUARY 24, 1888)

While Maggie and Charles entertained in modified southern style, they dressed in the code of the West.

> Here on the place we just need enough to cover our selves decently. When Dr. B. comes home he puts on an old pair of corduroy pants all out at the seat and has an old pair of low quartered shoes he wears without socks. I have in the way of clothing 2 calico dresses, 2 pair of $1.25 shoes & 2 pair of stockings & 2 skirts, but fortunately we dont need much in this country if we stay at home. (MAY 14, 1888)

Maggie missed the southern dress and wrote Pa wistfully that she was past her "day of romantic secrets and beautiful clothes"—this at age thirty-four.

With the settling of their life-style, relations improved between Maggie and Charles. Charles complimented Maggie, calling her the "mainspring of the place" (JULY 31, 1887)—a compliment Maggie admitted she deserved. Both confessed in letters to Pa that they were getting so well-fixed in New Mexico that they doubted they would ever consider returning to Virginia. When Charles was in between runs, he worked beside Maggie on ranch chores. The two joked about who was the more skilled "milker." In relaxed tones, Maggie commented that they were an "old settled couple." (AUGUST 25, 1887)

In the genial glow of those days, Maggie at thirty-five became pregnant again. Although during her pregnancy Maggie was conscious of death as an ever-present shadow ("if I should live," "if I should die," SEPTEMBER 11, 1887), still, her general mood was not morbid or depressed. Charles showered attention. "Anything I ask he does." Anticipation prevailed. On October 6, 1887, Maggie gave birth to a healthy boy whom they named James Albert (names celebrating men on both sides of the family).

Particularly pleased, Pa (Washington James) addressed a welcome note to his namesake:

> I heard of your arrival a week or two since. I avail myself of extending a *hearty welcome* to you as a citizen of our planet & hope you will ever be as you were in your arrival "a little ahead of time," in that case you will never be *left* by the train. Oh how I wish I had you in my arms a while. I would squeeze your little bones so much. (OCTOBER 23, 1887)

Maggie wrote anecdotes about her son, underscoring her delight in him.

> Albert is beginning to notice when I lean over the cradle. He jumps & throws up his hand & laughs; he has blue eyes & they are straight [Mattie's had been crossed, a result of illness]. . . . He has a long head or rather a long face with a double chin. He is just his papa over. (JANUARY 20, 1888)

> Albert is getting brighter every day. He is such a comfort to me. (MARCH 21, 1888)

> Albert squeels and laughs a great deal & is perfectly happy when he can get hold of his papa's whiskers & pull; so is his papa, who thinks there is no boy like his. (MAY 14, 1888)

As Rincon life stabilized, Maggie and Charles suggested to Pa (who had suffered severe financial loss) that he let Dannie, age twenty-one, try his fortune with them in the West. Negotiations stretched over months, with Pa finally giving permission. As days passed, Maggie watched the road from Rincon for the figure of Dannie to loom up. One day, seeing a figure of Dannie's stature lumbering along the railroad track, Maggie ran to meet him hollering welcomes—only to find her "Dannie" to be just a neighbor. Embarrassed, Maggie wrote Pa, "they all laughed very much at me." (MAY 27, 1888) That was mid-May 1888. Not until late June did Dannie finally arrive, having traveled, as he emphasized to Pa, "2,704 miles." (JUNE 24, 1888)

Dannie's letters to Virginia assumed the tone of the tall tale expected of males on the frontier. He told Pa of the catfish in the Rio Grande "that weigh from 75 to 100 lbs." (JULY 11, 1888), one of which just escaped Dannie's line. To that note Maggie appended her own remarking that he was "most too sanguine about catching fish." He described the adobe dwellings of New Mexico: "You ought to just see these mud houses with a garden on top of them & a ladder to go up on to chase the chickens off.

Things are not as shaby as you think they are." He closed his first letter home: "Give my regards to who think enough about me to ask, and tell them the indians have not got my scalp & dont think they ever will." (JUNE 1888)

Accustomed only to stable rivers like the James and the Rockfish, Dannie was unprepared for the erratic behavior of the Rio Grande. A typical eastern greenhorn, he envisioned big money in fishing, but Maggie had to write Pa in August:

> Dannie is not doing anything now fishing. He spent all the money he made on those he did catch for fishing tackle & lumber for a boat to go at it in earnest, when the river went dry or so near it there is no use trying to fish.

Dannie further detailed the strange river and land:

> Places in the Rio Grande that were bout 6 feet deep 2 weeks ago is dry land now. If you would like to stomp around after pole cats come out here. Doc & me killed 5 in less than 5 minutes not long ago. Well I will have to close as the bugs are about to eat me up, lots of em here. (AUGUST 12, 1888)

Charles and Dannie made good companions, Maggie calling them "just two big boys" who would never grow up. For over a year, Charles and Dannie hunted and fished like vacationing sportsmen. Maggie complained that she had more work to do than anyone else when Charles was away.

> I tell you it is awful hard on me to be all alone as I am when Dr. B. is gone. If I had some one to watch Albert which is so much trouble now, just beginning to crawl. We have fire places & he gets up to the hearth & eats dirt. I also milk 3 cows myself & have to go some distance to the cow pen. I sometimes bundle him up put him in his little 2 wheeled cart Dr. B. made him & pull it with two buckets to milk in. (NOVEMBER 19, 1888)

Dannie was little help. Still toying around with unsuccessful money-making schemes, he generally lounged around the house or fished. When the roof needed patching, Maggie, not the men, was the one who had to climb up and fix it.

> Every room in the house is wet & I suppose I will have to carry dust on the roof to stop it or hire tramps to. I have not a shoe to turn water and have more out door work than any one. (NOVEMBER 25, 1888)

But if Maggie felt the burden of too much work, she at least felt the security of Charles's steady income and the ranch's regular produce. And she felt her own efforts generating income; for once she had a modicum of economic control over family direction.

The ricochet of fate would not leave her content for long. In July 1889, Maggie had written Pa: "We have one of the best titles there is to 80 acres of the best land the sun ever shone on." However, in November of that same year, she had to begin her letter to Virginia with the glum admission: "Well we are afloat again." Charles had lost his job with the railroad for selling the fish Dannie had caught without license. Maggie spelled out the disaster:

> Dr. B. was removed. I think the reasons were for breaking a postal law forbidding the postal clerks "trafficking." There was quite a fuss about Dr. B. selling those fish (not by the department at the time) but by the butchers. They wanted Dr. B. to pay license; but he did not have to. Never-the-less they got very mad (& so did I). I said there would be trouble come of it for I had read the law carefully: but D.A. said "OH! you just want to keep me from making anything" So it went on. Then the authorities threatened to seaze them saying they were not healthy, then I just said Dannie you will have to stop or ship them in your own name. So he stopped. This is the way it was done. D.A. & pardners caught the fish & shipped them by the same train Dr. B. went on & to C.A. Brown then Brown sold them when he got there. All Dr. B. got out of it was 10 cents each way for a lunch. The last lot shipped [was] nearly all spoilt before they were sold. The department have given no reason for Dr. B.'s removal but just a day or so before it came a letter making inquiry about the fish did come. Well we will mortgage or rent the place and leave for some place perhaps Washington State. (NOVEMBER 2, 1889)

After this debacle, Dannie began working on a state crew constructing bridges across the Rio Grande. For Maggie and Charles the frenetic search for "home" that had marked their early years resumed. Maggie again wrote letter after letter to Pa with her dreams of a home in Virginia "with a big family room where all can all gather together and enjoy each others society." (DECEMBER 9, 1889) If she felt some relief that failure would at last force Charles to return to Virginia, she was wrong.

In order to sell, the ranch needed a proper ditch to divert water from the river. However, the task involved more than simply digging a diversion canal. First Charles had to establish water rights both to his source and then to the path across intervening property. Though he battled hard in court for these rights, he lost major decisions, which Maggie complained were caused by an overweight of Mexican jurors.

Maggie pressed Charles to sell for whatever he could get and to return to Virginia where family help could support them in a fresh start. Charles pacified her with a promise that "any property bought in Va is to be bought in my name." (DECEMBER 12, 1889)

Complications dragged on, and Maggie realized they were caught in the "territory" for an indefinite time. The depressed tones of her early years returned. Christmas was a repeat of the poverty days. There was no money even for gifts for little Albert. "Mrs Byron sent Albert some little toys & the merchants up town gave him a few little things & that is all he got. It did not seem like Xmas to me." Then with a sense of foreboding, Maggie

The Browns' impressive home in Bridgewater, Virginia, shown in winter. It was an imposing place built to accommodate a life of gentility and the comings and goings of a large family and circle of friends.

noted the appearance of a new disease: "We have *all* been real sick think [it is] the new disease 'La Grippa' or Russian Influenza." (JANUARY 3, 1890)

Only anecdotes about two-year-old Albert sparked life into Maggie's letters.

> He hunts up the old boards, takes the claws of the hammer, pulls the nails out & then straightens them & does it right. Then they are for use to him in chairs, the floor or anywhere he happens to strike. He seldom mashes his fingers. If he does he don't cry. (MARCH 14, 1890)

Pa, the skilled carpenter and smithy, would have looked proudly on such a grandson—a "real boy." Maggie, herself, delighted in that son.

> I wish you could see Albert. He is a gay boy. He is rolling around me now. He talks both Mexican & English [and] says most any thing. (APRIL 9, 1890)

Albert's compelling personality, however, did not revive the unproductive ranch or put money in Charles's empty coffers. Thus when Dannie took up residence in La Mesa some thirty miles southeast of Rincon and urged Maggie and Charles to rent a fruit ranch there, they sprang to the possibility. In April Maggie confirmed to Pa their latest uprooting:

> We have about decided to go to La Mesa, just as soon as Dr. B. can get off from a case he is waiting on. They are going to commence a new Methodist church there the first of May. They are very anxious for Dr. B. to come down. (APRIL 9, 1890)

With her amazing resilience, by July Maggie was bubbling with plans for lucrative projects there in La Mesa, bubbling with almost the kind of enthusiasm characteristic of Charles in his Colorado mining camp days. In her letters she began even to *sound* like Charles. From their new place in La Mesa, she outlined fine schemes for her favorite brother, W.J., to come from Virginia to be partner with her in farming:

> Now there is "big money" in an early vegetable garden. I will get the ground, Dr. B. says he will plow it & you & I will go in halves on all expenses & divide the profits. If we manage things right we ought to clear from $200 hundred to $300 hundred dollars a piece next year [and] can commence shipping things

> in March. . . . We will try to get you out as soon as possible. Let me hear from you *at once*. (JULY 27, 1890)

The extant letters come to a sudden halt. From July 27, 1890, to August 1, 1892, no letters remain. Certainly letters were written.

The stark facts of the time between late 1890 and mid-1894 come, not through letters, but through records in the family Bible and from a reminiscence of Mary Gose (the Browns' only child to survive to adulthood). On December 22, 1890, Maggie had given birth to a second son, John Daniel. His birth must have seemed a harbinger of a good change of fortune. The La Mesa prospects then were promising for the fruit business. Charles's medical practice was building. The arrival of another son must have made Maggie and Charles certain that life was at last favoring them. But, within a brief five days in March 1891, fate reversed to tragedy.

In early March, the entire family was striken with that "new disease"—"La Grippa" or "Russian Influenza." First Maggie and Charles were confined to bed, nursed by a caring Mexican woman. Then the two boys were stricken. Mary Gose's memoir recounts:

> Albert caught it first, then Johnnie. Albert was terribly ill with it and Maggie realizing he had a very short time to live said, "Oh, Albert, do you have to leave us?" He looked up at her and said, "Yes, Mama, and Johnny too." Johnnie was not yet sick at that time, yet in five days both children were gone.[17]

V. Where Home Is, *1890–1930*

The desert seemed determined to stop them each time they came up. Childless again, Maggie and Charles wearily moved back to Rincon, not to the waterless ranch but to the town, where Maggie dug into the process of being equal provider with Charles. While Charles tried to pull his fortunes together, randomly applying for positions as physician with the railroad and with the Mescalero Indian reservation, spending much energy, too, in trying to buy and sell mining stock and real estate, Maggie brought in a steady income from a small hotel and lunchroom.[18] In fact, she was replacing Charles as the provident force in the family.

But Maggie was also battling a catastrophic sense of failure. In her attempts to have children between 1892 and 1893, she had one stillbirth and one miscarriage. Finally, in June of 1894, Maggie gave birth prematurely to a baby girl, weight at birth a scant two pounds. That one child, Mary Augusta, was the only one of Maggie and Charles's seven children to survive to adulthood. While western demography claims a low fertility rate for pioneer women, the statistics simply cannot reveal, as they would not for Maggie, the children who died, the pregnancies that failed, the graveyards with small stones marked "S[till] B[orn]."

The only details of the new baby come from Mary Gose's typescript of apocryphal-sounding anecdotes:

> It was 114° in the shade on the day that I was born. I suspect that was one reason for my premature birth, for mother herself was cooking over a hot stove in that heat. I weighed two and a half pounds. I was so tiny that the wife of the manager of the Harvey House took me all over town and showed me to anybody who would look at this phenomenally small baby. A gambler slipped his ring over my wrist, they later told me. And another put a silver dollar on the end of my nose and it covered my eyes, nose and mouth—hardly sanitary! Being a rather large-boned woman, she put her elbow in the crotch of my thumb and the tips of my fingers came to the tip of her thumb. She even took me into the saloons to exhibit me.[19]

Sounding more tall tale than truth, the account may have been told to underscore the tiny baby's near miraculous birth. On the other hand, the incident could hold as much truth as fiction. Having lost six children, Maggie may have felt that no care of hers could preserve a life predestined for early death.

Only a handful of letters remain from 1895 to 1896, and most of those concern Charles's business. A rare one shows Maggie's intense concern about her frail baby daughter:

> I am real uneasy about her. I notice her throat is a little swollen. She is a little treasure. . . . I will send a little picture of her. She had had a spell of croup & we had this [photograph] taken by a traveling artist. It is not very good. . . . She is so sick now I cant hardly do anything.
>
> (DECEMBER 26, 1895)

A tragic undertone in the note may escape the twentieth-century reader, accustomed to the frequent taking of "cute" baby pictures. For those of the nineteenth century, a photograph of a sick baby formed a part of the "last rites"—something done before it died. It was a heartsick Maggie who mailed that likeness to Virginia.

In the 1890s, the feverish dislocation of the Browns' former years gained momentum again, as did the grasping after still unfulfilled dreams of home and success. Charles pressed on for the fortune promised by the western venture, aligning himself with all manner of mining speculations.

That effort to realize mining profit made Charles *and* Maggie excited at news from their friend (and fellow Virginian) Burt Ruple as he prospected "like hell" in the rugged Sierra Madre mountains around Ortiz, Sonora, in Mexico. In gratitude for some medical favor from Charles, Burt promised the Browns a big share of any strike he should make. "I owe my life to you and when I wear diamonds you have got to wear larger ones. My life down here is hell and worry but things are coming my way." (OCTOBER 8, 1898)

Burt's letters rang with the heated frustration of the isolated mining camp.

> Even now I am eating on my face and bumming stamp money. You write as often as you can, it cheers me up to hear from you. I cannot write often. I am between the "devil and the deep blue sea" all the time.
>
> (NOVEMBER 8, 1898)
>
> There are only a few mines that have been developed in this country and they have paid seven million dollars in three years. If we could only develop a property like that we could buy a few acres back in Virginia and take things easy. Beans, beans, beans, how would some hot cakes go with a little butter made by Mrs. B.
>
> (UNDATED FRAGMENT; CONTEXT PUTS IT AFTER NOVEMBER 8, 1898)
>
> Sunday night two of them [Yaqui Indians] passed my camp and one of them said to the other that he was going to fire at my camp fire, which was nearly out. My bed was about fifty feet from the fire and when he spoke I cocked

> my rifle. He heard the click and walked into camp with his hands above his head and asked me to take a drink out of a bottle. I told him it was bad medicine to monkey with a *Gringo* and that he came as near being a dead Yaqui as he ever could until he died. . . . You see a man is none to safe here.
>
> (UNDATED FRAGMENT)

Abruptly, in June 1899, Burt's letters stopped. It was not until 1901 that Maggie and Charles discovered that Burt Ruple had died in Nogales, Arizona, in the summer of 1900. Maggie wrote numerous letters tracking down Burt Ruple's widow and Burt's mining agent in Chicago. It took her three years to find them. Her pursuit of Ruple was to get from his heirs or from his estate the money to return "home." Some twenty years into their marriage, the tables were turning: Charles was following Maggie.

With renewed passion, Maggie negotiated "deals" to get them back to Virginia. She tracked down genuine possibilities, pressuring Charles to withdraw cash from his mining investments there in New Mexico and herself bargaining for property in Virginia. The westering years had spelled for Maggie only failure, and she was fighting to relocate in Virginia, propelling the family east with the same frenetic quality that had marked Charles's push west. In the summer of 1900, Maggie engineered a whirlwind trip to Virginia to investigate purchasing Clermont, a place adjoining Pa's property, which a friend had alerted Maggie to in 1893. When that enterprise failed, she arranged for Charles to rent his old family home in Bridgewater, Virginia. After the death of his mother and the settling down of his sisters in Staunton, the place had been managed by a distant cousin. The cousin tried to dissuade Charles from taking the old place, warning that the rent was high and that no concessions could be made even to a family member.

But Bridgewater in Virginia proved another failure. Charles—the gentleman doctor—if he could not press strangers for his fees was unable to press friends. Maggie rented Clermont and took the family there. But the deed could not be cleared in court, so when the lease was up in 1903, Maggie herself decided the family would return to New Mexico. They had been in Virginia barely twelve months.

Back they moved to the ranch that they still owned in Rincon. From there Maggie assumed control of the family's destiny, continuing to fight by mail for the plantation property she wanted in Virginia. In 1906, the battle for the land was won and the purchase of the Clermont plantation in Cumberland, Virginia, was made in the name, not of Dr. Charles, but of Mrs. Martha M. Brown.[20] After twenty-seven years and twenty-four moves across Colorado and New Mexico, back to Virginia, and back again to the Southwest, the Browns returned to make Virginia their "home."

They had crossed the country no less than four separate times: over the low plains, into the high deserts and the Rocky Mountains of Colorado, down into the valleys and mesas of New Mexico, Charles out to California, then both back to the fertile valleys of Virginia, again to New Mexico and again to Virginia—some 16,000 miles! Twenty-seven years of being nomads, putting down and packing up, being defined and redefined by the changing earth. The final coming "home" brought them back to where they started.

Though Charles returned with no fortune, he had the accoutrements of respectability. He came home as one who had been "out west." He had braved the unknown, slain his dragons, and come out whole. Maggie's and Charles's dreams, it would seem, should have been brought to closure.

But there was a flaw yet. The dream would not come together, and it had nothing to do with money or deeds or landscape.

In Virginia, Maggie and Charles rankled at the pressing closeness of

Dr. Charles Brown holding unknown infant, circa 1915, Clermont, Virginia.

family members. Sometime in 1917 Charles wrote to their daughter, Mary, who was teaching in a nearby town:

> We must sell this place and get out for jealousy and envy are doing us untold damage and we must get away from your Mama's people. I feel that all of our trouble comes from them. Of course land is going up fast but can we live through this eternal turmoil. Sometimes I blame it on one some times on another, but I some times think its all of them.

The family of memory across vast distances was easier to handle than the claustrophobic nearness of real relatives. Years of isolation and loneliness ingrained in Maggie and Charles a need for space that was irreconcilable with the culture of a southern community.

Maggie and Charles had locked into a pattern of mobility that had come to define them. In that crucible, scratching out a living in a hostile environment, they had learned the rhythm of uprooting. Movement had become a pain to which they had become accustomed and without which they hardly knew themselves. What an old-time friend in New Mexico

Maggie and Charles Brown in their later years, with their daughter, Mary.

wrote Maggie about himself curiously characterized the final posture of Maggie and Charles:

> I am a derelict in the zaragosa of the sea of life—*homeless*. (JULY 26, 1909)

They, too, had lost the habit of home. In searching for permanence, they had turned into wanderers.

Unbelievably, Maggie began to look into ways of trading long-sought-after Clermont for property in the West; in one of Charles's final letters, he was speculating on a gold mine in Colorado.

Only a year before she died, Maggie was planning a trip for herself and Charles to California to see the oranges and to escape the "dismal damp of Virginia." In her last months she fired a barrage of protest to her senator opposing treatment of conscientious objectors in Alcatraz. Her sympathies were for those who were misfits and objectors. The afternoon before she died, she restlessly walked several miles to glimpse oxen plowing a field. One late March evening in 1920, Maggie died in her sleep. She was sixty-four years old.

For the ten years in which Charles survived Maggie, his daughter, Mary, became his companion on the Clermont plantation. Together they hunted, fished, read. Mary's mention of that time rings happy and content. Charles, she noted, had spoiled her when the family was in New Mexico, leaving parental discipline to Maggie.

When Charles died in the winter of 1930, Mary became a teacher of the deaf. But she separated herself from the families of both parents—the Kellers and the Browns. She inherited none of her mother's dreams of the fixed center that was family. For a time, she too was "on the road," teaching the deaf in New York and in Idaho, even visiting briefly in New Mexico. Out of her childhood, she seemed to inherit a preference for solitude and for silence. She married when she was in her early forties, but the marriage ended, after a brief year, in divorce. When she returned to Virginia to work with the deaf there, she lived alone in the Cumberland area, seldom meeting with relatives.

Something of the unresolved quality of Maggie and Charles's lives haunted her, and in her later years, Mary Gose became obsessed with trying to resolve her parents' inchoate directions. She managed to retrieve over four hundred pieces of the correspondence of their westering years, writing her own commentary on their letters, arguing with each of them, deciding now for one, now for the other.

The Keller family, in the generations after Maggie and Charles's restless journeying, congratulated itself on the way it stayed rooted in the Cumberland Valley of Virginia. "Nobody *wants* to move away. No other place tempts us," boasts one of Maggie's great-grand-nephews. Each summer, since 1937, hundreds of Kellers from that area gather for a family reunion. They are landholders, bankers, educators—stable, proud Virginians.

Curiously, only Dannie is clearly remembered of the family's "westerners," in the flamboyant dress he affected, his holster, gun, and "lingo." His "tall tales," however, induced no other Kellers to trek west.

If the myth of the West was the promise of fulfillment, the reality, at least for the Browns, was different. In the ghost towns of two states, Maggie and Charles left the graves of six children, melancholy markers of their relentless moving. The places in which they staked their sometime abodes—Bonanza, Poncha Springs, Villa Grove, Rincon—have all become ghost towns; the Brown's presence was wiped out, as if they had never been there at all.

The Kellers gathered at a family reunion, Cumberland, Virginia, circa 1930. Maggie's brother, Dannie, who built his New Mexico life into legends, is the tallest male figure in the right-hand section of the photograph.

Notes

1. *Bureau of Immigration of Virginia Registry and Descriptive List of Virginia Lands*, advertising publication (Richmond, Va., 1879), p. 1.

2. B. C. Keeler, *Where to Go to Become Rich: Farmers', Miners' and Tourists' Guide to Kansas, New Mexico, Arizona and Colorado* (Chicago: Belford, Clarke & Co., 1880), pp. 99–100.

3. Sara K. Gillam, *Virginia's People: A Study of the Growth and Distribution of the Population of Virginia from 1607 to 1943* (Richmond: Virginia State Planning Board, 1944), pp. 52–53, 116–18. See also G. Thomas Ingham, Esq., *Digging Gold Among the Rockies, or Exciting Adventures of Wild Camp Life in Leadville, Black Hills and the Gunnison Country* (Philadelphia: Hubbard Brothers, 1883), pp. 431ff.

4. Duane A. Smith, *Colorado Mining: A Photographic History* (Albuquerque: University of New Mexico Press, 1977), p. vii.

5. Mary Augusta Brown Gose, typescript, p. 9.

6. Ibid.

7. Keeler, p. 63.

8. Ingham, pp. 271–72.

9. Bertram Wyatt-Brown, *Southern Honor: Ethics and Behavior in the Old South* (New York: Oxford University Press, 1982), pp. 230–31.

10. For extensive study of legends associated with Montezuma and the Pecos region of New Mexico, see John Kessell, *Kiva, Cross, and Crown: The Pecos Indians and New Mexico 1540–1840* (Washington, D.C.: National Park Service, U.S. Department of the Interior, 1979).

11. Howard Roberts Lamar, *The Far Southwest, 1846–1912: A Territorial History* (New York: W. W. Norton & Co., 1970), pp. 146–50.

12. *New Mexico, the Land of Opportunity* (Santa Fe, 1914), pp. 223–24.

13. *Bureau of Immigration of Virginia Registry*, p. 2.

14. Max Frost, ed., *New Mexico, Its Resources, Climate, Geography and Geological Condition: Official Publication of the Bureau of Immigration* (Santa Fe: New Mexico Printing Company, 1890), p. 116.

15. Gose, typescript, Clermont section, p. 13.

16. Such attitudes of being merely transients, visitors from elsewhere, characterized miners and their families in the West during the later nineteenth century. The goal was acquisition of quick wealth rather than settlement. A letter Charles Brown received from Hubert Poole, an oldtimer in Bonanza, Colorado, underscores this migratory pattern. Poole mentions nearly fifty people who were part of the

Bonanza boom in 1880. Only four were still in that area in 1915. Hubert Poole, Bonanza, Colorado, to Charles Brown in Dillwyn, Virginia, January 7, 1915.

17. Gose, typescript, pp. 185–86.

18. During the frontier boom periods, one of the most lucrative businesses for women was that of providing room and board. For more on women's success in this enterprise, see July Roy Jeffrey, *Frontier Women: The Trans-Mississippi West 1840–1910* (New York: Hill & Wang, 1979).

19. Gose, typescript, p. 186.

20. By the mid-nineteenth century there was a trend in Virginia, as in some other eastern states such as New York, to appoint women as executors of their husbands' estates. See Mary Ryan, *Womanhood in America from Colonial Times to the Present* (New York: Oxford University Press, 1980).

3. The Nehers and the Martins in North Dakota

1909 – 1911

Wild flowers were blooming. He picked a bouquet of showy golden peas and added several stalks of blue beardstongue. . . . He felt newly hopeful [as] he arranged the flowers in an empty syrup pail. Perhaps this God-forsaken country held more blessings than one realized.

PAULINE DIEDE, *Homesteading on the Knife River Prairies*

In the summer of 1909, two families of Baptists, whose ancestors had left Germany and traveled two thousand miles to live in Russia, reversed the direction of their migration and set out for America. They had little money, eight children among them, scant knowledge of English, and little more than an envelope with an address in Eureka, South Dakota. The families of Ludwig Neher and Fred Martin traveled from Odessa to Hamburg, and from Hamburg to Montreal, Canada. From there they boarded a train that took them through Chicago and then left them off in North, not South, Dakota. Their first American winter was spent in an empty boxcar, twelve adults and children, one woman pregnant, one infant seriously ill.

The families settled near the Knife River, where the best land was already taken. With little real knowledge of farming, they wrestled with bare hands on a land of unrelenting hardships. Women and children worked like animals, and the men struggled against their own anxiety and fear that they might die on this American frontier. The families survived the first seasons, meal by meal, with food provided by neighbors who saw their desperate need.

They secured their land, but the struggle was framed with bitter memories at the same time it was mixed with pride.

I. The Neher and Martin Families in Germany and Russia

The story of the family of Ludwig Neher and his brother-in-law, Fred Martin, is told by Pauline Neher Diede from conversations with her father and her uncle. The family history begins, as it were, in a colony named Freudental in the Odessa Valley of southern Russia. Over the course of several generations the Nehers had migrated from Germany to the remote Tiflis area of the Caucasus. They were Chiliasts, also known as Separatists, later calling themselves Baptists. Germans had migrated to Russia since the eighteenth century, when a manifesto of Catherine the Great of Russia in 1763 invited colonists to settle in exchange for free land, freedom of religion, exemption from compulsory military service, and other privileges. These were desperate journeys, escapes from conscription and poverty in Germany to even more harsh and primitive conditions in the unsettled "new" land. The journey was especially hard on women and children. "Many a pathetic story has been told of a woman hitched to a rough wagon filled with clothing and food, with a wailing child on top of the load, and a four- or five-year-old running beside, the mother pregnant as well." (P. 7)[1]

Ludwig Neher was one of only a few of his parents' children to survive the first journey, for several died along the way: "One after another was buried in a hole and covered with clay, the little graves filled with clods ('bola') as was the German custom, and wild flowers or sweet smelling herbs planted at the graves." (P. 8) Most Germans migrating to Russia chose Bessarabia in the Ukraine, somewhat less remote than where the Nehers settled. In response to Catherine's 1763 manifesto some 20,000 families from Hesse, the Rhineland, Baden, Alsace, Bavaria, and the Palatinate settled in fourteen mother colonies on the lower Volga river near Saratov and Khibyshev.[2] Two thirds of these immigrants were Protestants, one third Catholic. Over the first few years, through hot summers and cold winters, crop failures, and marauding outlaws, many died. Even so, enough settlers adapted and survived, so that in time colonies expanded.

While remaining distinctly German, and seldom intermarrying with Russians, these colonists nevertheless acquired Russian habits. They built underground homes to live in until they could acquire lumber and used underground root cellars and summer kitchens in the Russian manner. A "summer kitchen," Pauline Diede describes, was an "annex" built near but not usually attached to the main house, "to keep the big house clean, cool and free of flies during the summer months."[3] Germans from Russia wore sheepskin coats and felt boots, they cooked borscht and other Russian foods, and they took numerous Russian loan words into their dialect. They mixed *mischt-holz*, or cakes of manure and straw, for fuel. Retaining the German tradition of glorifying work, they kept to themselves and enforced their separateness in a land tenure system called *dorf* (a village commune) that apportioned land only to males. Many of these traits distinguished the Germans from Russia from other settlers on the American continent at the turn of the twentieth century.

The fortunes of Pauline Neher Diede's grandparents generally conformed to this description of the lives of Germans who settled southern Russia. The marriage of her father's parents, which begins the Neher story, was an attempted rescue from great poverty. One day Ludwig Neher

> entered the home of a Baptist minister and found a family desperate for food and clothing. Typical of pastors' families, they nearly starved for doing as the Good Book said about taking in wayfarers and giving them bread, even if their children were left with practically nothing to eat. Here Ludwig met the minister's daughter, Julianna Zimmer, who was anxious to get away from the destitute conditions of her family. She married Ludwig in the hope of a better future. (P. 9)

But in supposing that a farmer always would grow enough to eat, Julianna would be consistently disappointed.

The Nehers first lived in a new colony, Sofiental, where Ludwig built winter huts. Then they moved to a resort town, Karlstal, where Ludwig worked as a gardener for a Russian nobleman. Their first child, also named Ludwig (Pauline's father), was put to work feeding the hogs from the refuse of the nobleman's estate, and he learned to snatch partly rotted apples from the hogs to assuage his own hunger. His "hog days," as he remembered them, were filled with floggings from both the hog overseer and his own father, his punishment so severe that sometimes his mother cried for him. Ludwig always thought of his mother differently from the way he remembered his father. Pauline Diede writes:

> Ludwig remembered his mother as hardly having an idle moment, always working with food, weaving, mending, knitting, gathering and shelling grain, and doing all the jobs women were expected to. When Julianna had a bit of time, she would teach her children scripture and German. She brought up six living children: Ludwig II (my father), Jacob III, Wilhelmina, William II, Anna, and Daniel. (PP. 11–12)

The childhood of Fred Martin, who married the sister of Pauline's mother and joined the Nehers in the journey to America in 1909, was if anything even harsher than Ludwig's.

> I grew up a semi-orphan in Russia, for my mother died when I was but a child. My father remarried and my stepmother tried to get me out of the house. I had to work as early as I can remember. I often think how cruel she was, for she did not even want me to come home for a visit for fear she would have to share an extra piece of bread. Today as I think of it I realize I was not the only young boy treated that way. Cruelty was part of discipline in those days. (P. 77)

Strictness and deprivation marked ordinary growing up, and the younger Ludwig experienced more of both in the Russo-Japanese War. Even though German colonists had settled in Russia with the understanding that they would not be conscripted, they were drafted for the war with Japan. This is what happened to Ludwig: "Cossacks had been riding through village streets picking up young men without serving them notice. Mothers cried and screamed at them. Ludwig hardly had time to say good-bye to his mother and gather up his belongings. His mother shoved into his bundle the warmest pair of underwear [without which] he would have frozen to death." After a battle, Ludwig helped to save the life of a wounded friend "whom he carried to a pond. Here he washed his friend's wounds and fetched him drinking water in his cupped hands. Ludwig often spoke of that man's miraculous recovery, for after two days and nights in their hideout, a peasant woman appeared, as out of thin air, dressed in rags, bringing a kettle of cooked grain and a spoon. She came from a village nearby, and must have heard their moans." (P. 12)

At the end of the war everyone in the family left Karlstal. Ludwig's father was no longer able to work as a gardener, and he took his family back to Germany. It was time for Ludwig to set about finding a wife. The manner of his marrying conformed to the customs of the times, but it distressed him later to think about it.

> Ludwig was now of marriageable age, and approached the village marriage broker whose business it was to keep track of suitable young women. When a girl's breasts developed and she had become well trained in indoor and outdoor labor, she was ready to be married. It was thought a disgrace for a younger sister to be married before an older one, so some marriages were apt

Ludwig Neher II and Adam Wolf upon their discharge from the army after serving in the Russo-Japanese War, 1904–5.

> to be hurried. Ludwig's marriage broker took him on a rough wagon ride from Freudental to Groszliebental to call on the George Steinerts. There Christina was home, busy shoving bread out of the clay wall oven. The bread was light and smelled good; Ludwig ate some and liked what he saw of Christina. A week later the two were married and settled with Ludwig's parents in an already overcrowded household. (P. 13)

Christina's sister, Sophie, also had made an "arranged" marriage, and her husband, Fred Martin, several times spoke about that rather ruefully: "Ours were the kind of arranged marriages that were proper in those days. Many couples hardly knew each other. Your mother and father were an example, for neither knew more about the other than first impressions." (P. 25) Within those marriages of "strangers," Sophie bore nine children; Christina eight. Lena, Sophie's eldest child, had primary responsibility for the younger ones. It was Christina's third daughter, Pauline, the first to be born in her parents' own house of sod, who took it upon herself more than fifty years later to write down the story of the two families' migrations.

These stories, by Pauline Diede's own account, came mainly from conversations with her father, Ludwig Neher, and her uncle, Fred Martin. The men spoke of their own lives—the exhausting physical labor required by subsistence farming; the anxiety of a move with infants and small children; the responsibility for the happiness of others. They were ashamed of being poor, baffled at finding themselves in a country where they could not speak the language, and angry that they were held in such low esteem. The men said they felt dislocated and friendless, and they also spoke as though they regretted what they had done.

Extracting the details of the lives of the women—Sophie, Christina, Lena, and Pauline—and trying to assess how they affected their families and how they viewed themselves are not easy tasks. For all the family lore, these mothers and daughters were all but hidden in the stories they themselves told. Sophie and Christina and their daughters were hidden because the Germans from Russia kept to themselves. They also were hidden within their own families, in ways typical, to varying degrees, of rural populations generally. In the settler generation women were not expected to act independently of their husbands; they were to help in farming or whatever work the men had chosen, to raise as many children as they could, and otherwise to behave inconspicuously. The particular women we are speaking of were hidden further by the fact that their stories emerge through the words of the men they married—Fred Martin, Sophie's husband, and Ludwig Neher, Christina's—both men admitting that because of their arranged marriages, they "hardly knew" their wives. What the women thought or felt about their experiences in their own right largely has to be inferred. The lives of Sophie Martin and her daughter Lena, and of Christina Neher and her daughter Pauline, were hidden in poverty, and in the customs and values of their cultural heritage. But we can try to listen for their voices in the account of the family's migration and the first two years in North Dakota that was compiled by one of the daughters, Pauline Neher Diede.

II. The Journey West, *1909*

Conscription into the Russian army in violation of Catherine's manifesto, along with the political disturbances that led to the Russian Revolution of 1917, convinced many like the Nehers and Martins to leave. These families were relatively late emigrants, for Germans had been departing in increasing numbers from their settlements in Russia over the previous twenty or thirty years for many of the same reasons as had drawn their forebears to southern Russia in the previous century. As early as 1870, Czar Alexander II canceled some of the privileges the manifesto had accorded to Germans, and thus precipitated the second large German migration, this time to the grasslands of Argentina, Canada, and the American Great Plains.[4]

American railroad companies advertised energetically in the German-settled regions of Russia. Unlike many foreign immigrants who lived in the East or Midwest before they made permanent homes in the American plains and western states, Germans from Russia came directly to the grasslands west of the Mississippi. Those who went to the Dakotas typically rode the Chicago, Milwaukee & St. Paul Railroad as far as Yankton, South Dakota, then continued north by wagon to Aberdeen and Eureka, and crossed the Missouri River into the south-central counties of North Dakota. As railway lines expanded, more of the trip could be completed by train. Settlers began arriving in Yankton in 1874; by 1880 they were moving toward northern South Dakota; by 1884 the first Germans from Russia had settled in North Dakota. This movement went "across the grain" of more usual east-west migration patterns in the United States, and "outward expansion of Germans from Eureka averaged almost ten miles a year for the first decade of North Dakota settlement.... At the peak of immigration, special trains of twenty and thirty cars of immigrants arrived at regular intervals at the Eureka station."[5] Between 1887 and 1902 Eureka claimed to be the largest wheat producer in the region, the harvest of 1892 of three to four million bushels of grain being loaded onto 165 trains. Eureka also became something of a retirement community when Germans returned in old age to the town from which they felt they had begun the American venture.

These Germans who came from Russia through South to North Dakota were for the most part from the Black Sea region in the Ukraine. They were people who aspired to owning land, and most came as family units.

Leaving Russia was not an easy decision. Fred Martin pointed out that leaving Groszliebental meant leaving a relatively prosperous community, where his wife's family were well-to-do, and where church and school meant educational opportunities for children. His ambivalence was tied also to Sophie's reluctance.

> Sophie thus was reluctant to give up these advantages. I, on the other hand, had been an orphan and very poor, and Sophie felt that I was beneath her. . . . I knew that although emigrating meant going into the unknown, it also would mean greater security for my boys and a way of avoiding their conscription into the Russian army, reason enough to take the venture even against my wife's opposition. (P. 14)

Fred Martin had not served in the army, but he and others knew what service as a foot soldier could mean, and his older children were approaching the age when they would have to go. Fred decided to leave against Sophie's wishes with little cash and seven children, only the two older ones able to work. Ludwig Neher did not want to repeat his army experience; he had little money and his wife had just given birth to their first child. The men planned the trip together; their wives apparently had little say.

The journey occurred in several stages and took several weeks: by horse-drawn wagon from Groszliebental to Odessa; by train from Odessa to Hamburg, Germany; by ship to Montreal (rather than to New York, where most German-Russians landed); by train from Montreal to Chicago, then to Ashley, North Dakota; and finally by horse-drawn wagon to their first boarding place in Ashley. The odyssey, so typical of thousands, now seems astonishing in its audacity and fragility: two families together, with small children and infants, no knowledge of the language, geography, or customs of the country they were traveling toward, no experience beyond the agricultural villages they grew up in, and little money. The trip gave Fred Martin pause to dread the thought of what he was doing and what he unwittingly had subjected his family to. Between Odessa and Hamburg,

> the train was crowded, as bad as a stock car of hogs. Children were perched atop sacks and bundles so closely they hardly had elbowroom, and they set up a howl. The palms of their hands were saucers into which was thrown a piece of bread and "schpeck," or salt-brined pork. . . . No toilet facilities except on the premises of a train station. Children rebelled and cried and were shoved, shouted at and slapped, even more by train conductors than by parents. I even felt like slapping my wife because she constantly scolded me for choosing this ordeal for the family. (P. 15)

On board ship, conditions were worse:

> One or another of the boys was bawling most of the time, especially George. It took a lot of impatience for me to hit a child, but one night I had had it. In anger I got up, struck a match, and lit the kerosene lamp on the wall. My eyes focused on the ceiling quite accidentally and I saw a mass of crawlers squirming and creeping into crevices. I examined George's body and found bedbugs crawling about, his body covered with red blotches, and then I knew why he was crying. (P. 16)

Fred Martin left the kerosense lamp burning all night to keep bugs away and to comfort the child.

The journey shocked Fred; he blamed himself for subjecting his family to the appalling conditions on board train and ship. During a violent storm on the sea trip, he caught hold of one of his boys just as the child was about to be swept overboard. If such a voyage was supposed to include an element of daring, Fred admitted to more anguish than one would expect of an ambitious adventurer: "I was at one of my weakest points on the entire journey. I shivered from fright. I stood on the deck with my hands and arms outstretched shouting, *'Gott, bring' uns doch zum land'* ('God bring us yet to land'). I didn't know where to go, for I was terribly seasick. . . . This was the time I wished we could have turned back. I felt guilty that I had brought my family into such an ordeal. My spirit was at its lowest ebb." (PP. 16–17) The Martin family were not alone, of course, in their suffering. Fred told of a child in another family who had died and was buried at sea: "Little Andrew was forcibly taken from his screaming mother and his body put into a gunny sack." Fred feared for his own infant daughter, Mathilda, who was ill. The crowding, seasickness, bugs, and lice made him think that what he was watching his children endure was worse than anything he had experienced in his own childhood.

> But as I watched what my boys were going through, right then I felt they had it even worse. . . . People can be more cruel to children than to animals. . . . I too got hard with my children at times, but then I remembered my hard lot as I grew up and decided my children needed better treatment. Then I would cry and become tender, wipe dry my eyes and hope again that in a few days we would step onto American soil. (PP. 18–19)

Whatever his hopes, Fred Martin saw all around him greater indications of difficulties than success. When they debarked in Montreal, he said, "I did not feel excitement but anguish. The children looked pale and wandered about in a straggly manner." Even a routine health inspection could mean doom: "If any family member was afflicted with disease, you were sent back. A woman at the other end of the ship had lost her mind, and I knew the family had no chance of getting through. I looked at that man's cross, and considered mine light." The Martins and Nehers passed inspection without anyone's detecting that Henry "was breaking out with measles. Your father [Ludwig] wrapped him up in a blanket and carried him to the port's camp, where we were stalled for a number of days. A U.S. inspector discovered our trouble and said, 'For measles you would not be sent back to Europe. Keep your family here. Do not take them on the train in this condition.' We were delayed for over a week and were lodging in a ship's tent from which we could see the Atlantic Ocean to the east, but I kept my eyes focussed to the west, where land was." (PP. 18–19)

In Montreal, where they landed and where they boarded a train for the Dakotas, "one of the first blessings was milk for the children, and another was their being able to run free. What a relief, yet what an uncertainty." (P. 19) Space, in the new world, is a recurring theme in these accounts—a sharp and sometimes frightening change from the cramped quarters on board ship, the crowded housing in sod and wooden shacks, and the crowded Russian village they had left. They hoped for greater space, physically and emotionally, and relief from oppressive intimacy. In Montreal, much of the pleasure Fred and others found came from the ability to "run free," and at times, as we shall see, the prairie landscape afforded such freedom. But perhaps the other side of such new freedom was uncertainty, a second recurring theme, as both families strained to learn English, understand social expectations, learn new farming technologies, and make a home for themselves. As best he could, Fred kept his gaze to the west. Once on the train, he said that "the autumn scenery was spectacular. The vast land gave us revived hope for better things."

But uncertainty took hold more often than not. The Martins' two-year-old, Mathilda, grew weaker. In Chicago there came some small relief.

> A good elderly immigrating mother who wore Russian clothes came to our assistance; at least we thought she could help. She gave our little Mathilda a good smear with homemade ointment that she had brought from Russia, and she uttered a meditation and exercised the child's opposing legs and arms together, releasing bodily tensions. Then she wound a wide cloth around her abdomen, admonishing us to cover her well for a sweat. It did Mathilda some good, as well as the rest of us, for she fell asleep and slept and slept. (P. 19)

Uncertainty plagued them in the very basic matter of travel arrangements. With no one in the group able to speak English, and their German dialect scarcely intelligible to German-speaking people, the Martins and Nehers depended on the name of the town—Eureka, South Dakota, written on an envelope—to get them where they wanted to go. However, the train had reached Medina, North Dakota, considerably to the north, before the conductor remembered to let them off. They had no idea where they were or what they should do. Someone directed them to the livery station, and the liveryman found them lodging for the night among Catholic families. Fred, remembering old rivalries in Russia, thought it surprising that they should be helped by Catholics. To his relief, "the [Catholic] women made no fuss, for they were all religious people. Their homes seemed to us fit for a king's family. Pictures of Holy Mary and Jesus hanging on the cross adorned the parlors of these homes and I wondered whether that was something we could look forward to. Must we be Catholics to become so prosperous?" (P. 20) The next day they started south in the liveryman's wagon pulled by "his well-fed horses," and Fred Martin enjoyed again some of the "relief" he had glimpsed in Montreal: "This was the first time I was relaxed enough to focus on the prairie land. It was rolling plains country with homesteads perched about, showing patches of turned-over prairie soil, indicating that the land was being farmed." When they reached Ashley (to the southwest of Medina), the driver thought he had taken them far enough: "We found ourselves moved into a train boxcar. Again, kindness was shown to us in our hour of need. Immigrant people were all around us, and God, how we thank them." (P. 21) Stationary boxcars were first homes for some settlers.

III. The Boxcar Winter, *1909–1910*

The boxcar confined them to a small and not very clean space, and the families made do with traditional peasant methods. There were no trees for fuel, and so the boys were sent to gather *mischt*, or dried cow manure, but even that was scarce because other settlers were gathering it too. They acquired some manure from a farmer, and, Fred explained, "We handled it as we had in Russia, working in weeds, twigs and pieces of wood to make dried fuel cakes that we stacked close to the door of the boxcar so as to keep watch on it. We also were introduced to some new fuel possibilities, dried corn cobs, that we had not had in Russia." (P. 22) The boxcar for the twelve of them, even with the stove and cornhusk mattresses that they found, hardly made for comfort. They fashioned a toilet from a grease can, "and near it a box of corn husks for toilet paper. We thought that a luxury. Corn and a certain wide-leaved sudan grass were new crops that fascinated me. We had none in Russia. Only better established farmers dared raise corn and sudan grass. What a challenge." (P. 23)

But as the weeks wore on, living in the boxcar, Fred said, was "worse than a coyote hole." Christina was pregnant again and could not hold her food down. An attempt to send one of the children to school failed, making the families feel even more like strangers and more than ever "inferior" to people around them. The new venture appeared to offer very little hope for a better life after all, and the Martin family's failure to present even one child for schooling seemed like a severe setback to joining American culture.

Russian immigrants at the railroad station at Bismarck, North Dakota. The treeless plains of the prairies resembled the steppes of their native land.

> There was an American school in Ashley. We saw how lively the children in the school yard appeared, and we thought we had better get some of our middle boys started. Fred, our third child, would be the one to start, for we needed Lena and John to help gather manure fuel and dig coal for the oncoming winter. Lena placed a hunk of bread and an apple in a syrup can for Fred's lunch. He was told not to eat the apple before noon, the one incentive to get him going. But Fred barely reached the school ground when some older boys piled on him and called him a "Rooshen." Fred knew not a word of English and had no way of defending himself, and so arrived at his boxcar home beaten and bawling, less from bruises than from having his apple taken away. . . . Poverty and the lack of variety of food kept growing children always hungry and quarrelsome. The biggest squabbles among boys were over stealing each other's apples. They were plain starving for lack of nutriment.
>
> (P. 24)

Virtually every day's experience hinged upon whether someone did or did not get fed. Children were always hungry, and much of the "cruelty" Martin speaks of regarding discipline concerns denying them food, or not being able to give them enough to eat. Neither family was prepared for encountering basic issues of survival. The residents of the Russian village were unacquainted with starvation, even though as a child in Karlstal Ludwig remembered helping himself to apples meant for hogs. Now, in what was supposed to be a new land of opportunity, hungry men were snatching seedling wheat from their children. Fred Martin's reflections to Pauline Diede of his arrival are gloomy: "I think the journey to America and that first winter in Ashley were the hardest times of my life. I got into the habit of crying much of the time. Sometimes I was glad it was your father [Ludwig] who disciplined the boys, for it relieved me." (P. 25)

It was a winter of confusion, the men trying to control fears through often aimless violence in the name of discipline, treating children and animals about the same. Martin called these the "oxen days," except that his oxen were too unsatisfactory to use. "Those oxen were the most stupid, uncooperative, stolid animals I had ever encountered. I tried beating sense into them, as was the custom then. Being forceful at hitting, both humans and animals, was a part of playing the role of a man. A man could release his temper as well as show his power as boss." (P. 37) Unspoken in such reported conversations between Fred Martin and his niece Pauline Diede are direct references to the women—Sophie and Christina and their children and infants who were subjected to the outbursts of frightened men trying to assert themselves as "boss." A poignant note of regret often enters the conversations Pauline Diede reports of her uncle and her father. In their youth these men, brought up in a stern paternalistic and military culture, tried to conform to the "role of a man," sometimes with harshness. But in their old age they tempered accounts of those days with regret. Fred Martin sounds sad when he tells of deprivation; he did not brag about hardships he had surmounted through "manly fortitude."

In February of that first winter, the weather suddenly turned deceptively warm, and Fred Martin and Ludwig Neher decided to make a trip to Bismarck to register at the land office for a homestead. They got there on foot, by short wagon rides and train, but when a snowstorm following the warm spell locked in the entire region for miles around, they slept on the floor of the train depot, huddling against the stove. They slept next to men Martin referred to as "freight-train bums," one of whom stole Ludwig's loaf of bread. Someone brought a kettle of grits: "We were like hungry pigs around a trough." Ludwig, when the storm let up, procured more grits and a can of sardines, which was a new wonder: "Nowhere in Russia was food preserved in a can; this was new to us. The depot man opened the sardine cans with a sharp knife and poured the contents into a dish. All this went on in the freight room, out of sight of the bums." They saved the can "for all kinds of uses." Always they depended on the provisions of others: "Your Pa took to his feet and knocked at doors of Bismarck homes, bringing many a loaf of bread back to the depot. So then we had bread." (P. 27) The trip to the land office disclosed that the only land still available was near the Knife River. Fred went to the Walths, friends of his wife's in Richardton, who he hoped would take him to see the land, and Ludwig returned to the families in the boxcar.

The Walths represented to Fred Martin all he had heard promised about American prosperity, because there was no shortage of food in their household. "I was taken in with open arms. O, that good soup that soothed my hunger. The Walths also were Germans from Russia and had immigrated some years earlier. Seeing their plentiful food, clothing, and comfortable home, considering the times, my whole being surged with new hope." He was amazed to be told that the calendar on the wall came free from the druggist: "Was this what America had to offer?" (P. 28) The Walths took him to a family named Jaeger, "High Germans," who lived near Martin's allotment. Fred Martin's discomfort returned: "I felt inferior, for their talk showed they had had more schooling than I. They had class, and I began to understand how many people had come from other European countries besides Germans from Russia." But the Jaegers welcomed him warmly. "Frau Jaeger reheated some 'schpaetzla' soup, and how it warmed my whole being." (P. 29) To be fed and be warm were the hallmarks of prosperity in this America.

With the advice of the German family, Martin picked out land and sites for houses, realizing, however, that the "true" Germans had maneuvered him onto less desirable ground, for they did not want these new immigrants any closer than could be helped. From then on, the Martins and Nehers felt they were looked upon by German, Irish, and other settled families in the vicinity with pity and scorn. Even when they were shown considerable charity and kindness, they said again and again, they felt "inferior." Not only were they looked down upon by other European immigrants, but unlike the many Germans from Russia who had been arriving since the late 1870s and who settled in homogeneous communities, the Nehers and Martins found themselves in what could be called a mixed neighborhood, with few other Germans from Russia close by. They had risked the journey in late summer, too late to plant a crop before winter, and they arrived after the best land had been taken. They were short of cash, could not speak or read English, knew next to nothing about weather, soil, and agricultural conditions in the northern plains, and possessed few skills necessary for farming. The wonder is that these families survived at all. Tenacity and the help of others saw them through.

> Helping out was a must in those days. People understood that if a wayfarer asked for bread and a place to lay his head, it was a holy obligation. Anyone who did not respond to the needs of others was judged harshly in strong language and fitting verses from the Bible. There was a closeness among Germans from Russia homesteaders. They took it as their mission to share bread with the hungry even though they had little for themselves. (P. 30)

One of the troubles for which these families badly needed help was the poor health of two-year-old Mathilda. In Ashley, neighbors offered an assortment of cures: "One grandmother and midwife supplied herb treatments and gave the child the sign of the Holy Cross, a healing belief in the Catholic faith. We Protestants used the method we called 'brauching' "—a folk healing that combines herbs, massage, and incantations from the Scriptures. (P. 23) Fred Martin was grateful for the attention: "Again I must say thanks to the good people who gave us herbs, teas, goose lard and liniments to smear the sicknesses away." (P. 31) But in spite of prayers and herbs, Mathilda died, adding grief to the hardships of that first boxcar winter in Ashley. Much of the child's care rested on Lena (short for Magdalena), the eldest of the Martin children.

> Magdalena, then a teenager, had played the role of an adult since she was a child, for we placed weighty responsibilities on her. In those days, it was customary to expect the impossible, especially from a girl. Lena had to watch the younger ones. . . . So many of us crowded into so small a space caused friction. One evening Lena was lifting her very sick little sister from one arm to the other when the child's body went limp, the ebb of life gone out. Little Mathilda had died in Lena's arms. (P. 23)

The death was hard on Lena, whose existence in the boxcar was unimaginable. She lived in continual anxiety and distress.

> We were crowded together like coyotes and their young in a hole. You can imagine Lena's turmoil: she was in her adolescence, with no privacy whatever, and we did not even recognize a girl's needs. We shrugged off having any kind of conversation to explain to her the stages of human development. In those days, everything was shameful. The less said and the more children were kept in ignorance, the better. Lena went through a hard time in her growing up years. All in all, we expected too much of her. (PP. 37–38)

With her parents harried by the daily struggle to find enough food and fuel dung cakes, Lena was left to nurse her dying sister, her own life and her own needs obliterated in day-to-day emergencies. As her father awkwardly suggests, she had begun to menstruate, an added humiliation. Not even her mother could give her information or privacy or reassurance.

In the "coyote hole" there was no intimacy; there was only hunger and irritability. On the broad expanse of North Dakota people were locked together in a dark and cold boxcar for the winter.

IV. Spring in an Abandoned House, *1910*

In the spring of 1910 Nehers and Martins—four adults and seven children—moved from the Ashley boxcar to their claim, spending some days with the Walths in Richardton, and seeing more examples of persons who, in their eyes, miraculously were achieving the immigrant dream. On the way from Ashley to Richardton they stopped at the Roth farm where, Fred said, "I had my first experience in America of sticking two fingers into a calf's mouth to help it suck up milk. I remember how I longed for my family to be so fortunate as to have milk and daily bread and such housing as the Roth family had." (P. 31) The going was rough from that farmstead to Richardton, even supplied as they were with a last meal of dumplings and potato soup and fried pork and six loaves of bread. "The little children cried. It helped that the bigger boys could romp along and throw an occasional dirt clump at the horses to get them prancing faster. The oldsters were cranky, to put it mildly. What a trip." The prosperity he saw among such families as the Walths and Roths "gave me hope," Fred said, "but how I longed to be settled with my restless children and discontented wife." In Richardton once again they were housed by neighboring families, "but we felt unsettled . . . like parasites, eating, as we were, at others' tables. I say it was the providing God that inspired families to help out, or we would have starved." He admired the gardens, including often "a 'bashtaan,' or row garden, of potatoes, watermelons and pumpkins. The good supply of stored vegetables in root cellars in the Richardton area made me hope I could provide as well for my family." (P. 32)

In April the two families crowded into an abandoned house on their land and began to plow and plant grain under the supervision of the "Herr" Jaeger who had helped them find the allotment. Jaeger, Fred said, "was a master, and I followed his every admonition, and he seemed to want to be treated that way." Both families became dependent upon the Jaegers, and Fred Martin cautioned his brother-in-law to refrain from "hollering back," pointing out that not only would it be politic to get along with them because they were neighbors, but that Mrs. Jaeger was the local midwife and soon would be needed at the Nehers': "I told him more than once to hold his mouth, we needed the Jaegers." (P. 33)

The relationship between the Jaegers and the Groszliebental families, especially the Nehers, emphasizes how fragile newcomers' survival could be. The Jaegers were "true" Germans who came directly from Germany, and they had arrived in the area early enough to acquire the best farming land. They possessed sufficient money and expertise to make them comfortable. They had a "summer kitchen," which meant that they were living in expansive quarters and in hot weather could cook in what was not much more than a shed so as not to heat up the rest of the house. The families endured an ambivalent relationship, the Jaegers feeling the continuous call to charity, and the Nehers feeling "inferior," as they so often said, to benefactors who not only were more prosperous but were considered culturally and socially superior. "True" Germans, they learned, thought they were better than "Rooshans." The Nehers had arrived with one child, Matilda (having the same name as the Martins' child who died); she was born in Russia and was now fifteen months old. On May 6, 1910, during a fierce evening thunderstorm, Christina gave birth to Ottilia. Fred Martin described the harrowing event:

> The older children were crowded into the wagon box at night, and I paced around outside telling the boys to go to sleep. The two littlest children were in the shack, along with Sophie, Ludwig, and Frau Jaeger. Your mother was screaming in pain, and thunder and lightning squalled with an occasional crack. We could not go into the shack, so Lena, the boys and I huddled together under the wagon and sat on a "stroh-sach" (straw-filled cloth case). Luckily we had the old horse blanket the Walths had thrown in when we left them, and now it sheltered us in that downpour. We put our heads under it, but it didn't take long before we were sitting in water. The boys bawled, and Lena was screaming in fright, she, who usually was the one to stand as a brave scold to keep the boys in shape. But not that night. This is how Ottilia (later called Tillie) was born. Your Pa always said that North Dakota's first thunderstorm brought her. (P. 34)

Fred distributed soaking wet children to various neighbors, where they remained for several days, and again received food from other families. After the baby's birth, Mrs. Jaeger took Christina away to live in her summer kitchen, hoping to give her a brief respite from her husband lest he make her pregnant again. It was social control, and it was one woman's means of reaching out to protect another.

Desperate as they were, Martins and Nehers, the men competed between themselves. Fred was jealous that Neher's wife, her pregnancy and the birth of her baby, won him their neighbors' pity and help: "I felt a twinge of envy that your father had fallen into that kind of luck. I am only human. Yet all in all, it was the dear God that did not forsake him, for Ludwig had so little money, and there was nothing for it but people had to help out, your parents had so little to start on. Not only did we have no help from the government, but we knew nothing about the rigors of North Dakota weather." (P. 34) Here Fred touches on issues not often discussed in the history of western settlement. Real estate offices, the major purveyors of information, seldom discouraged immigration by providing accurate descriptions of western topography and climate. Furthermore, the requirement that each homesteader "prove up" and be physically residing on the land for a certain portion of the year meant that families were scattered about the countryside. Each family meant to secure for itself the largest amount of land, free from neighbors close by. For immigrants who had come from agrarian villages, the dispersal of households meant a drastic change in living habits. The isolation of settlement was also different from the habits of local Indians, who, although they were nomadic on the plains, always moved together in groups. Lonely foreigners found that life on the vast prairies held little time for coming together, little enough center for communal life.

"At every turn there was a need. I cannot describe our dilemma," Fred said. The plow he had bought had no horse to draw it, nor was there one to borrow because everyone else was plowing as well. A neighbor rancher, Matt Crowley, came with his horse and his plow to break the land for Ludwig to plant hay and to construct a sod house. Crowley also broke sod for the Martins. "Sometimes I felt like wringing Ludwig's neck," Fred said, "but that day I almost kissed him. He knew a few words of English and somehow made himself understood to the Irish-English Crowleys. And on the way back to the Crowleys' ranch, Ludwig even managed to get Matt to break up another patch of his 'hee' (high land). So he was ahead of me again. It seemed to me his poverty repeatedly worked in his behalf, but I was eternally thankful anyway that Ludwig saw to it to have some of my homestead prairie land broken up." (P. 35)

They seeded oats and wheat by hand and planted gardens with seeds neighbors gave them—pumpkins and potatoes. Work was unremitting, for children as well as adults. The Martins began cutting sod to build a house closer to their own land, and the boys helped. "The boys used to run across the prairie to take messages back and forth or bring me things to eat. The boys did many other things too; they were born to toil. In those days children were not accustomed to much playing. From the time they could romp, they worked." (P. 36) While Fred was building the sod house, the family lived in the shanty and caught rainwater off the roof. They were crowded, and found also that the shanty

> sat on what became a pond. My Sophie hauled me over. . . . Our shanty floor was one big bed at night. There was a lot of bawling at night, particularly the night we had several inches of a downpour and the floor gradually submerged in water. Everybody was up and around and in a stand-offish mood. As many as possible crowded into our bed. Some of the boys perched atop the table, cuddled into the straw mattress. . . . The next morning everything was wet, even my spirits. This was one time I considered going back to Russia, but I did not say so out loud. (P. 37)

Fred Martin had spoken with his niece, Pauline Neher Diede, not long after his wife Sophie died; his memories may well be colored by her illness and death, for he said a good deal about Sophie's unhappiness, and even suggested that it may have been foolhardy of him to have left Russia when he did:

> The spring of 1910 was our most difficult time as pioneers on the prairie. I hardly slept. My temper was short, for I realized my family's survival depended on what we could grow on the land. . . . But to be spending my accumulated wealth gained in the most prosperous period in Russia, with seven children and a dissatisfied wife, spelled extreme suffering for me. I admit I cried out my tensions and worked like a beaver. I often shouted to God for help: *"O Gott, du muscht helfa"* ("O God, you must help"). (PP. 35–36)

And when his shack sat in water, Sophie screamed at him. "Deep down she loathed everything about America and never stopped thinking about the Groszliebental life. It is odd we even slept together, but we had no other choice." (P. 37) The constant pressure of daily emergencies, coupled with crowded living, alienated family members from one another; it certainly did not, by Fred Martin's account, bring them closer together. It appears the more poignant that in his old age, Martin should be trying to reconstruct what Sophie thought of it all, when at the time, he admitted, he had felt little obligation to listen to her objections. All in all, Fred Martin's summary reflections are a long way from the hopefulness, the bravery, and the sense of daring that immigration, and certainly western settlement, were supposed to evoke: "Often nothing made sense to me, and it was a good thing that I had no time to think about it nor to listen to Sophie's reproaches. We were stuck on this prairie and had to endure it and hope it would be kind enough to produce food. . . . We were so lacking in tools and items for changing the rugged prairies into productive farm land that when I think back to our first year on that coyote land, I can hardly keep from crying." (P. 39)

They persevered because they had no alternative. Fred moved his shanty farther up a hill, and he and Ludwig constructed dams to keep the water away. Lacking a "stone boat," a sort of sled pulled by horse or ox for carting stones away from a field, Martin's boys carried stones for the dam. Food was so scarce the children ate grass and plants, and the only water they had was from the creek. They developed diarrhea and worms. The local druggist advised them to dig a well. Maybe God helped a bit, for when the Martins dug a well, it was a success.

> Bitterman [another neighbor] was summoned to use his willow twig, and he found a location easily as some mysterious force turned the willow fork downward. If he was under some higher power, it was not the devil, that I knew, for the devil would not have wanted us to have water. . . . Some people laugh and don't believe in water witching, but I crossed my hands over Bitterman's and experienced myself the magic pull of the willow twig, a feeling I can't describe except to say it is one of God's many blessings, a miracle of the prairies. (P. 40)

Water appeared at only twelve feet and, possibly another miracle, it brought some happiness to Sophie. Fred said, "The water came fast and clear. I tasted it and drank myself full. That was one time I saw Sophie smile. It was a day I'll never forget." (P. 40)

Sophie did not smile often. Her sadness made Fred Martin aware that he had made decisions she was obliged to agree to whether she wanted to or not, such were the customs of their culture. In rare moments, they came together in shared sympathy. Pauline Diede retells one of her uncle's stories:

> One early morning in late May Martin took a stroll around the hill and up to the high flat where Nature greeted him with a good feeling. The sun had barely risen and cast a golden glow over hills and valleys. Ample showers had made everything green. Wild flowers were blooming. He picked a bouquet of showy golden peas and added several stalks of blue beardstongue, an attractive bouquet. Perhaps this God-forsaken country held more blessings than one realized. He felt newly hopeful as he presented the fresh wild flowers to his moody wife, and she too showed an early morning exaltation of spirit. She always had been fond of flowers. Martin fetched water from the dam in an empty syrup pail, arranged the flowers in the can, and set them on a flat stone close to the garden. It added color to the whole place, and Martin felt elated. (PP. 50–51)

How can we interpret Fred Martin's story or appreciate the experiences of the two families? Fred was amazed that he had lived long enough to tell his tale to his niece, and by then he had changed his mind from the time when the stories were taking place. He spoke with Pauline about matters that could not have been easy for him, and perhaps not possible to speak of at all with Sophie, or with Christina and Ludwig. Sophie's death not long before these conversations gives them an elegiac tone. Like so many settlers, Fred Martin was ignorant of America. He was at the mercy of people like the train conductor and the liveryman who decided on their own where the end of the line should be. Behind his words we barely glimpse Sophie's life, she who, like her sister Christina, had come from a village where parents and other relatives could support her growing brood of children. There, the husband who was half a stranger need not have been her sole companion; here, she had no one but a sister who sometimes appeared even less competent than she. In this otherwise detailed account there is little comment about the relationship between the two sisters.

Yet a family's survival depended not only on the men but upon the labor of women and upon their miraculous capacities to give their families something to hope for in desperate times. Pauline Diede writes about the women remembered from Russia:

> A woman in those days had few rights and kept her needs to herself, often in desperation crying out her troubles only to another woman, though cautiously so, that she not be discovered in her laments. Ludwig spoke often of his mother with tears in his eyes, overcome by emotion and homesickness so that his statements were short as he let out a sob. What he remembered most about his mother was seeing her on her knees praying, her hands outstretched to the heavens where God was. Julianna Zimmer had a hard lot, as did most women in those days. But somehow she gathered the grace of endurance and patience and taught her family to follow her "Heiland" (Lord). She gave her children something else as well, good minds and an incentive to learn. Even though her children were denied school, Julianna taught them scripture and how to read and write German. (P. 11)

This same woman "knew the future in Russia was bleak for her children" and therefore did not stand in the way of their leaving. More particularly, she continued to represent to them everything they had valued most in their past, and she was remembered as a source of comfort from that long-ago place, almost as if women lavished upon their infants the tenderness denied them in their own lives with their husbands. Before the families left Russia, "Matilda [the eldest Neher child] was delivered by Grandmother Julianna and consequently was cuddled by both grandparents." "Cuddling" warmth is a strong element in the tradition of almost any European immigrant group, yet among Nehers and Martins, once they arrived in North Dakota, it appears to have been scarce. The loss of community and grandparents meant a loss of precious fondling and caressing. Other families report experiences similar to the Martins' and Nehers'. For instance, William Julissen, an artist living in Grand Forks, writes:

> Ours was not such a severe situation as the Nehers', but it still amounted to constant drudgery and lack of laughter and life's comforts along with the hard winters, childhood diseases and dreaded two-seater meditation shack back by the alley. For many nights we kids and the folks would sit around the kitchen table with its kerosene lamp after supper quizzing my father about his 23 years in the Russian army, into which he was "recruited" as a 15-year-old captive Estonian boy. My mother often sang and talked sadly about her work as a girl in the Salz (the Russian fields), which broke her health and left her chronically ill all her life. And even to their ends in 1948 and '50, our questioning my father about his Estonian past brought silent curses, and of my mother's village life and girlhood, tears.[6]

Given their many difficulties, it was not easy for husbands and wives in the Martin and Neher families to establish any closeness or even to endure each other's company. Fred spoke of Sophie's "stand-offish" moods and of her "haul[ing] him over" in desperate times. The men felt obliged not only to make the decisions to migrate, then plan and execute the journey, buy land, see to housing and provisions, but also to control unhappy wives and children, who were miserable with disease and hunger. Fred and Ludwig were themselves hungry most of the time and had an obsession with food and eating. Irritably, they competed with one another, and lived like "coyotes and their young in a hole."

Ludwig Neher began with less money than did his brother-in-law, and he didn't have children old enough to work. Ludwig's previous experience feeding hogs on the Russian nobleman's estate did not teach him the skills he needed to begin a homestead farm. His wife, Christina, had grown up in a settled and prosperous agricultural village, and although she knew how to bake bread and thresh grain, she was unprepared for the isolation, poverty, and hardships of living in North Dakota. The children were often beset by disease and accident. Ludwig and Christina had little time and less energy to pay attention to them. Neither state nor church helped support these families; instead, what aid they did receive came haphazard from other households in the vicinity.

In 1910, the first year on the Knife River homestead after the winter in the boxcar near Ashley, Ludwig ran out of money. One day, on the spur of the moment, he set off for the homestead of the better-established rancher Matt Crowley, where he negotiated the loan of a cow and a horse, promising to pay for them eventually. He wanted the horse to hitch to his plow, and the cow, who was about to calve, for her milk.

> Crowley noticed that he was hungry and invited him to the cowboys' bunk house for beef stew simmering on the cast-iron range. . . . And so he let him go home with a full stomach, riding his horse and leading a prospective milk cow on a length of rope attached to a halter, and carrying a syrup-pail of well-water for good measure. (P. 45)

The cow brought Ludwig's family comfort and assurance, as well as milk.

> Soon Bossie had a calf. At first she allowed herself to be milked easily. Neher sat on a stone while he milked. He felt the firm udder. Then Bossie kicked,

> throwing him off the stone. It took a while for the two to trust each other. After a time, Bossie made the stone her stopping place when she wanted to be milked, and Neher bragged about how clever she was, and how now he could offer extra milk to the Bittermans. He could skim the cream and make butter. Each morning he filled the syrup can Crowley had given him, had milk to drink all day, and also had enough for the calf. (P. 45)

Almost every memory Ludwig Neher recounted mentions food. When he and Fred bought horses from Matt Crowley's father, Jeremiah Crowley, Neher "smelled something good cooking. Johanna Crowley had made extra biscuits, and although she would have preferred that the visitors were Scandinavian or Irish-English, she was glad of any company." Another Crowley son, Jack, was less hospitable toward begging Germans from Russia: "Jack realized their need, but could not take his eyes off what was happening to the stew. Neher's plate of biscuits was covered with beef gravy, to which he had helped himself, and there was very little left for Jack." (P. 47) One day, feeling particularly discouraged after a disagreement with Fred, Ludwig visited the rest of the Martins, where "Sophie offered him a bowl of soup that he devoured in haste. She noticed he had been crying." Sophie suggested Ludwig visit Christina (in the Jaegers' summer kitchen, where she had been invited to live after the birth of her second child). He went to Christina, and when he left the next morning, Jaeger offered him a rabbit trap, and "Frau Jaeger gave him carrots and potatoes from her root cellar, and Christina added bread she had baked, much nicer than any bread the German woman could bake." (P. 48)

It seems remarkable that fifty years later, when Ludwig Neher recounted these times to his daughter Pauline, he remembered so exactly individual foods and particular meals, and where and how he had acquired them. As anxious as he was about getting enough to eat himself, we can only imagine how the women felt—Sophie and Christina, pregnant and hungry, never having enough food for themselves or for their husbands, managing by miracles to have enough bread to keep the little ones from crying.

On a trip to Bismarck for tools, the men went into a store, growing "hungry just thinking about those little fish in the oblong cans, but [they] had no money for such luxuries. [Neher] bargained for them anyway, leaving the store manager to wonder whether he would ever see his money. Thus Ludwig enjoyed his second can of sardines as he had before in

Bismarck during the storm. He talked unfalteringly, as if the sardines had given him strength." (P. 53) On his way home from this trip to Bismarck, Ludwig stopped again to see Christina at the Jaegers' summer kitchen, and when he left, Frau Jaeger "sent Neher to the house for her husband to give him left-over supper, and Neher filled up on stew of liver, carrots, and dumplings. It didn't taste like his mother's cooking but his stomach needed food." (P. 55) Then, "early the next morning Frau Jaeger called Neher over for a big bowl of barley cereal" and told him it was time to remove his family from her summer kitchen because she would be needing it. She felt bad at turning them out: "Regretting what she had said, Frau Jaeger made up a pail full of potatoes, carrots, and beets from her root cellar for Neher to take along, but reminded him to bring back the pail" (P. 55)—generosity was wed to thrift. When in a few days Neher came to pick up his family, Jaeger "asked his wife to cook up a soup and send along a supply of carrots, potatoes and anything she could spare for those poor people." (P. 57)

The Jaegers were not the only family to provide food for the Nehers. Their very survival, in fact, appears to have been a community challenge. Once in their sod house that Ludwig had been building while Christina was housed in the Jaegers' summer kitchen, another neighbor, Elizabeth Boehler, brought over contributions. Christina grew to feel more warmly toward her than she did toward Mrs. Jaeger—personal encouragement as well as food was what these families craved. Elizabeth Boehler "shared a corner of her root cellar, and pickled watermelons and cucumbers in a small barrel for the Nehers as well. Fortunately her garden produced heavily in 1910, and her root cellar was filled amply" (P. 63). One day she visited, bringing cooked vegetables,

> and Christina mixed a bit of lard, and a little flour and some onion slices, added water, and brought it to a boil for a thickened broth that Frau Jaeger called flour soup. This time Mutter Boehler added some of the chopped vegetables, dill, onion and beet tops. The result was a mixture of high and low German soups, or so Ludwig called it. It was good. Mutter Boehler discovered that Christina had a knack for making something to eat out of almost nothing, and she took a dipperful home to her ailing husband. (P. 64)

V. Preparing for Winter, *1910*

That summer of 1910, when he realized he would have to supply himself with coal (a soft surface lignite) for the winter, "Ludwig began with a visit to Matt Crowley, who he found had just made a large beef stew, and aggravated as he was by the visit, Matt dipped out beef and potatoes which Ludwig ate hungrily," and when Crowley left the room, Ludwig "helped himself to a little more stew." (P. 65) Later, a sign that the two families might achieve some prosperity after all was Christina's being able to reciprocate by feeding others. In August of 1910, neighbors provided threshing machinery and Sophie and Christina cooked a meal for the threshers.

> Well, there was bread. Christina had done wonders, letting the dough rise again and again after punching it down, and placing loaves in large well-greased bread pans. All Christina needed, besides the everlasting yeast the Frau Boehler had given her, was a couple of handfuls of sugar, some salt, a bit of warm lard, and good milled flour, and she turned out eight massive loaves of golden brown bread. She gave credit for the well-risen bread to Sophie's wonderful cast-iron stove with its large oven. "*Du wa-aischt gar-net wie glicklich du bischt*" ("You do not know how fortunate you are"). By comparison, Christina felt all the more her own family's shortages. (P. 73)

Pauline Diede's account seldom quotes her mother explicitly, as it does her father and uncle, but a major portion of their history in fact centers on Christina, a woman who felt "shortages" throughout her life. Almost nothing in Christina's life in North Dakota appeared joyful.

> [Ludwig's] marriage to Christina by "Koopla," the arranged marriage, was not meeting his expectations. When he had first gone to her home with the marriage broker, they had found her placing raised bread dough in the oven, and four huge loaves of freshly baked bread were already on the table. Ludwig thought that if she could bake, they could eat, and she was attractive to look at as well. Men wanted their wives to be like their mothers, but Christina

> Steinert was not like Julianna Neher, especially in her intellect. Christina came from a progressive dorf [village], but other than Lutheran religious instruction [Ludwig's family were Baptists], she had had little schooling, and could not read or even write her name, unlike her older sister Sophie. This displeased Neher, because in Russia you were somebody if you knew how to read and write. His mother had taught him to write, read, and memorize scripture. (PP. 47–48)

Christina came to the marriage with high hopes—and girlish illusions. "It had not occurred to Christina, when she married the dashing soldier, that her childbearing years would be spent in such poverty. Her parents had been well off, and her dowry was good enough, but the money she had inherited had been used for [the] travel costs of immigration, and Ludwig had not received soldier's benefits from the Russo-Japanese War." (P. 69) Life had moved too quickly for Christina—from the safety of *dorf* life, with parents and grandparents, to the poverty and desolation of that strange journey and strange new land. By the time she tried to settle in to the homestead promise in North Dakota, Christina was exhausted, and preoccupied with bearing and caring for her children. Children were born in too rapid sequence, her daughter asserts, because men were unwilling to practice birth control, which, in rural areas, typically meant abstinence. (Despite Fred Martin's remarks about it being a wonder he and Sophie even slept together, the Martins had two more children in North Dakota.) Pauline Diede writes:

> Scriptural injunctions to "multiply" too often were the excuse to ignore common sense in birth control. Some who followed Biblical pronouncements literally thought there was nothing wrong with a surplus of children and were convinced that God will provide and that other people would help out families with many children and many needs. Every household had to be ready to feed a distressed neighbor who brought his throng of kids. (P. 74)

The issue of family planning even came up between the two families. While Christina was recuperating from the birth of Ottilia in the Jaegers' shed, Fred Martin rebuked Ludwig for wanting sexual relations with her so soon, and Ludwig became irritated, complaining that he felt unhappy at "not having his wife with him: '*Die natur verlangts*' ('Nature demands it')." Fred was not sympathetic—Ludwig's first child was a little over one year old, and the second less than two months: " '[Your wife] is better off where she is [in the summer kitchen]. Do you want to make her pregnant again?' Neher answered that it was fine for Martin to talk, he already had a good number of children" to work beside him clearing the land (P. 46).

The first time Ludwig visited Christina at the Jaegers', Mrs. Jaeger tried to prevent his having sexual relations with Christina. "Today Frau Jaeger was even more high-strung, for she knew why Ludwig had come and she did not want this already bereft young woman to become pregnant again. She ordered Christina to keep the baby sucking to prevent impregnation, and told Ludwig that Christina was still in the menses from childbirth and he should abstain. (*'Du sollst "fast" haben'*)." (P. 48) When Ludwig again stopped to see Christina on his return from the Bismarck trip with Fred, he found the children sick and Christina distraught: "Neher wanted comfort for body and soul and the warmth of a woman, [but] Frau Jaeger appeared, giving her usual stern admonishments." (P. 55)

When the Nehers departed the Jaegers' farm for their own homestead, Frau Jaeger "advised Neher one more time, as he left, to watch out lest he get his wife pregnant too soon again." (P. 58) She succeeded only a short while. When Elizabeth Boehler visited Christina she found her again *in andere umschtaenda* (in a family way): "*Ach, mir sen do-e for desz, mir weiver* (We are here for this, we women)," she said. (P. 85) Seventeen months after Ottilia, in October 1911, Christina gave birth to Pauline, the daughter who recounts her story. Just hours before the birth, their home was threatened by a prairie fire.

> Autumn was dry, and fire broke out in the Elm Creek neighborhood, one that took days to control. Men, women and children were summoned to help fight it. Neher hitched Bay to the stoneboat and upon it set a barrel of water along with a number of gunny sacks. Christina dipped a gunny sack into water, and struck at the advancing flames, doing as the neighbors did. But her back ached and she became aware that her unborn child had dropped considerably since the day before, a sign that she would soon deliver.
>
> Ludwig fetched Frau Jaeger and the two arrived in time for the good midwife to deliver the premature baby on October 10, 1911. Frau Jaeger named the baby after her own daughter, Pauline, and because she was convinced it would die, she performed proxy baptism, then wrapped the three-pound child in swaddling cloths which she had brought along. She injected into her mouth droplets of sweetened camomile tea. Frau Jaeger's daughter Pauline came to

> help Christina, who was to remain in bed for nine days, according to the belief that nine days was the time it took for the body to recover from childbirth. (P. 85)

And Diede adds, after describing her own birth:

> Ludwig and Christina had their first three babies in a period of two years and seven months. Then Elsie was born May 20, 1913; Louise on October 19, 1914; and finally a boy, Edwin, on December 21, 1916. By this time a kitchen built of lumber had been added to the regular sod room. The Martins had two more children, Martha and Albert, and the Nehers two more daughters, Anne and Clara. Babies came often, for it was considered necessary to raise a large family in order to have help with the work, even though mothers craved more time between births. (P. 85)

That meant nine children for the Martins (counting Mathilda, who had died) and eight for the Nehers.

Work was the overriding settlement experience. Work was not simply an occupation or the record of achievement—work strained the limits of physical strength. The work of women and children was performed with their bare hands. When Pauline Diede describes her mother fetching two buckets of water, we see not only how exhausting such a seemingly simple task could be, but also how the chore made connections among work, child care, and family relationships. The episode occurred shortly after Christina's arrival at the sod house following her confinement and her brief respite in Frau Jaeger's shed.

> Christina's first days on the homestead were hectic. Among many other things, she needed water for drinking and cooking. Ludwig had told her about the new well that gave water steadily. There was plenty of it, but using it for drinking and cooking was something else. Christina did not find it tasted as good as the water at [the] Jaegers'. Ludwig had been drinking from the well, but not steadily, and had suffered no ill effects. But Odeela [Ottilia] developed diarrhea, and there was nothing like toilet paper or changes of clothing to take care of her. Frau Bitterman was summoned. She said there was too much salt, potash, and soda in the water, and bid Christina to take clear water from a creek hole and boil it for camomile tea. Elizabeth Boehler, who lived not far away, grew a lot of camomile in her garden, Frau Bitterman said.

> Christina was glad that there were a few older women living nearby even if she did not have the security of Russian dorf life, where older people lived among the young, and where grandmothers had the last word as long as a man was not around. Christina needed help, for she was afraid. The Nehers had a barrel and two pails they had borrowed from Martin for water, and it was Christina's job to keep these filled so that the staves would not shrink from the rims and the barrel go to pieces. She needed clear good-tasting water to cook with and to make camomile tea. Over the hill to the south she found a water hole that had formed a pool of clear water (except for water insects on the top). She scooped water out with the dipper she had brought from Russia, then tied a cloth over the pail to strain out the water life. Then she had to lug the two pails full of water over the hill. Little Dilda [Matilda] ran along close by, rubbing her eyes, crying from the mosquitoes, and wanting her mother to carry her. Christina could not very well carry both pails and the fifteen-month-old as well. So she sat Dilda on her shoulders, expecting the child to hold on. But she had scarcely hoisted the two pails and taken a few steps when Dilda let go and began falling. Quickly Christina dropped one pail of water and grasped the frightened child. It took a long time to reach home and a lot of water had been lost, but Christina was glad to have what was left. . . . She had had enough of hauling water and now had to nurse the baby and her breasts were limp. There was hardly anything to cook, and everyone was hungry. . . .
>
> But there was not time enough to worry. While the sun shone, there was hay to make for winter feed for stock. But the two babies wailed most of the time probably because they did not have enough to eat and were uncomfortable in their itchy clothing. Christina was not prepared for living on the prairie alone, so unlike what she had known in the Russian dorf. She had two babies and a man she scarcely knew and she felt, all in all, thrust into chaos.
>
> (PP. 60–61)

Out of such chaos, exhaustion, and undernourishment, Christina Neher nevertheless managed to construct some ties of her own.

> Having Mutter Boehler as her closest neighbor made Christina feel secure. She was more open with her than with anyone else in expressing her feelings, and less intimidated by her than by Frau Jaeger. She appreciated all that Jaegers had done for her, and she wished she could be like the high Germans, but always felt inferior. Christina was a submissive person, but when she was with Mutter Boehler, life in those hills became more endurable even though it was never like the dorf where everyone minded everyone else's business. She grew to love Mutter Boehler, who encouraged her and gave her credit for what she did. (P. 64)

Intimidated as Christina felt among the Jaegers for having to accept food and lodging from them as well as listening to strictures about her sexual behavior, she nevertheless played a crucial role in her own family's economic survival. For example, she was the one to instruct Ludwig about threshing. However primitive her skills, it was Christina who knew about farming. Her daughter Pauline documents her work:

> Tortured days followed. Christina carried armsful of wheat down the hill to the threshing platform. Not wanting to wear out her only pair of shoes, she tied rags around her bare feet to protect them from cactus stickers. Ludwig borrowed a sledge hammer to beat out the wheat, then Christina carried armsful of straw into the yard, for if even a few heads of grain remained, they would be good for the cow. They had prepared a site for a round strawstack the night before at some distance from the haystack, so that if one burned, the other would not catch fire. Ludwig was beginning to learn about precarious North Dakota weather, that lightning could strike and start fires. Christina called on God to preserve their crop, for they needed every grain. Ludwig thought her behavior odd, although he remembered his mother also praying out loud, but that was different. He thought Christina weak, for he did not himself think that he needed God that badly. Christina sensed his mockery and had the nerve to tell him that he ought to become a convert. In Russia Christina had been to a revival meeting at her Lutheran Evangelical church, calling on her loving Saviour to redeem her from sin and promising to take Him into her heart. That is why she talked out loud as though God were right beside her, and often cried as well when she was very tired. (P. 68)

Rural life is supposed to be peaceful and farm work ennobling, the idealized setting for family concord. But for these families work was brutalizing. Neither Christina's skill, nor her expert knowledge about how to construct a threshing floor, spared her from hard labor.

> Every time Ludwig picked up the pitchfork that he had bought on time at his last visit to Hebron, he thought of how fortunate he was to be able to use something that handy, and how lucky he was that the lumberman trusted him until fall. Christina had to use her open arms and ten forked fingers to grasp armsful of ripened wheat and carry them to the gumbo floor. Then to rest herself she led Bay [the horse] round and round to stamp out as much of the wheat as possible. Then Ludwig would take grain ears and stalks to another stack, and they would sweep wheat and chaff into gunny sacks, the sacks and broom also having been placed on charge lists of Hebron businesses. (P. 70)

Certainly Christina was crucial to the threshing, and indeed the entire harvesting operation, contributing both labor and expertise, but Ludwig understood that as the man he was to be in charge. In later years, describing Christina's breakdown when the care of her children became too much, he felt sympathy for her plight. Ludwig's words came through his daughter, who wrote them down.

> Although Christina did not complain of her extreme fatigue and sore back, one evening she developed convulsions, and Ludwig did not know which way to turn. Both babies were screaming. He went to the Boehler homestead for help. . . . Good Elizabeth Boehler was willing to walk all that way in the night, declaring that Christina was being killed with work, that it was not human any more, and that she was to stay in bed until she got back her strength. . . .
>
> It was no wonder that Christina had been brought to a state of complete exhaustion by her ox-like labors, malnutrition, and worries about her little ones. She also was homesick. (P. 71)

In the first years of settlement there was, of course, a great deal of work to be done, none made easier by the lack of roads and social services, the scarcity of hired help, and, for many, an awful poverty. Nevertheless, among Germans from Russia, work took on a prominence that cannot always be attributed entirely to these conditions or to the nature of the tasks. There is an obsessive quality in the dedication to hard labor that one does not find among most other settlers of the period. Christina illustrates this bent when she went to work on a henhouse, again without tools—stooping, hauling buckets on foot, and making "gumbo" of mud for masonry. She was also pregnant with Pauline.

> Christina used a flat sharp-edged stone to loosen and scrape gumbo, cupped the silty soil into a pail, then lugged it over prairie hillocks, often spilling some on steep hills. She had reason to rest, lying down on prairie grass, and fancying the clouds were baby-carriages, for she knew she was pregnant again and worried that she would miscarry. (P. 84)

For Christina and Sophie and their children, physical demands were relentless: neither childbearing nor childhood was protected in the settlers' struggle to survive. The women and children were subject to the men, and the men were driven to distraction in their anxiety to provide for their families in a land that bewildered and perplexed them at every turn. The need to appear masterful was the inverse side of fear.

> This was a way of life that now cannot be described to fourth, fifth, and later generations. There was general abuse of minors in the family, children and wives, and it was considered discipline according to the Bible. (Of course such severe discipline did not prevail in every settler household.) Nevertheless the man in the family held all the rights, often making things hard on women folk. (P. 84)

Later Pauline Diede writes, "Most settlers were disciplinarians." She quotes Frau Boehler, who befriended her mother: "Females were for that, young or old, they were slaves, of inferior rating, and were subject to any kind of treatment due to a man being insecure about what life held in store for him and his family." (P. 86)

Children worked as soon as they were able, and always they were at the mercy of hunger, disease, neglect, and emotional as well as physical punishment. In this narrative, childhood hardly appears as the distinct life state celebrated by the middle class since at least the nineteenth century. Pauline Diede remembered well what it felt like to be little. Her descriptions of childhood episodes, both those she remembered and others she had been told of, dwell sometimes on disgusting details—neither childhood nor poverty supported gentility.

> I remember my two older sisters and me sleeping on a splintery board floor in the northwest corner of the sodhouse, and I remember crawling onto a tick that had rustling stuff in it. We three children had a feather filled cover and I sucked and chewed on one of the corners of that quilt. The three of us fought—each one wanted to suck a particular corner. Finally we felt each other's warmth and went to sleep.

The basic care of infants was also unsettling:

> I also remember Ma holding baby Louise on her lap and feeding her something in a spoon. Nearby stood a container of "kindes brei" (baby mush). It was a flour and water or milk mixture which was simmered on the stove to a sauce-like consistency. Ma took a spoonful of it and swished it around in her mouth,

> then fed it to the baby. Every midwife recommended that the brei should first be mixed with the mother's saliva before being fed to the baby. It was considered the proper way, and no worse than the baby sucking from a mother's breast. Even as a child of four years, it made me gag.[7]

Poverty was a list of humiliations. Children in the Martin and Neher households did their part begging. Ludwig remembered: "Our boys had a way of running about and showing their hunger. Some of the more established immigrant families realized our dilemma. One day our oldest son, John, brought me a large hunk of fresh bread soaked in chokecherry syrup, and it was good." (P. 22)

At first the parents were not aware of the potential dangers of contaminated water. The boys, Fred said,

> would simply lie flat on the ground and drink from a pool, swallowing what gave them intestinal worms. . . . [They] ailed and lost strength, but it was not hard to guess what was wrong, as those pinworms in the intestinal tract acted up, especially at night. Mrs. Bitterman [the local midwife and herbalist] investigated. She greased her forefinger and reached into the rectum of one of the boys, grabbing hold of a nest of worms. She boiled up a bitter drink that caused vomiting. (P. 39)

The parents' search for medical help for ailing infants tells something about both folk medicine and childcare: "[The] Nehers lived in no more than a squat on the prairie, hardly fit for babies. Odeela was colicky and screamed at night, and Dilda followed suit. Mrs. Bitterman smeared their bellies and exercised their arms and legs, and the babies fell asleep." (P. 5) Most farm women were accomplished herbalists. Elizabeth Boehler grew "plants for many uses: medicine, perfume, and insect repellent. . . . Gardens were her specialty, and she would talk out loud to vegetables, encouraging watermelons and pumpkins to grow fast, and she was an expert with herbs, knowing just which ones were mild for children, and which stronger for older people. She felt called on to help others." (P. 63)

One morning Ludwig summoned Elizabeth Boehler out of bed very early after a night of the baby's screaming, having decided that "Odeela needed to be 'braucht.' " Pauline Diede explains also about a practice of tightly binding infants' abdomens and wrapping them "so that no fresh air could reach them. . . . Women believed in such practices and passed them down from one generation to the next; for most women, that was the extent of their education." One night there had been a thunderstorm, and when Ludwig and Elizabeth Boehler arrived at the Nehers', they found the house very smoky from a downdraft, and Christina with Dilda, who had been coughing. "When Ludwig and Mutter Boehler arrived, Odeela had stopped whimpering, but Mrs. Boehler, noticing how pale she was, brought her outdoors for air to revive her." (P. 64)

And sometimes neighbor women, versed in the lore of "the old country," were dangerous too. On one occasion, "instead of removing the band around the baby's abdomen covering her navel [Mrs. Bitterman] tightened it, and despite the heat, wrapped the child even more, in the belief that air, whether summer or winter, caused illness. She was only acting according to what had been passed down to her from elder-women in the old country. She performed 'brauching,' rubbing with vinegar and fat, moving the baby's arms and legs in rhythmic motions while she said a holy meditation." This time she wrapped the child again, but instead of sleeping, Odeela fell into convulsions. Christina and Ludwig took her first to the Martins', where they got a team and wagon, then to the Jaegers', "dismissing Frau Bitterman to walk home alone dejectedly and wondering what she had done wrong." Along the way, "Christina loosened the naval band and other wrappings, giving the baby more air. It was the right thing to do, even though it violated old wives' practices." Mrs. Jaeger treated Odeela for what she called infected lungs: "She placed a heated bag of oats in a woolen sock on the baby's chest, replacing it with another when it cooled. She bathed the infant in cool vinegar water to cut the fever, and in a few hours Odeela fell asleep, having been fed an oatmeal 'brei' or pap." (PP. 68–69) Mrs. Jaeger responded with special warmth to this child she had delivered and sent the parents home with an extra baby bottle.

Pity was the primary emotion the Neher infants evoked from other adults. The time Matt Crowley helped Ludwig dig coal, he stopped at the Nehers' house.

> On this visit, Matt met Christina and the two little ones for the first time, and noticed the bare circumstances under which this poor shy woman had to carry on, the family's actual destitution. He caressed Dilda, running his fingers through her hair and set her on his knee as he squatted on the ground, the rancher's usual position for accommodating a cup of coffee. Dilda loved the attention, chattering away in German baby-talk. She guided the friendly stranger indoors to see her baby sister Odeela lying in a wooden box lined

> with a straw-filled mattress. She had a little pillow Frau Jaeger had made with fine feathers of prairie chickens. Matt Crowley was touched by the sight of these children. The baby was tightly wrapped in swaddling clothes and sucking on its fist. He reached for the baby's other hand when Dilda pulled it out of the tight wrappings. He opened the tiny fingers and wrapped them around his forefinger, feeling its softness. He was moved by the pathetic one-room house and the family's struggle to survive, and he was not sorry to have taken time to try to help. Although Matt Crowley could neither speak to nor understand Mrs. Neher, he showed her that he admired her, for she was a good looking woman. But Christina was ill at ease, and wished that she had some of her good sweet bread to serve with coffee as she would have done in Russia. (PP. 65–66)

And when he came to cut the Nehers' grain, again "Matt walked over to the house to look at the children. Odeela sucked on his finger and Dilda pulled on his pants. He had nothing to give them except affection and pity, thinking that next time he would carve a toy for them to play with." (P. 67)

> The winter of 1910–1911 was one of the most lonely times, a true initiation into the rigors of Dakota winters. The winter before, having twelve in the boxcar at Ashley was crowded, but there was company along with the hardship. Now Christina complained of feeling ill from the smoke and foul air in the one room with dirt walls and a stove giving out puffs of smoke. Rubbing clothes on a washboard, rinsing in water from melted snow and then slowly drying them piece by piece, such labor got the best of her good nature. She was irritable and scolded a lot and had little patience with the little ones.
>
> (PP. 81–82)

VI. The Later Years, *1911 and After*

Christina and the babies were not the only ones to resent the immigration venture. Ludwig, like his brother-in-law Fred Martin, had deep reservations as well. More often thoughts of Russia came to him when he was unhappy. On the day he bought the horse Bess from Jack Crowley, he was so homesick that he "sat on the stone near his unfinished sod house, eating his brined side pork and bread. He fell to his knees, clutching the stone, and screamed." (P. 47)

Another time, after one of his visits to Christina in the summer kitchen, carrying home a box of Mrs. Jaeger's supplies, "he kept thinking about the fertile level fields of Russia and wishing he were back, even though he did not like the Russian government that had no respect for German colonists. . . . He felt the hopelessness of turning over prairie sod into productive soil when he had nothing to work with and was discouraged at every turn. His mother would tell him to pray, but he knew supplies would not come with prayer." He also knew that his mother would have said, "Son, you cry. But God will supply. What is there in your box? Food? Then thank God for it." (P. 49) After a thunderstorm that Ludwig thought had destroyed the oats he had scythed, "he stretched his arms to the eastern horizon and called on his mother, using her familiar words: *'Nim den Heiland in dei herz un laz Im dich staercha un fuehra'* ('Take the Lord into your heart and let Him strengthen and lead you')." (P. 62)

When news came of his father's death, Ludwig felt more homesick than ever for his mother: "Nothing made him give way so readily to tears as the mention of the word 'mother,' for thinking of her brought tender memories and homesickness for Russia herself. . . . Ludwig recalled the time his father was assigned the worst of Russia's silty, clay land, where they could not raise enough wheat to chew on, and now here in America he had only hills and stones for his allotment." (P. 71) The second spring, 1911, Ludwig despaired of being able to plow his wheatfield with his one-horse, one-share plow. He went to Matt Crowley, "and for the first time Matt saw Ludwig cry," and of course helped him. (P. 83) In the last pages of her book Pauline Diede writes, "I have heard both my father and Uncle Fred Martin say that they would rather forget those terrible first winters of homesteading. *'Mir kenn's gar net mit worta erklaera; diez waren verachten zeita'* ('We cannot explain in words; those were desperate times')." (P. 86)

In the midst of their doubts and their homesickness, the two families vied with each other. Fred Martin felt superior to Ludwig because he had more money and felt he was a better manager, but he also was jealous of what he thought was Ludwig's use of poverty for his own gain. Ludwig learned English more quickly; that, and his more outgoing manner, Fred thought, gave him unfair advantages.

The men felt their lives tied together, and yet, like brothers, each resented the "advantages" they saw materializing in the way of the other; they competed throughout their lives for the crumbs of luck that might be found along the way. Once, it occurred to Fred that he had the money to buy the horse that Ludwig, with no money to pay for it, had borrowed from Matt Crowley. But Fred "knew this was an evil idea that had a way of creeping into his thinking in bad times, for he could not play that kind of trick on his brother-in-law." (P. 50) However, he could not have been very serious, for he confided his thoughts to Ludwig. And "when he let Neher in on the idea, Neher complained again that he was the one who had made preliminary negotiations, and that Martin was reaping the benefits while he had nothing. . . . Neher even claimed that Martin had been able to continue making money while he, Neher, had had to serve in the Japanese war; it wasn't right. Martin only smirked." (PP. 58–59)

This rivalry survived into Pauline Diede's own childhood, for she recalled, "the Martin family continued more prosperous than [the] Nehers. With a good supply of teenage boys and girls, Fred and Sophie Martin had better workers and more land and more stock. They enjoyed luxuries, like wax candles at Christmas which the children in my own family were denied. I remember Martha unwrapping red tissue paper and finding a lace trimmed pettycoat. It wasn't so much the pettycoat I minded, but the rustle of the bright colored paper." (PP. 85–86).

Although rivalries and hard times persisted, the families' extreme desperation softened when they established houses, tilled fields, and built ties within the community. And as they relaxed even a little, they grew to feel a renewed concern for religion. The men particularly had got out of the habit of religious observance. When Fred was struggling with recalcitrant oxen, he once cursed them as damned asses (*ihr verdamte Esel*) even though he "had pledged himself to the Lord at a revival meeting in Russia." (P. 46) "[One] Sunday his conscience bothered him. He remembered how in Russian dorfs Sunday was deemed holy," yet people around him were not going to church. Fred Martin "found himself praying again for help," and he decided "from then on to have a simple Sunday afternoon prayer and Bible reading," a plan that pleased Sophie and Christina. (P. 78) The women helped organize religious services, and gradually other German from Russia families joined, "some trudging over snow, others on horseback or by horse-drawn stone boat." It sometimes took more time to get there than to conduct the service, "but they were together." These services were religious in the deepest sense. Anxiety, physical danger, loneliness, emotional strains among family members and between husbands and wives were woven into the service. Release and pleasure came

The children of Fred and Sophie Martin: (FRONT ROW) Emelia, Albert, Martha; (BACK ROW) George, Fred, Lena, John, Henry.

from the simple art of group singing—all these elements were important to the occasion.

> The group sang, to a rhythmic beat, evangelical songs they had memorized in the old country. A leader kept the singing going, for hymn books with music were not common in those days. They discussed scripture openly, and a convert [new member] was apt to admonish others of their sins. Women went to their knees and cried their woes out to God, but if a woman spoke of her man's abuse, she was scolded then and there. These people realized how much they needed help beyond themselves. Getting together was their one human contact to ease loneliness. They were soothed and gained strength to endure another week. (P. 81)

These services allowed emotional expression, the enjoyment of company and song, but they also served to reassert men's physical power over women as part of the process of readmitting God's spiritual power.

Pauline Diede describes as well, albeit briefly, better times. She remembered that her father could also be pleasant: "When he was rested, he often became a different person. It brought out his sense of humor. He was a smart man, no doubt with his mother's brains, able to figure things out more quickly than most people." (P. 80) Sometimes he and others found moments of relief in landscape and countryside, as Christina did in the spring of 1911, when she "took two-year-old Dilda for a walk while baby Odeela slept, and she felt invigorated by being outdoors." (P. 83) There were other pleasures:

> The wholeness and fruits of the great outdoors, the times when Pa bought each of us a pencil box with a few crayons out of the goodness of his heart; the times he told stories that made everybody laugh; the times Ma hovered over us as we lay in high fever, bending over and saying, "*Ach, du liebes kind, du bischt ja so krank*" ("You dear child, you are so sick"). Once there was nothing to eat but corn meal mush swimming in fat and Pa said if he couldn't eat it, then the children couldn't either. . . . As we grew older, there were times spent around the organ, and how Pa relished singing along with his children; the times Pa taught us German scripture and led morning devotions; the many good meals Ma prepared from scratch. She taught us to be neat and clean. (P. 86)

But a better economic situation did not give the children leisure.

> Our clan of growing girls were brought up to strict hard work, especially the two eldest, Matilda and Ottilia, who became field workers. They were expected to do as much work as a man . . . hauling hay and pitching bundles for the threshing machine. . . . I . . . was chore girl to help mother with domestic work, which I did not like, and often was slapped by my mother. I much preferred being outdoors, and was very curious, traits that brought much trouble to my relationship with my mother. (PP. 86–87)

The family finally succeeded in buying a neighboring farm and moved into the three-room wooden house, "a luxury for my mother." But the luxury of a real home did not make work disappear: "All of us cleared stones from new broken fields, and manured barns, part of the hard manual labor that was every-day work for us. We were raised strictly, scraping and digging coal, digging fence post holes and throwing hay up the barn stairs, and we grew up as did many children on the prairie." (P. 87)

Pauline Diede's narrative ends: "My father acquired two sections of land in Mercer County, North Dakota, brought it into cultivated grain fields, and lost practically everything during the Depression. All that work, and for what? For [the] children, life promised better. On the whole we had good country schooling and the advantages of an open and free life on the prairie where we learned to work, to pray and to forgive." (P. 87) How free was the life she describes, with dirt, cramped quarters, hunger, poverty, and lack of easy access to schooling, medical care, or sociability? At the least, her narrative maintains, they were spared the Russian Revolution, grounds enough, perhaps, to account for her patriotism, and the closing words of her story: "America is a great country. Yes indeed."

The Neher-Martin narrative recounts deprivation, hunger, and near starvation; men who lacked understanding of the women and children in their own families. It includes coarse details: bedbugs aboard ship and in the boxcar mattresses, worms in army sauerkraut, worms in a child's rectum. And Pauline Diede does not remember, she says, much affection coming from her mother: "Our Ma had very little time for her [a sister, Elsie, who slept in a box and cried a lot] since there was another baby that constantly yelped or whimpered. . . . I cannot ever remember Ma taking time to hold me. . . . It seemed so many pioneer mothers had no time, nor patience, nor ability to reason. There was no time to talk or teach, only punish when something went wrong."[8] In newspaper columns, Pauline Diede has detailed the exhausting work of children: milking, washing clothes, cleaning house, and ironing, in a constant war against dirt.[9] Her mother worked even harder at housecleaning when they moved from the sod structure with its dirt floor and walls into the poorly insulated frame house. "Prairie women judged every woman ruthlessly on how her wash looked. Ma was no exception; she was sure her reputation as a homemaker rested on the number of wrinkles there were after the tedious task of ironing."[10]

Much of the suffering of such women was undeserved, and their contribution undervalued.

> Pioneer mothers, like my own, journeyed through life meeting hardships and denials, many dying of a broken heart for want of a word of praise, and few knowing how much they had left behind. These women endured indifference, seldom hearing a word of approval or kindness. What do I remember most? I often found my mother crying, and wonder whether she cried of fatigue, craving a word of recognition, gratitude, or praise. She was deprived of these, through lack of knowledge, through our pride or plain indifference, and I have lived to regret that I did not speak more loving words when she was still alive. . . . Not only did she look after her household and the hundreds of duties there, she was expected to be first hand help with outdoor work. Her day began at dawn and did not end until the small hours. The family's livelihood often demanded of a woman something beyond human endurance. Cooking and sewing for large families turned women into old ladies before their time.[11]

What can we know of these families? In their first two years in North Dakota they were hardly touched by community institutions: schools, churches, welfare agencies, hospitals, or government or private organizations. Although some of the children eventually did go to school—articles Mrs. Diede wrote for the Hebron, North Dakota, *Herald* describe that one-room schooling—the Martin child's initial attempt ended in futility. He was sent only because he was the least useful child at home, but he lacked the language, the stamina, and even the food in his lunch pail to continue. Such poverty does not cement closeness; husbands and wives in both couples claim scant acquaintance. The rule of the men meant that when men needed the sympathy and companionship of women rather than their wifely subservience, women and men both lacked the language and gestures to achieve that communion. Women like Christina and Sophie could only "follow" their husbands; they could not look for friendship in that direction. As for children, families felt too crowded sometimes even to appreciate who was there: Ludwig held a newborn daughter with a feeling close to surprise; their mother was too harried to caress her babies. Memories of child life were of bodies huddled together: Pauline and her sisters under quilts, the many Martin children on top of a table during a flood. And always the commitment to staying alive, to preparing soil for crops, spending no more on household comforts than just enough to keep people able to work. The quest was for food, for something to eat.

Between 1909 and 1911 these families kept together because they could not afford to be apart—separation would have endangered their physical survival. Separately, they would have starved to death. The "coyote hole" way of life meant proximity at a crude level, but not necessarily intimacy or affection; crowding made amicable relationships more difficult. Even so, the women saw to "family," to the small recurring habits, the private gestures and personal kindnesses. These sustaining qualities were what Ludwig missed in his mother, the "cuddles" the grandparents gave the first children before they left Russia. On that exhausting journey with the buckets of water, Christina left the youngest infant unattended in the house, but she strained herself to carry both the toddler and the water. Neighbor women, when they gave food and household goods to the Nehers, were not merely doling out charity. Their gifts matched their sense of what was needed: rags for diapers, boxes for storage, herbs for soup. For all her impoliteness, Mrs. Jaeger was thinking of the family's survival when she tried to shame Ludwig from impregnating Christina. She also was thinking of making them more like herself, more "American."

The lives of children have improved over the centuries, partly because parents have grown increasingly sympathetic to children. Puritan parents did their best to beat the evil out of their children, but since then most parents have come to see children as progressively less threatening to social order, and have treated them correspondingly more gently. The "cuddles" the older Martin children remembered from their grandparents in Russia attest to such gentler attitudes.[12]

Nevertheless, historical changes do not move at the same rate for all persons, and the progressive history of childhood has advanced at uneven rates, even back-stepping for children in such families as the Martins and Nehers. Rural and farm children have been slowest to benefit from changing attitudes as well as from the improved medical and social care that increasingly became available to children in more urban communities. The Keating-Owen Act of 1916, "An Act to Prevent Interstate Commerce in the Products of Child Labor and for Other Purposes," was struck down as interfering with interstate commerce—"The goods shipped are of themselves harmless," an argument that sounds like the one about guns not killing people. Children under fourteen would have been prohibited from working; between ages fourteen and sixteen they could work only eight hours a day and six days a week and only between six in the morning and seven at night. The publisher of the *Southern Textile Bulletin*, David Clark, spoke for those who opposed any child labor legislation when he said in Senate testimony against the 1916 bill that even though mill work could not be said not to harm children, children who worked in mills appeared to him to be "better looking people than the first generation that came from the mountains. . . . My theory is that the work in the mills is not as hard or as injurious as the work on the farms. The promoters of this bill have not the nerve to include the farms or even to refer to the farms."[13]

Whatever the national debate in the early 1900s, child protection legislation is not a subject the Martins and Nehers say anything about. To the contrary, in 1911 Fred Martin put out to labor two of his children in a manner that child labor protectionists would have prevented if they could. An Irish neighbor, fed up with improvident German-Russians settling near his ranch, made a suggestion to a newly arrived farmer in "the Golden Valley" to the north of the Martins' farm. The man was looking for draft animals and was told, "There, way down on the south side of the first long hill another Rooshen has settled with a bunch of kids. You might get a couple of them if you buy them each a pair of shoes." The farmer took this advice and found Fred constructing a shed for his animals. Magdalena, John, and the other children were hauling stones for the foundation. Pauline Diede recounts:

> The man pointed out that while Martin had more than enough children to get his work done, he needed two because he was not yet through with his threshing, would Martin give him a pair? This cunning dealer had come at just the right time, for Martin had grown impatient with his children, and right on the spot, without even consulting Sophie, he hired out Magdalena and John. His word was command.
>
> Packing the children's clothes was no problem, for they had little more than what they wore, and both were barefoot, good enough reason for a quick

agreement and a resolution on the employer's part to buy them each a pair of shoes for the winter when he sold his wheat. Quickly Magdalena and John found themselves in the stranger's wagon, with hardly a decent goodbye and rather frightened to be leaving their brothers so suddenly. Sophie was highly perturbed to think that her oldest children were taken away and gone she know not where, and she gave way to scolding: "*Noch net a-mol do-oter waz saaga, so gscheid sin sie. Wel-ar a-a mann isch*" ("Not telling me anything. He thinks he is so smart, just because he is the man").

The weeks that followed were a terrible ordeal for the two Martin children. The work was treacherous and far too hard. For Magdalena it was never-ending; milking one cow after another tortured her because her hands were weak. At her own home she worked steadily, but also had chances to sit on the shady side of the house and dream a bit about her beloved grandparents so far away who had caressed her when she was a little girl. Now there was no such thing as a gentle human touch. Yesterday she had been a small girl, and today expected to take on adult responsibilities. She often screamed at this crude man who only told her to hurry up, there was much work to be done before bedtime. And the homesteader's wife was no better, an obstinate and filthy woman, in a mulish way always ready for an argument. Most of her energy went to angry outbursts, swinging her arms and screeching that Magdalena and John would not get their new shoes if they did not show more will to work. Nights were the worst times for the Martin children, for, when they ought to have been getting much needed rest, they were plagued by bedbugs. The house was foul with dirt, a perfect place for bedbugs to thrive. Magdalena remembered the bedbugs on board ship, and how upset her mother had been, and now she reacted similarly. She was frightened. If she had known the way home, she and her brother would have started right then.

One Saturday evening the slave-driving man threatened to beat John for crying, saying he was not worth having around. That night John got sick. He cried and cried and cried, and Magdalena shed tears as never before. First the bedbugs, and now her brother in such a feverish condition was too much for her. She cried aloud for her parents, and the "pig woman" as she called her told her to be quiet and go to sleep. Magdalena was horrified by these people's filthy dress, house, and yard, and even by their language.

As if by second sight, Sophie had not given her Fred any peace the whole time her children were gone. She nagged and scolded. That Saturday night she had a premonition that something was very wrong with her children, and she said she was going to them if she had to walk. Fred gave in, and early Sunday morning the dispirited Martins made their way northward with a wagon and team, inquiring along the way for the whereabouts of the family. There was not much conversation between them, for Sophie was greatly troubled about her children.

By Sunday morning John's fever had subsided but he was subdued. He blinked his half-shut swollen eyes and ignored the stern order to eat the grits before him as he sat close to his sister at the table. John spent most of the forenoon sitting by the side of the sod house petting the bedraggled and half-starved dog who craved affection as much as food. The dog let out a low growl when the man and woman left with their team and buggy to a church service, where they would have much to reckon for. Magdalena was scratching her bedbug sores. Suddenly, Doby, the dog, perked up his ears, then barked and ran south where there was a wagon approaching on the horizon. John ran to the windmill and climbed it. He started to cry. If it was his parents, it would be for gladness; if it was not, he would cry for grief and homesickness. He saw that it was his father and mother, but, now insulted and angry, he clung to the high windmill, his hands clasped to the shaft. "*Ach Gott, kind, komm doch runder*" ("O God, child, come down") Sophie called out to him as she descended from the wagon, holding out her hands to him, looking up and pleading that she had felt a warning that all was not well with her children.

Sophie wrote a note in German, informing these strange people that they had taken the children home with them. The Martins drove home at a fast pace, Magdalena in the back of the wagon hearing those two dirty people scold and scold, and John between his "*Baba un Mama*," feeling their warmth and security. Both Magdalena and John suffered emotionally. They had been torn too soon from their home in Grozsliebental, and the harsh conditions of the past year made them grow up too quickly. The homesteader appeared at the Martins' some time later to say that he was disappointed in his two hirelings, especially at what he called the evil boy who was not worth anything. There was an argument, but he handed Martin a few dollars which purchased Magdalena and John each a pair of shoes. (PP. 74–77)

This story of indentured children shares some elements with fairy tales: the ominous farmer and wicked wife; children sent off the parents know not where; their eventual poignant rescue. It also resembles a fairy tale in what is left out—nothing is said about how parents and children reconciled themselves to each other afterward.

Rural poverty has been less well understood than urban poverty; one might almost infer that poverty in a rural setting hardly exists, because two of the concomitants of urban poverty—crowding and lack of food—presumably do not exist for rural people, who have land on which to grow food, and all outdoors to move around in. But as the Nehers and Martins demonstrate, living space in the country can be excessively crowded and unsanitary, and "all outdoors" can mean being cut off from neighbors, from help, and from support. Furthermore, to harvest a garden you have to have been there to plant it, with seeds, equipment, and suitable soil. And you have to know how to do a lot of other things besides: how to build housing, supply clean water, arrange sanitation, find fuel, and so on.

Excruciating poverty was the primary condition governing the lives of the Martin and Neher families between 1909 and 1911. They had not nearly enough money to sustain farm and household in anything like reasonable comfort and safety, and consequently they had little thought to spare for their children. When children were not labor and economic assets, they were nuisances, and seldom objects of protection. And as for women, Christina's case may be extreme, but is probably not unusual. Even though she was the one who knew how to make gumbo mortar for the henhouse, thresh grain, and devise soup out of flour and not much else, her skills did not lessen her work. Her convulsions after threshing and her premature delivery of the third child after a day beating wet rags onto burning grass fires attest to what it cost her to emigrate from a relatively comfortable Russian village. As years went by, with increased prosperity, a frame house (and more children), Christina did less field work and restricted herself to the house and milk barn. She may then have enjoyed somewhat greater autonomy. Competing with neighbor women for the whitest wash, while that sounds like an incongruous burden to put upon oneself, nevertheless was more a matter of her own choosing than was competing with bedbugs. Certainly work for her never ceased, but as obsessive as her domestic discipline of her daughters sounds, it represented a way of living less desperate than the one that called so often for *brauching* screaming infants.

The tough-times-but-we-made-it chorus to so many pioneer reminiscences, often sung by the children of those first settlers, implies that country living, however stark, makes people good; it brings them close together, it nurtures strong affections and family ties. Hardship is said to build character, but it did not cement closeness. Both Martin and Neher parents had married through the offices of a matchmaker and claimed to have gained little intimate acquaintance as the years went on. Parents were distant from their children, even if they could not get away from them. Fred Martin often spoke of a "coyote hole" way of life, typified by the bedful of infants sucking on the same blanket. There is no reason not to take Fred Martin at his word that he was motivated, as he expressed it, by "hope for a better land for our children and ourselves," yet the immediate effect on children of these extraordinary removals was, at best, a precarious survival. Children for the most part were overlooked. "We did not even recognize a girl's needs," Fred Martin reflected years later about his eldest daughter.

The poverty of women is made worse by their children, and any child is bound to suffer whose mother is poor. The legacy is complicated and full of contradictions. Pauline Diede, by recounting without adornment the daily happenings among her relatives, makes it difficult to deny that heritage of poverty in the settlement of the west. Yes, it was done for the children, and yet in spite of the strong appreciation with which the book closes—"I have no regrets, nor illwill. More important that they chose America! A thousand thanks and tears of joy"—the contents of the book reckon the cost, and it was considerable.

It is little wonder that it was difficult for Pauline Diede to record her family's move to the North Dakota homestead. Even when she was little, adults were not eager for her to learn about her background, sensing the shame in so much poverty. Three months after she had interviewed her father, he died, and, she writes, "In my sorrow I dreamed of him incessantly and determined to write out his story." Her uncle, Fred Martin, was preoccupied with caring for Sophie, who had suffered a stroke, and only after her death was he "more ready to engage in interviews." From these men and other neighbors, Diede obtained fruitful interviews, but details of the women's lives she found more difficult to reach: "Only when I asked Uncle Fred about his marriage with Aunt Sophie would he not open up." Except that she scolded and was unhappy about having left Russia, Fred said little about his wife. Sophie's sister Christina likewise is shadowy behind the stories men told: "My mother also spoke to me, but briefly, of those experiences." (P. 5)

Pauline Diede mentions a number of reasons for writing her book. "Germans from Russia were not valued enough," and she certainly has added to information about a little-known ethnic group. She wanted to instruct her children and grandchildren, to whom the book is dedicated, so that they and other young people would understand something about "a way of life that now cannot be described." (P. 184) She also wants to celebrate her own growing up, her appreciation for the countryside and for the efforts her parents made on her behalf, feelings she expresses in patriotic fervor: "I love every part of the Knife River prairies. America is a great country! Yes indeed."

Yet America was a country that might well have let these families starve. Having lured settlers onto land, the "country" did nothing more. There was no public transportation in rural areas, no schools or hospitals; no agency other than real estate companies provided information about farming conditions and agricultural methods appropriate to the northern plains.

Writing about her family's experiences, Pauline Diede was willing to search out and reveal more information than most accounts do. Some of her story remains shrouded in the contradictions: Germans from Russia have been neglected in history, and they were despised when they came as an impoverished minority. But how such ostracism and hardship are to be turned into a heritage that descendants can be proud of is not clear. The experiences are there, and somehow affirmation must be wrung from them. Ultimately, the goal of the Martins' and Nehers' journey was achieved—they established themselves on homestead farms and their children moved into American culture. Although the Nehers lost their farm during the Depression, and did not feel their own lot had improved from the days in the Russian *dorf* ("All that work, and for what?"), the fact that their third daughter some seventy years later wrote, in English, the story of those troublesome years seems proof that they had attained the American Dream—a place in the middle class.

And yet much of this moving story concerns those family members who did not come near to achieving the dream. Poverty, physical weakness, possibly psychological disorder, and estrangement from her husband were Christina's share in the New World. Of her sister Sophie, who also baffled and frightened her husband, we know even less. These women, and Lena as well, remained outsiders, unassimilated immigrants in their own families, let alone in the land toward which they must have journeyed with silent hope.

Pauline Diede, like so many children of immigrants of her generation, pivots between her several cultures, displaying the aspirations and the sufferings of a migration halfway around the world. She describes longing still for the "cuddles" of her Russian grandparents whom she was born too late to know, and she is repelled by remembering the smell and touch of "suck nodes" in the crowded bed in the crowded shanty. She expresses anger at the violence that controlled women and children in families, the fear of men that women lived under, and the fear of the environment, of injury, of failure that men tried to hold at bay. There is regret for the lack of feeling expressed among family members, and the small humiliations that came from lack of privacy and from ignorance and silence about sexuality. Her accounts leave us feeling saddened that there should have been such suffering at a time and in a country that elsewhere enjoyed mounting prosperity. And yet Pauline Diede's writing makes no attempt to resolve the contradictions between the "harrowing experiences" she described and her insistence that "America is a great country! Yes indeed."

The purpose of this book is to praise. The sufferings it records, like the stigmata of saints' lives, are intended to appear nearly impersonal—to the glory of something higher, country and prosperity if not God. There is no bragging about hardships, nothing to make us think anyone was strengthened by misery; if anything, we watch the parents weakening with each emergency. The praise comes for the survivors, now, in the present, who, Pauline Diede appears to be saying, hallow the land that gave rise to their suffering, precisely because they are here, still, to tell

The Neher family in the late 1920s: (FRONT ROW) Edwin, Ludwig, Clara, Christina, Anne; (BACK ROW) Matilda (born in Russia), Ottilia, Pauline, Elsie, Louise.

the tale. In the mind of such resisters there is no contradiction between praise and suffering. We are not intended to be saddened by the exhaustion, the inarticulateness, and the general unhappiness of these protagonists. But we cannot help it. Pauline Diede is eloquent in telling what neither she nor we actually want to know: that for all too many, the settlement experience may well have come to a bitter trade of lives for a pair of shoes.

Notes

1. Pauline Neher Diede, *Homesteading on the Knife River Prairies*, ed. Elizabeth Hampsten, with an introduction by William C. Sherman, published under the auspices of the North Dakota Germans from Russia Heritage Society (Bismarck, N.D., 1983). Page numbers following quotations are to this edition.

2. These movements are described by Timothy J. Kloberdanz in "Plainsmen of Three Continents, Volga Germans' Adaptation to Steppe, Prairie, and Pampa," *Journal of the American Historical Society of Germans from Russia*, Summer 1982, pp. 29–37.

3. Since 1981 Pauline Neher Diede has been writing columns under the title "Prairie Echoes" for the Hebron (North Dakota) *Herald*, a weekly newspaper. These are based on reminiscences of her childhood and anecdotes from that period. This quotation is from the column for June 8, 1983.

4. Those participating in this second movement searched for lands as similar as possible to those they were leaving in Russia. Thus, from settlements of the Volga Germans, for instance, Kloberdanz recounts, scouts set out in 1874 for the Great Plains, and returned with a pound of Nebraska earth and a handful of prairie grass, souvenirs that persuaded 1,500 Volga Germans in the summer of 1876 to leave Russia for Kansas. Similar excursions began in 1877 for Argentina and in 1893 for western Canada.

5. William Sherman, *Prairie Mosaic: An Ethnic Atlas of Rural North Dakota* (Fargo: North Dakota Institute for Regional Studies, 1983), passim. William Sherman has mapped foreign, Native American, and other North American settlements in North Dakota county by county. The maps locate where people of various groups

lived, and the text describes the development of towns, churches, schools, and other institutions affiliated with each group.

6. Letter to Elizabeth Hampsten, October 30, 1983.

7. Diede, "Prairie Echoes."

8. Pauline Neher Diede, "A Settlement Childhood: Work," *Plainswoman*, February 1982, pp. 10–13. This quotation is from p. 12.

9. Diede, "Prairie Echoes."

10. Diede, "A Settlement Childhood," p. 13.

11. Ibid.

12. See, for instance, Robert H. Bremner, ed., *Children and Youth in America: A Documentary History* (Cambridge, Mass.: Harvard University Press, 1971); Neil Postman, *The Disappearance of Childhood* (New York: Delacorte Press, 1982); and Lloyd DeMause, "The Evolution of Childhood," *Journal of Psychohistory* 1, 4 (Spring 1974): 503–75.

13. Bremner, p. 709.

4. Families and Frontiers: A Reading for Our Time

Home is a notion that only nations of the homeless fully appreciate and only the uprooted comprehend.
WALLACE STEGNER, *Angle of Response*

Frontiers have always held special significance in American history. In 1893, Frederick Jackson Turner called our frontiers the most distinctive factor in the American experience, setting their egalitarian stamp on our democracy and character.[1] *Frontiers transformed the first settlers into grand individualists and gave rise to a national folklore. Frontiers nurtured concepts of "the strenuous life" and Manifest Destiny and of the political expressions of those attitudes. There have been farming frontiers, ranching frontiers, mining frontiers, frontiers of space, frontiers of thought. For more than three hundred years, expanding frontiers have been part of the American heritage.*

However frontiers may be described, however explored, something curious happens when frontiers are considered in the context of families. The field between them is immediately charged, for a frontier suggests that which is expansive and unlimited, and family implies boundaries. The terms do not come together. The American Dream is the vision of new possibilities and unexplored opportunities. But it is also "a dream of the Pilgrim's homecoming—a vision, finally, not of voyages . . . but of safe arrivals."[2] *The American Dream may be a home of one's own, but an endlessly expanding horizon does not bring it closer. Frontier and family—the drama that is played out between them is enacted anew in each generation of our history.*

A frontier is first and above all the space beyond the last settlement, an unconstructed region with no organizing systems—no maps, no roads, no outposts. Frontiers are volatile environments in which men do not control the natural world and are subject to chance encounters. The sudden blizzard that swept in after a warm day in North Dakota; the Columbia River that rose over its banks to flood crops; flash fires that burned mining shacks like so much tinder; Indian wars—"If you should not get enney Letter from us for six Months you can Think that we are All kild"—the men who might set upon you and take your gold and your life; accidents, childbirth, illness, catastrophes of every kind, these were the commonplaces of frontiers. Worst of all, what is won one day is wiped away the next. A frontier may toss us about with little care, and family is little or no security against its capricious impulse.

More than geography and environment, frontiers have had other dimensions. Jefferson imagined the frontier as the land of the yeoman farmer where men and earth are bound to each other in the benediction of fruitful labor. The image of the Garden holds family and land and inheritance in balance. Generations are tied in a sedate and orderly progression. The frontier as Garden was conceived in the imagination of a Virginian and shaped by the Enlightenment. It was the idea carried by the Malick family from Pennsylvania to Illinois and then to Oregon Territory. Frontier as Garden was the dream of Maggie Brown before it withered and died in the desert of the Southwest. It was the classic vision that empowered Ma Joad in Steinbeck's *The Grapes of Wrath* and still drives political ideology and farm programs with powerful and compelling memories of pioneers and sober family farms. It is what the poet Wendell Berry calls "The Gift of Good Land."[3] The vision resonates through our history. It is a dream of order and of blessing.

But American frontiers have also been places of more irreverent dramas. Perhaps the righteous officialdom of the Puritans created the need for breathing space, expansion, experimentation. Perhaps those dark sermons inspired the defiant will to test whether hell and damnation truly followed upturning the accepted order. However that may be, the outlying rim of settlements has also been the place for breaking bounds, and the raw humor of the Ohio River boatmen could be heard through the Gold Rush as the frontier became the place of Carnival.[4] On the wildly disordered frontier, the unexpected came to pass; frontier was a world of "fool's day" where hunger, desperate effort, and fear could be transformed by hilarity. On the frontier as Carnival—as Mardi Gras—one wore different faces and lived different lives that needed no accounting. The Carnival frontier was the place of high stakes and low jokes, a place for buffoonery and swagger, where cowboys and Indians played deadly games with breakneck courage. This was the frontier of Abigail's children, where eccentricity expressed the Carnival attitude. Shindel's bathos and sentimentality could be turned off at will; misfortunes were merely one of the "hands" in a game of cards. Jane married men her mother considered shiftless, "mean," and "dirty." And Susan's elopement and her attachment to the traveling players proclaimed her view of the frontier as a place for comedy.

For all its pain, the frontier was also a place of Carnival to Charles and Maggie Brown. Gambling and speculation filled the mining towns with people who came to be transfixed by the wonders of magicians. Sleight-of-hand tricksters, wizards, musicians—one might think they were in short supply there in the cold tents of Colorado and in the baking adobes of New Mexico, but they were surely present, performing behind the surveyors' offices, singing at the door of the land agent. And even though people went hungry waiting for the next display that would astonish, though they were cold and wet waiting for miracles, they did not go home.

Finally, frontiers have worn darker aspects, of heartbreak and loneliness and desperation. Walter Prescott Webb said in 1957 that western history is "brief and it is bizarre." It is a place "full of negatives and short on positives."[5] Under all the promise there is something of the perverse. The Gothic frontier is the one usually hidden from memory. It is the record of human failure and the distortion of effort. On such a landscape we confront our own limitations and face the denial of our dreams of bountiful blessing. The Nehers in North Dakota lived like coyotes with their young in a "hole." Their frontier years were spent in isolation and poverty and exhaustion. Their frontier was not Jefferson's Garden, their labor was more humiliating than ennobling. On those western lands where families were strewn haphazardly about, people lived alone and terrified. On that unforgiving frontier a man doubted everything he had believed in. Such landscapes and such despair inspired the black humor of Mark Twain's *The Mysterious Stranger* and *Pudd'nhead Wilson*. Such thoughts were set down in Melville's *Pierre* and *The Confidence Man*. Those who survive their Gothic frontiers, like the old man in Hemingway's last novella, retrieve a trophy that may be only a skeleton.

These are the frontiers that transcend geography, but they are not less real. The landscapes that appear as the Garden, the Carnival, and the place of Gothic austerity are chameleon. Like the shadow play, they intend to deceive. One man prospers, another dies. Abigail's vision of sober Christian order on the western frontier was as clear and as palpable as the vision of her children who followed a piper in a hat with clamoring bells. In all their different aspects, frontiers have framed conflicting images and bid us test which will hold our own future.

Each of our families—the Malicks, the Browns, the Nehers and Martins—tested the frontier and were tested by it. The census of Clark County in Oregon Territory shows that in 1850 there were forty-four families like the Malicks. But one decade later, only nine of the original families were still there. Thirty-five families, 80 percent, vanished.[6] Perhaps, like Abigail and her children, they suffered too many losses and disappeared. The "persistence rate"—the number of settlers who remained in place into the second and third decades—was only 20 percent.[7] In Colorado and New Mexico Maggie and Charles Brown left no mark of their passage, but they were not much different from the other men and women in the mining stops of the Southwest. Their shadows pass through ghost towns where modern-day tourists wander through empty streets and houses, snapping photos, and paying a kind of cultural tribute to transience. The descendants of Ludwig Neher have left the land.

Frontiers "provoke the disappointment seen in the inarticulate, but very meaningful, response of transience."[8] People moved because success on a frontier was a promise rarely redeemed, and because "real opportunity was largely beyond the reach of the overwhelming majority of the people who participated most directly in this much fabled land."[9] Migration can be read as the statement that a family was in one place at one time, and that at another time, it was somewhere else. Or migration is the design of a new direction, another vision of what life might be and where it could lead. Sometimes it is the mark of failure.

In all these aspects, American frontiers have been the history not only of "conquests" but of the constant "wash" of families who do not put down roots, who choose to "move on." "In Buffalo [New York] for instance, founded in the late 1820's and the 1830's, the average length of residence during the 1850's remained only 6.2 years. Established male heads of households, the most stable population cohort, remained only 8.8 years. . . . Newburyport, Massachusetts, a rapidly growing manufacturing center, experienced a 65% transient rate between 1860 and 1870; over half of Newburyport's population moved again between 1870 and 1880."[10] In San Francisco, Denver, Omaha, and Atlanta in the last decades of the nineteenth century, the total number of *different* people at any one time was five to ten times the total population of any one city. And in Albuquerque, New Mexico, in the 1960s and 1970s, one sixth of the total population represented in-migration to replace one sixth of the population that moved *out.*[11]

American cities, like frontiers, are giant "sieves" for a flow of moving people who sort themselves into collections of tract houses and shopping malls, then vanish without warning. Behind the icons of stability—the churches and the schools and the neat houses—families keep moving through.

Some families remain in place. "They are the ones who provide the continuity and the cohesion necessary for communal life."[12] They are the Albrights in Illinois and the Kellers of Virginia, and even John Biles's family in Portland until 1902.[13] "Every advance of the frontier left behind [some] families . . . who intended to remain and prosper where they were."[14] But this has been the weaker tendency, less characteristic of the mood and the inclinations of Americans. As a people we have not chosen to live long on a single landscape. The desire to move is the national condition; we are fired by the vision of "elsewhere," the dream of some other *place* "where the past can be discounted and the future shaped at will."[15]

Centuries of frontiers make "moving on" a common expression of American family life. Whether by covered wagon or moving van, leavetaking means the unmaking of home.

In hundreds of years and generations of uprooting, Americans have assumed that families were strong-growing plants. Set them on any landscape, anywhere, and they will take root and grow. But a family is a fragile assortment of human needs. In all our migrations, our families come apart. We leave a parent here, a sister or a brother there, somewhere else a child. The family continues as best it can, but it is less than, and different from, the family that arrived.

Because frontiers are given to chance and to change, they would seem the wrong place to search for truths about family history. A family on the frontier is "an ephemeral, perhaps a paradoxical institution," set upon a landscape "doomed to extinction probably within the space of a generation."[16] Certainly our stories of frontier families, in their letters and reminiscences, provide a small and idiosyncratic sample out of which to propound ideas about American family life. "In this age of statistical sophistication, it is a bold historian who builds any case upon three [or four] examples."[17] But quantitative history, however broad and imposing and authoritative, is history without nuance, "the raw outlines of the model house . . . with none of its evocative domestic trim."[18] These frontier families are somehow familiar; they hold discourse with us. They lead us beyond the statistician's chart and show us the effects of change over time. They tell us something of the process by which families on distant landscapes survive or die.

The first thing these small histories show is that the journey itself is part of the complex destiny. More than the interval of time it takes to get from one place to another, or the space between two points on a map, the journey is a wily antagonist. Seasoned travelers like the Malicks prepared carefully for their travel from Illinois to Oregon Territory, and then watched helplessly as their seventeen-year-old son drowned at a river crossing. Their eldest son, with his pockets full of gold, disappeared in California on his way home. Forty years later, another journey led two Virginians, Charles and Maggie Brown, through the desert towns and mining camps of New Mexico and Colorado that promised them riches first here and then there, always just beyond reach, always just down the line. Like the "spirit spout" of Moby Dick that led the sailors of the *Pequod* across the oceans of the world, the road lured them on until they could no longer stop when they wanted. In 1909 the Nehers and the Martins, who had the longest journey to find a new home, watched on deck of their ship as another immigrant family put a dead child "into a gunny sack" and buried it at sea. By the time they arrived in North Dakota, they were full of fear of what this vast country might demand of them. The journey—the first act in the drama of frontiers—set its mark on those who tried its distances. It changed all who started out.

Once a family reached the frontier—the rich landscape of Oregon Territory, or the desert of New Mexico, or the austere expanse of North Dakota, it did not matter which—once there, each family struggled to survive. Abigail Malick was endlessly inventive in keeping her family together and in meeting the needs of her restless children. She provided care for the temporarily indigent and for orphans, living quarters for widowers, shelter for divorced and deserted wives, hospice for transients, nursing care for the convalescent and, ultimately, home care for the insane. Her home was hospital, asylum, orphanage, bank, rest home, school, and site for cottage industry—sewing and dairying.

Like Abigail, Maggie Brown baked bread and raised chickens and took in laundry. Her husband, the gentleman doctor of Virginia who knew little or nothing about mining or irrigation or capital investment, became a down-at-the-heels miner, a prospector, and a part-time carpenter, housepainter, mail clerk, railroad man, and speculator.

In North Dakota, the Nehers and the Martins were foragers, forced to take the kernels of wheat from their children in order to plant a crop against the coming season, "selling" a "pair" of children to lighten the burden of mouths to feed at table. No one could say the families did not exert every effort to adapt to a frontier life.

But frontiers put forward conditions that went beyond geography; frontiers entrapped human frailties. The Malicks found land richer than their expectations. Abigail came to love her land on the Columbia River. Her crops and her gardens and her orchards were her passion and pride. They almost redeemed the deaths of her husband and her children. This land would be her grand legacy. But her surviving children despised their inheritance, broke from family, and wandered from home. Without the children, Abigail lost the land. Nothing worked out as she had planned.

On the southwest frontier, Maggie and Charles Brown found a brutal landscape of lizards and horned toads, where grinding poverty and miscarriage turned Maggie, in her mid-thirties, into an old woman with bad teeth and a stooped walk. Blown this way and that, reaching for the place where surely they would "strike it rich," intending always to go "home" to Virginia, Charles and Maggie became vagabonds. Even when they did not believe its promises, they could not take the frontier out of their lives.

The families from Russia wrestled with the unforgiving prairies of North Dakota, lived in a boxcar and then in a "coyote hole" with their children, and were driven to the wall of endurance and of sanity. Even children were made for toil and abuse, their lives so different from those born into American families—Abigail blowing soap bubbles in the doorway with her grandchild, Maggie's vaulting pride in little Mattie. The work of the immigrant families was "something beyond human endurance," beyond the explanation of words. They survived, but frontier America was not as they dreamed.

Given the character of frontier experience, given its instability and its hardship, why have Americans ventured again and again into that disordered space? What is there in the core of American history that has drawn so many westward in such endless pursuit?

The answer lies beyond geography; beyond owning the land or the riches that land may hold. Like the French Foreign Legion, frontiers have offered the space to separate from failure and the place to escape domestic despair. When Henry David Thoreau wrote, "The old have no very important advice to give the young. Their own experience has been so partial, and their lives have been such miserable failures,"[19] he spoke of generations breaking apart. Although Thoreau's "West" was Walden Pond, his message was that family rebellions are real and they are powerful. Frontier children do not duplicate the family arrangements of their parents. "The unsettled atmosphere . . . inspired the young to design their own life strategies."[20] Frontiers allowed "husbands to escape from family responsibilities . . . [allowed] runaways, elopements, divorces. . . . There were abundant frontier opportunities to break free of family restraints."[21] The description is not about the frontiers of Oregon or California or New Mexico, but of Oneida County, New York, in 1790! As Americans we have been "dis-assembling" our families since we came to this land. Our migrations have been our rebellions "against the father no less than against lord or priest, against the husband no less than the father."[22]

Historian Mary Ryan speaks of "the potential for conflict and change [that] gently quaked beneath the foundation of the . . . New York frontier."[23] A half-century later, those generational conflicts were no longer gentle. They had become so powerful that distance alone absorbed their violence.

Shindel rejected his mother's life with defiant passion when he left the farm to work in the mines; behind him Jane went mad and Susan eloped, divorced her husband, and joined a troupe of traveling players before she was sixteen! Even the reliable and stable John Biles had run away from home to join the army when he was seventeen. His parents did not know for twenty months where he was. Charles Brown put two thousand miles between himself and the nagging of his mother and his sisters, who felt that his inadequacies as a son and brother, more than the defeat of the Confederacy, diminished their lives. The frontier players cut themselves free from family with savage intensity, and they tolerated few other boundaries on their lives.

Frontiers absorbed them all. Behavior that was bizarre in traditional communities was merely eccentricity on an unformed frontier. The dramatic gestures of the Malick children did not seem especially different from the behavior of other young people. Shindel's departure from the farm was common enough in a region where commerce and mining developed alongside agriculture. More important, it was commonplace in a region where parental obligations did not rest heavily upon young men. Even Susan's eloping at fifteen was unremarkable when other young women were flying the flag of romantic love in order to break free from the family. She went on, as Mrs. Levant Molton (until her husband was killed in an accident), as though nothing extraordinary had occurred. Even Jane's "insainity" was not so unusual she could not remarry and settle down to being a stable wife and mother. Frontiers absorbed the erratic; they gave wide place to idiosyncrasy and dissipated the passions that exploded within families. "[Ordered systems of life] are for the period of carnival suspended; above all, the hierarchical system and all the connected forms of fear, awe, piety, etiquette, etc., are suspended, i.e., everything that is determined by social-hierarchical inequality among people, or any other form of inequality, including age is suspended. . . . People who are in life separated by impenetrable hierarchical barriers enter into free, familiar contact on the carnival [frontier] square."[24]

Frontiers absorbed passions the family could not contain, transforming the eccentric into the norm. But frontiers also changed those who lived there for a lifetime. Perhaps this was the most poignant aspect of the frontier experience, this radical separation of vision. Abigail, who thought of herself as the bulwark of stability, by the time she was an old woman was a study in contradictions. Through all her letters filled with exhortations for news of kin, for photographs, for seeds, for scraps of clothing to keep the fragile ties of family alive—through it all—Abigail maintained a stubborn refusal to live with her own children. She refused to connect with the family in Illinois when it could shelter her in old age. She died where she wanted to be, in her own house, on her own land—among strangers. She yearned for family, but she resisted them too; she preferred the lonely bastion of her solitude. In the same way, after twenty years in a desert that practiced illusions to while away eternity, Charles and Maggie Brown found the closeness of their Virginia family intolerable. They had grown away from the home they spent so much of their lives wanting.

More than geography, more than social class, more than ethnic origin, discontinuity marked the frontier families. Whether from Pennsylvania or Illinois or Virginia or Russia, dislocation altered—and sometimes shattered—the families who struggled to redeem America's promises. Living "on the edge," in an environment unsettled and uncharted, the families grew separated not only from the homes they had come from but in the very homes they created. In the oppressive closeness of their boxcar days, the Nehers and Martins were men who did not know their wives, close kin who chafed at one another, children who were strangers to their parents and to themselves. Clinging to the great arm of a windmill, a child thrust out of his home so that the others might survive was an emblem of the frontier's alienation, where hardship and confusion, frustration and fear made people—even parents—do desperate things.

Families were not nurtured by frontiers. Quite the opposite; people within the same family rarely "saw" life in the same way. They had different angles of vision. Little on a frontier "came together." Like the pictures in a kaleidoscope, vision was shattered into myriad forms and unfamiliar shapes.

Through all the uprooting, and amid all the change—perhaps because of it—families on the frontier yearned for the home they left behind. Living precariously, sometimes desperately, on the perimeters of change, they longed for an image of home outside of time. In the daily deconstructions of their frontier lives, they escaped from family only to yearn to see it woven back together. Abigail wrote letters for fifteen years, telling herself that her daughter would join her, that she would hold her grandchildren again in her arms. Rachel Malick, on the eve of her wedding, remembered her sister's home in Illinois: "I imagine your Neat White rooms and your Neat kitchen and your nice looking stove and all your bright Things and that dark eyed man reading a newspaper at the table." A remembered tranquility not touched by time. Maggie Brown remembered "Pa" as he had been, her sisters and brother when they were children, and all of them in a home where no one grew older. Ludwig Neher, a grown man who brought his family to the New World, would "shout to God for help," and when God did not answer, "he stretched his arms to the eastern horizon and called his mother. . . . Nothing made him give way so readily as the mention of the word 'mother.' " Settled on the new landscape, sometimes at the risk of life itself, each family longed for what it left behind. Isolated from its past, each family had willed its own separation and yet longed for home as it was remembered in the heart. But the family left behind was not the family remembered. Even the peaceful kitchen of the Albrights in Illinois was split by discord, and when Michael's father died, there was a lawsuit between brothers and sisters over land to be disposed of by inheritance. When Maggie returned to Virginia, Pa was not eager to have her back and the "children" of memory were grown men and women, strangers who did not welcome an "intruder."

The vision of home was a longing for life as it could never be, a vision of time without change. Formed for the road, men and women on wild and lonely American frontiers dreamed of home as the still point of all their departures.

In a nation where the frontier defines the future, in a culture that rewards mobility and "newness," family must be subversive of all that we are taught to desire. Family, with its definitions and continuities, its interdependencies and acceptances, thwarts the craving for freedom and self-definition. The space of an uncreated frontier beckons and promises escape from the tyrannies of family obligations and compromises. Some untried geography sets us free from failures and unfulfilled promises. In three hundred years of westering, generations upon generations, families have been "dis-assembled" so that we can stretch toward the new possibilities. Frontiers grow us for separations and they have given us a language and a moral philosophy for our acts. As Americans tumbled across the continent, in makeshift wagons, jalopies, vans, pick-up trucks, later on trains and jets, each heart held to the belief that there was a new chance to erect a city on the hill, to strike it rich, to leave a better future to the children. But with each move, some image of childhood and the fabric of affection is torn loose, some part of ourselves is left behind.

Given cultural traditions that "define personality, achievement, and the purpose of human life in ways that leave the individual suspended in glorious but terrifying isolation,"[25] it is something of a miracle that families have survived at all. In all our history, we have been prodigal, giving families freely to frontiers, assuming always that a family could be transplanted anywhere, and in any permutation. Set it down however one will, it will grow. But in all our westering, on all our frontiers, families have come apart, splintered. Our families are short of roots and of branches.

The "dis-assembled family" is our accommodation, over time, to frontiers. We seldom grow to maturity within the circle of our grandchildren; the "network of kinship has narrowed."[26] "The ideal of the self-reliant individual leaving home is . . . passed from parents to children through ties that bind us together in solitude as well as love."[27] And once the children leave home, "even the relations between parents and children are matters of individual negotiation."[28] We have learned to want that which is unformed, the empty space in which to construct our own lives, beyond the limitations that come with generations that touch. We lose the habits of home and the heart to care.

Against this background, "keeping the family together" has been the special charge of women. Family histories are recorded in their hand. It is the women of these stories who become our companions; theirs are the voices we hear most clearly. Abigail Malick and Maggie Brown and Pauline Diede were weaving together families divided by lifetimes and by distances. But the obligations of home are carried out in a nation historically unsure that home is where it wants to be.

Each of these stories is, in its own way, a praise song to survivors. On frontiers which became Gardens of orderly progression and bounty, on frontiers which became Carnivals of chance, on Gothic frontiers that were bitter tests of endurance, those who survived were not always heroic pioneers so much as people whose lives were a sequence of false starts and mistakes. Their survival was due as much to luck as to strength of character. For those who struggled against terrible odds, the terrors of the years on the frontier blur but do not disappear. Having lost so much, having endured so many privations, survivors hold on to what is left with fierce passion.

In the comfort of our modern-day lives, we are kin to the frontier families who toiled and won few victories. We recognize ourselves on their lonely landscapes, as we know the loneliness of the diners and storefronts of Edward Hopper paintings. We carry our frontiers within us, the ambiguous spaces between people, the silent distances that keep us apart.

If we expected the stories of the frontier to reveal something of the future, we are left rather to ponder what was left behind—the "cuddle" of grandparents, the comfort of people in their own places. American frontiers leave a complex emotional legacy, but so does family. Family and frontier are the magnets of our minds, charged so cleverly that they force each other apart. The family gathered at the Thanksgiving table is caught in the Instamatic camera and then breaks into the "frontiers" of our private and separate lives.

The Navajo call themselves a wandering people. They imagine they are completing a circle that reflects the universe and they find blessing in unifying all things in an ordered world. Unlike the Navajo's, our journeys do not yield the benedictions of return. However much we yearn to come within the circle of home, we are also determined to escape its boundaries. In the end, we are caught between those magnetic poles, between the familiar dream of home and the dissonant shapes and sounds of frontiers. With the frontier families, we think of home from the distant landscapes of our journeys.

Notes

1. Frederick Jackson Turner, "The Significance of the Frontier in American History," in H. P. Simonson, ed., *The Frontier in American History* (New York: Frederick Ungar, 1920).

2. Myra Jehlen, *American Incarnation: The Individual, the Nation and the Continent* (Cambridge, Mass.: Harvard University Press, 1986), p. 15.

3. Wendell Berry, *The Gift of Good Land: Further Essays in Culture and*

Agriculture (Berkeley, Calif.: North Point Press, 1981); see also Berry, *The Unsettling of America: Culture and Agriculture* (San Francisco: Sierra Club, 1977).

4. The work of M. M. Bakhtin has been germane to this reading of the frontier in American culture. See, for example, Richard M. Berrong, *Rabelais and Bakhtin: Popular Culture in "Gargantua and Pantagruel"* (Lincoln: University of Nebraska Press, 1986), pt. 1.

5. Quoted in Donald Worster, "New West, True West: Interpreting the Region's History," *Western Historical Quarterly* 18, 2 (April 1987): 155.

6. *Federal Population Census for Oregon Territory, 1850–1860* (Washington, D.C.: National Archive Trust Fund Board, 1979).

7. "While communities in early nineteenth century New England were characterized by dicennial persistence rates of 50 to 60 percent of households, communities in the American West experienced rates of 30 percent or less. Sugar Creek [Illinois] was no exception to this western pattern. At least two thirds of heads of households moved elsewhere during the course of each decade." John M. Faragher, *Sugar Creek: Life on the Illinois Prairie* (New Haven, Conn.: Yale University Press, 1986), p. 50.

8. Robert A. Burchell, "Opportunity and the Frontier: Wealth Holding in Twenty-Six North California Counties, 1848–1880," *Western Historical Quarterly* 18, 2 (April 1987): 195.

9. Ibid., p. 178. "Dreams of wealth and economic security fired the imaginations of many Americans in the 1800s, but few actually rose from rags to riches." Gerald McFarland, *A Scattered People: An American Family Moves West* (New York: Pantheon Books, 1985), p. 240.

10. Carroll Smith-Rosenberg, "Bourgeois Discourse and the Progressive Era," in *Disorderly Conduct: Visions of Gender in Victorian America* (New York: Oxford University Press, 1986), p. 169.

11. Peter A. Morrison and Judith P. Wheeler, "The Image of 'Elsewhere' in the American Tradition of Migration," paper presented at a symposium on Human Migration, American Academy of Arts and Sciences, New Harmony, Indiana, April 1976, p. 4. See also George W. Pierson, "The M-Factor in American History," in Michael McGiffert, ed., *The Character of Americans*, rev. ed. (Homewood, Ill.: Dorsey Press, 1970), pp. 118–30.

12. Faragher, p. 52.

13. Mary Kelley Biles petitioned as a widow for the pension due John Biles for his service in the wars against the Indians, 1855–56. She described herself as a resident of Portland for twenty-seven years.

14. Berry, *The Unsettling of America*, p. 4.

15. Morrison and Wheeler, p. 12.

16. Mary P. Ryan, *The Cradle of the Middle Class: The Family in Oneida County, New York 1790–1865* (New York: Cambridge University Press, 1981), p. 10.

17. Anne Firor Scott, "Self Portraits: Three Women," in Richard L. Bushman et al., eds., *Uprooted Americans: Essays to Honor Oscar Handlin* (Boston: Little, Brown, 1979), p. 74.

18. Ryan, pp. 3–4.

19. Henry David Thoreau, "Economy," in *Walden and Other Writings*, ed. Brooks Atkinson (New York: Modern Library, 1981), p. 8.

20. Ryan, p. 57.

21. Ibid., pp. 21–22.

22. Pierson, p. 155.

23. Ryan, p. 20.

24. M. M. Bakhtin, *Problems of Dostoevsky's Poetics*, trans. R. W. Rotsel (Ann Arbor, Mich.: Ardis, 1973), p. 101.

25. Robert N. Bellah et al., *Habits of the Heart: Individualism and Commitment in American Life* (New York: Harper & Row, 1985), p. 89.

26. Ibid., p. 62.

27. Ibid., p. 89.

28. Ibid., p. 20.

PHOTOGRAPH ACKNOWLEDGMENTS

PAGES	
ii–iii	Photograph by Ben Wittick. Courtesy Museum of New Mexico.
9	Courtesy Colorado State Historical Society.
12	Photograph by Lorenzo Lorain. Courtesy Oregon Historical Society.
18–19	Courtesy Oregon Historical Society.
30, 31, 69, 94	Courtesy Mrs. Jackie Roszel.
46	Courtesy Lane County Historical Museum.
141, 153, 157, 162, 168, 169	Courtesy Mrs. Lolita Cox Smith. The Charles Albert Brown Collection is housed at the University of New Mexico Library, Special Collections.
171	Courtesy Mrs. Lillian Keller Peters.
180	Courtesy Mrs. Pauline Neher Diede and the Picture Collection, State Historical Society of North Dakota.
188	Photograph by Hiram H. Wilcox. From the Haynes Foundation Collection. Courtesy Montana Historical Society.
216, 227	Courtesy Mrs. Pauline Neher Diede.
237	Photograph by Stephen Castagneto, New York Times Pictures.

INDEX

A

B

C

H

I

J

K

L

M

O

P

R

S

T

V

W

Y